M000250607

أطلس السيرة النبوية

أماكن، أقوام، أعلام

Atlas on The Prophet's Biography

Places . Nations . Landmarks

© **Maktaba Dar-us-Salam, 2003**

King Fahd National Library Cataloging-in-Publication Data

Abu Khaleel, Shawqi
Atlas on the Prophet's biography: Places, Nations, Landmarks. /
Shawqi Abu Khaleel.   - Riyadh, 2003
292 p.; 14x21 cm
ISBN: 9960-897-71-0
1- Muhammad, Prophet life   2- Islam- History   I - Title
239 dc   1424/6425

Legal Deposit no. 1424/6425
ISBN: 9960-897-71-0

A Unique Publication for the First Time

Atlas on The Prophet's Biography

Places . Nations . Landmarks

An Authentic Collection of Information on Prophet's *Seerah*
with Maps, Illustrations and Pictures

Compiled by
Dr. Shawqi Abu Khalil

DARUSSALAM
GLOBAL LEADER IN ISLAMIC BOOKS

Riyadh, Jeddah, Sharjah, Lahore
London, Houston, New York

طبع هذا الكتاب بإذن من دار الفكر دمشق – سوريا

This book is translated, printed and published
with the permission of DAR-AL-FIKR, Damascus, Syria

First Edition: March 2004
Supervised by:

ABDUL MALIK MUJAHID

Head Office:

P.O. Box: 22743, Riyadh 11416, K.S.A. Tel: 00966-01-4033962/4043432 Fax: 4021659
E-mail: darussalam@awalnet.net.sa Website: http// www.dar-us-salam.com

K.S.A. Darussalam Showrooms:
 Riyadh
Olaya branch: Tel 00966-1-4614483 Fax: 4644945
Malaz branch: Tel 4735220 Fax: 4735221
- Jeddah
 Tel: 00966-2-6879254 Fax: 6336270
- Al-Khobar
 Tel: 00966-3-8692900 Fax: 00966-3-8691551
U.A.E
- Darussalam, Sharjah U.A.E
 Tel: 00971-6-5632623 Fax: 5632624
PAKISTAN
- Darussalam, 36 B Lower Mall, Lahore
 Tel: 0092-42-724 0024 Fax: 7354072
- Rahman Market, Ghazni Street
 Urdu Bazar Lahore
 Tel: 0092-42-7120054 Fax: 7320703
U.S.A
- Darussalam, Houston
 P.O Box: 79194 Tx 772779
 Tel: 001-713-722 0419 Fax: 001-713-722 0431
 E-mail: sales@dar-us-salam.com
- Darussalam, New York
 572 Atlantic Ave, Brooklyn
 New York-11217, Tel: 001-718-625 5925
U.K
- Darussalam International Publications Ltd.
 226 High Street, Walthamstow,
 London E17 7JH, Tel: 0044-208 520 2666
 Mobile: 0044-794 730 6706 Fax: 0044-208 521 7645
- Darussalam International Publications Limited
 Regent Park Mosque, 146 Park Road,
 London NW8 7RG Tel: 0044-207 724 3363
- Darussalam
 398-400 Coventry Road, Small Heath
 Birmingham, B10 0UF
 Tel: 0121 77204792 Fax: 0121 772 4345
 E-mail: info@darussalamuk.com
 Web: www.darussalamuk.com

FRANCE
- Editions & Librairie Essalam
 135, Bd de Ménilmontant- 75011 Paris
 Tél: 0033-01- 43 38 19 56/ 44 83
 Fax: 0033-01- 43 57 44 31
 E-mail: essalam@essalam.com
AUSTRALIA
- ICIS: Ground Floor 165-171, Haldon St.
 Lakemba NSW 2195, Australia
 Tel: 00612 9758 4040 Fax: 9758 4030
MALAYSIA
- E&D Books SDN. BHD.-321 B 3rd Floor,
 Suria Klcc
 Kuala Lumpur City Center 50088
 Tel: 00603-21663433 Fax: 459 72032
SINGAPORE
- Muslim Converts Association of Singapore
 32 Onan Road The Galaxy Singapore- 424484
 Tel: 0065-440 6924, 348 8344 Fax: 440 6724
SRI LANKA
- Darul Kitab 6, Nimal Road, Colombo-4
 Tel: 0094-1-589 038 Fax: 0094-74 722433
KUWAIT
- Islam Presentation Committee
 Enlightenment Book Shop
 P.O. Box: 1613, Safat 13017, Kuwait
 Tel: 00965-244 7526, Fax: 240 0057
INDIA
- Islamic Dimensions
 56/58 Tandel Street (North)
 Dongri, Mumbai 4000 009, India
 Tel: 0091-22-3736875, Fax: 3730689
 E-mail:sales@IRF.net
SOUTH AFRICA
- Islamic Da`wah Movement (IDM)
 48009 Qualbert 4078 Durban,South Africa
 Tel: 0027-31-304-6883
 Fax: 0027-31-305-1292
 E-mail: idm@ion.co.za

A Note from the Publisher

After the valuable presentation, *Atlas of the Qur'ân*, as promised, Darussalam is presenting *Atlas on the Prophet's Biography*.

This Atlas is also a compilation of the distinguished research scholar Dr. Shawqi Abu Khalil. The book is in Arabic language and published by Dar-Al-Fikr, Damascus. Dr. Shawqi completed this Book also after the careful study and research this great work required.

In this Atlas, the *Seerah* has been given in a brief form, and maps, explanatory diagrams and photographs have been added to show the places and directions of various events that took place in the life of the Prophet ﷺ. The maps and illustrations have been presented in chronological order.

Throughout the study of this Atlas, the perception and understanding of the *Seerah* of the Prophet ﷺ becomes very easy as if the past events are passing before our eyes in the form of imaginary pictures.

I must thank Mr. Muhammad Adnan Salem, owner of Dar-Al-Fikr, Damascus, for his cooperation and permission to publish the translation of the book.

We pray Allâh to make this work beneficial to all of us.

Abdul Malik Mujahid
General Manager
Darussalam
Riyadh
March 2004

Contents

INTRODUCTION

In the Name of Allâh, and blessings and peace be upon our master the Messenger of Allâh, and upon his good and pure family and Companions.

On the evening of Wednesday 28th Sha'baan 1422 AH (14th November 2001 CE), I stood in front of the *Rawdah* in Al-Madinah Al-Munawwarah, and I felt a wonderful sense of peace. The following Verses entered my mind:

﴿إِلَّا نَنصُرُوهُ فَقَدۡ نَصَرَهُ ٱللَّهُ إِذۡ أَخۡرَجَهُ ٱلَّذِينَ كَفَرُوٓاْ ثَانِيَ ٱثۡنَيۡنِ إِذۡ هُمَا فِي ٱلۡغَارِ إِذۡ يَقُولُ لِصَٰحِبِهِۦ لَا تَحۡزَنۡ إِنَّ ٱللَّهَ مَعَنَاۖ فَأَنزَلَ ٱللَّهُ سَكِينَتَهُۥ عَلَيۡهِ وَأَيَّدَهُۥ بِجُنُودٍ لَّمۡ تَرَوۡهَا وَجَعَلَ كَلِمَةَ ٱلَّذِينَ كَفَرُواْ ٱلسُّفۡلَىٰۗ وَكَلِمَةُ ٱللَّهِ هِيَ ٱلۡعُلۡيَاۗ وَٱللَّهُ عَزِيزٌ حَكِيمٌ ٤٠﴾

"If you help him (Muhammad ﷺ) not (it does not matter), for Allâh did indeed help him when the disbelievers drove him out, the second of the two; when they (Muhammad ﷺ and Abu Bakr ؓ) were in the cave, he (ﷺ) said to his companion (Abu Bakr ؓ): "Be not sad (or afraid), surely, Allâh is with us." Then Allâh sent down His *Sakinah* (calmness, tranquillity, peace) upon him, and strengthened him with forces (angels) which you saw not, and made the word of those who disbelieved the lowermost, while the Word of Allâh that became the uppermost; and Allâh is All-Mighty, All-Wise."

[Qur'ân 9:40]

﴿إِذۡ جَعَلَ ٱلَّذِينَ كَفَرُواْ فِي قُلُوبِهِمُ ٱلۡحَمِيَّةَ حَمِيَّةَ ٱلۡجَٰهِلِيَّةِ فَأَنزَلَ ٱللَّهُ سَكِينَتَهُۥ عَلَىٰ رَسُولِهِۦ وَعَلَى ٱلۡمُؤۡمِنِينَ وَأَلۡزَمَهُمۡ كَلِمَةَ ٱلتَّقۡوَىٰ وَكَانُوٓاْ أَحَقَّ بِهَا وَأَهۡلَهَاۚ وَكَانَ ٱللَّهُ بِكُلِّ شَيۡءٍ عَلِيمًا ٢٦﴾

"When those who disbelieve had put in their hearts pride and

9

haughtiness – the pride and haughtiness of the time of ignorance, then Allâh sent down His *Sakinah* (calmness and tranquillity) upon His Messenger (ﷺ) and upon the believers, and made them stick to the word of piety (i.e. none has the right to be worshipped but Allâh); and they were well entitled to it and worthy of it. And Allâh is the All-Knower of everything."

[Qur'ân 48:26]

And I remembered two lines of Arabic poetry which summed up this meaning, namely the descent of *Sakinah* (tranquility) upon the Messenger of Allâh ﷺ:

"His soul was immersed in grief, but it calmed down when we reached Al-Madinah.

How could it not feel at ease in the presence of the one on whom tranquility was sent down?"

My eyes filled with tears of humiliation and love for the beloved Prophet ﷺ. Whilst I was standing before his *Minbar*, I felt a strange and wonderful sense of tranquility, and Allâh inspired me to say words of supplication, of which I remember saying, "O Allâh, the life of Your Beloved is not merely the matter of ancient history, for history talks about past events, but we are writing about his *Seerah* (biography), and his *Seerah* is an example to be followed, and it will be kept alive until the Day of Judgement. So make me, O Lord, one of the servants of the Prophet's *Seerah*, so that the Muslims may benefit from that which I have devoted my life, namely studying the *Seerah* and writing about it."

I went back to Damascus, where for several days, every time I thought of the beloved Prophet ﷺ, my eyes filled with tears, especially since the first lesson after my return in the Graduate Studies Department was "The Prophet's *Seerah*: Of Whom Do We Speak?" on which occasion I said to my students:

We are going to speak about the Chosen Prophet ﷺ. The scholars have said that when a person is given many names, that is an indication of the greatness and high status of the one who is named, because when the Arabs hold a person or a thing in high esteem, they give him or it many names.

We are going to speak about Muhammad *Al-Amin* (Muhammad the Trustworthy), about *Ahmad Al-Hâdi* (Ahmad the guide), about *Sayyid Walad Adam* (the Leader of the sons of Adam), about *Nabi Ar-Rahmah* (the Prophet of Mercy), about *Khâtimun-Nabiyyin* (the Seal of the Prophets); about *Al-Mustafa Al-Mukhtâr* (the Chosen One), about *Al-Mujtaba* (the Selected One), about *Al-Hâdi Ash-Shafi' Sâhib Al-Hawd Al-Mawrud* (the Guide, the Intercessor, Owner of the Cistern to which many will come), about *Sahib Al-Maqâm Al-Mahmud* (the Owner of the Station of Praise and Glory), about *As-Sirâj Al-Munir* (the Shining Lamp), about *An-Nadhir Al-Bashir* (the Bringer of warnings and glad tidings)...

We are going to speak about the most perfect of human beings, with his great wisdom, his intelligence, his strong senses, his eloquence, his dignified movements, his good characteristics, his patience and perseverance, his forgiveness even when able to wreak vengeance, his generosity, his modesty, his courage, his easy-going nature, his willingness to help others, his sincerity in friendship and giving advice, his kindness and compassion to all people, his zeal for his faith, his loyalty and fulfillment of promises, his humility despite his high status, his dignified way of life, his trustworthiness, his refusal to beg from others, his sincerity of speech, his dignity, his chivalry, his asceticism and indifference to worldly gains, his fear of his Lord, his obedience to Him, his devotion in worship, his gratitude to his Lord and his turning to Him, his devotion to Him, his sincere faith, his trust in his Lord, and his living for His sake...

He combined all the noble characteristics and virtues. His attitude was the Qur'ân; he was pleased with what the Qur'ân is pleased with and was angered by that which the Qur'ân is displeased with.

1- The Qur'ân says of Mûsa ﷺ, who is one of the Messengers of strong will (cf. *Al-Ahqâf* 46:35):

$$﴿وَعَجِلْتُ إِلَيْكَ رَبِّ لِتَرْضَىٰ ﴿٨٤﴾﴾$$

"And I hastened to You, O my Lord, that You might be pleased."

And it says in the holy Book of Allâh concerning Muhammad ibn 'Abdullâh ﷺ:

$$\text{﴿ وَلَسَوْفَ يُعْطِيكَ رَبُّكَ فَتَرْضَىٰ ۝ ﴾}$$

"And verily, your Lord will give you (all good) so that you shall be well-pleased."

[Qur'ân 93:5]

What a great difference there is between the two.

2 - Allâh says concerning Mûsa ﷺ:

$$\text{﴿ قَالَ رَبِّ إِنِّي ظَلَمْتُ نَفْسِي فَاغْفِرْ لِي فَغَفَرَ لَهُ إِنَّهُ هُوَ الْغَفُورُ الرَّحِيمُ ۝ ﴾}$$

"He said: 'My Lord! Verily, I have wronged myself, so forgive me.' Then He forgave him. Verily, He is the Oft-Forgiving, the Most Merciful."

[Qûrân 28:16]

And He says concerning Muhammad ﷺ:

$$\text{﴿ إِنَّا فَتَحْنَا لَكَ فَتْحًا مُّبِينًا ۝ لِيَغْفِرَ لَكَ اللَّهُ مَا تَقَدَّمَ مِن ذَنبِكَ وَمَا تَأَخَّرَ وَيُتِمَّ نِعْمَتَهُ عَلَيْكَ وَيَهْدِيَكَ صِرَاطًا مُّسْتَقِيمًا ۝ ﴾}$$

"Verily, We have given you (O Muhammad ﷺ) a manifest victory. That Allâh may forgive you your sins of the past and the future, and complete His Favour on you, and guide you on the Straight Path."

[Qur'ân 48:1,2]

What a great difference there is between the two.

3 - It says concerning Mûsa ﷺ:

$$\text{﴿ قَالَ رَبِّ اشْرَحْ لِي صَدْرِي ۝ ﴾}$$

"[Mûsa (Moses)] said: 'O my Lord! Open for me my chest (grant me self-confidence, contentment, and boldness).'"

[Qur'ân 20:25]

And it says concerning the Chosen Prophet ﷺ:

$$﴿أَلَمْ نَشْرَحْ لَكَ صَدْرَكَ ۝﴾$$

"Have We not opened your breast for you (O Muhammad ﷺ)?"

[Qur'ân 94:1]

What a great difference there is between the two.

4 - It says concerning Mûsa ﷺ:

$$﴿وَيَسِّرْ لِي أَمْرِي ۝﴾$$

"And ease my task for me."

[Qur'ân 20: 26]

And it says concerning the Pure and Trustworthy One ﷺ:

$$﴿وَنُيَسِّرُكَ لِلْيُسْرَىٰ ۝﴾$$

"And We shall make easy for you (O Muhammad ﷺ) the easy way (i.e., the doing of righteous deeds)."

[Qur'ân 87:8]

What a great difference there is between the two.

5 - Mûsa ﷺ spoke to his Lord on earth:

$$﴿وَنَادَيْنَاهُ مِن جَانِبِ ٱلطُّورِ ٱلْأَيْمَنِ وَقَرَّبْنَاهُ نَجِيًّا ۝﴾$$

"And We called him from the right side of the Mount, and made him draw near to Us for a talk with him [Mûsa (Moses)]."

[Qur'ân 19:52]

$$﴿فَلَمَّآ أَتَىٰهَا نُودِيَ مِن شَاطِئِ ٱلْوَادِ ٱلْأَيْمَنِ فِي ٱلْبُقْعَةِ ٱلْمُبَارَكَةِ مِنَ ٱلشَّجَرَةِ أَن يَٰمُوسَىٰٓ إِنِّيٓ أَنَا ٱللَّهُ رَبُّ ٱلْعَٰلَمِينَ ۝﴾$$

"So when he reached it (the fire), he was called from the right side of the valley, in the blessed place, from the tree: 'O Mûsa (Moses)! Verily, I am Allâh, the Lord of the 'Ālamîn (mankind, jinn and all that exists)!'"

[Qur'ân 28:30].

But the Guide, the Leader of the sons of Adam, spoke to his Lord in heaven:

﴿عَلَّمَهُ شَدِيدُ ٱلْقُوَىٰ ۝ ذُو مِرَّةٍ فَٱسْتَوَىٰ ۝ وَهُوَ بِٱلْأُفُقِ ٱلْأَعْلَىٰ ۝ ثُمَّ دَنَا فَتَدَلَّىٰ ۝ فَكَانَ قَابَ قَوْسَيْنِ أَوْ أَدْنَىٰ ۝ فَأَوْحَىٰ إِلَىٰ عَبْدِهِۦ مَآ أَوْحَىٰ ۝ مَا كَذَبَ ٱلْفُؤَادُ مَا رَأَىٰ ۝﴾

"He has been taught (this Qur'ân) by one mighty in power [Jibril (Gabriel)]. One free from any defect in body and mind then he (Jibril — Gabriel in his real shape as created by Allâh) rose and became stable. While he [Jibril (Gabriel)] was in the highest part of the horizon, (*Tafsir Ibn Kathir*) then he [Jibril (Gabriel)] approached and came closer, and was at a distance of two bows' length or (even) nearer. So (Allâh) revealed to His slave [Muhammad ﷺ through Jibril (Gabriel) ﷺ] whatever He revealed. The (Prophet's) heart lied not in what he (Muhammad ﷺ) saw."

[Qur'ân 53:5-11]

What a great difference there is between the two.

6 - Mûsa ﷺ was sent to the Children of Israel, to his own people only:

﴿فَأَرْسِلْ مَعَنَا بَنِىٓ إِسْرَٰٓءِيلَ وَلَا تُعَذِّبْهُمْ﴾

"... 'so let the Children of Israel go with us, and torment them not'..."

[Qur'ân 20:47]

﴿وَءَاتَيْنَا مُوسَى ٱلْكِتَٰبَ وَجَعَلْنَٰهُ هُدًى لِّبَنِىٓ إِسْرَٰٓءِيلَ أَلَّا تَتَّخِذُوا۟ مِن دُونِى وَكِيلًا ۝﴾

"And We gave Mûsa (Moses) the Scripture and made it a guidance for the Children of Israel (saying): 'Take none other than Me as (your) *Wakil* (Protector, Lord, or Disposer of your affairs, etc)'." [Qur'ân 17:2]

But the Trustworthy One was sent to all of mankind, as a mercy to the worlds:

﴿وَمَا أَرْسَلْنَاكَ إِلَّا كَافَّةً لِّلنَّاسِ بَشِيرًا وَنَذِيرًا﴾

"And We have not sent you (O Muhammad ﷺ) except as a giver of glad tidings and a warner to all mankind."

[Qur'ân 34:28]

﴿إِنْ هُوَ إِلَّا ذِكْرٌ لِّلْعَالَمِينَ ۝ وَلَتَعْلَمُنَّ نَبَأَهُ بَعْدَ حِينٍ ۝﴾

"It (this Qur'ân) is only a Reminder for all the *'Ālamin* (mankind and jinn). And you shall certainly know the truth of it after a while."

[Qur'ân 38:87-88]

﴿وَمَا أَرْسَلْنَاكَ إِلَّا رَحْمَةً لِّلْعَالَمِينَ ۝﴾

"And We have sent you (O Muhammad ﷺ) not but as a mercy for the *'Ālamin* (mankind, jinn and all that exists)."

[Qur'ân 21:107]

﴿قُلْ يَا أَيُّهَا النَّاسُ إِنِّي رَسُولُ اللَّهِ إِلَيْكُمْ جَمِيعًا﴾

"Say (O Muhammad ﷺ): "O mankind! Verily, I am sent to you all as the Messenger of Allâh.""

[Qur'ân 7:158]

What a great difference there is between the two.

7 - It says concerning Mûsa ﷺ:

﴿وَأَلْقَيْتُ عَلَيْكَ مَحَبَّةً مِّنِّي وَلِتُصْنَعَ عَلَى عَيْنِي ۝﴾

"And I endued you with love from Me, in order that you may be brought up under My Eye."

[Qur'ân 20:39]

And it says concerning the Chosen Prophet ﷺ:

﴿وَاصْبِرْ لِحُكْمِ رَبِّكَ فَإِنَّكَ بِأَعْيُنِنَا﴾

"So wait patiently (O Muhammad ﷺ) for the Decision of your Lord, for verily, you are under Our Eyes." [Qur'ân 52:48]

15

In the latter Verse, the grammatical structure of the original Arabic is indicative of complete and comprehensive care.

8   The Most Compassionate (*Al-Ra'ûf*), the Most Merciful (*Al-Rahim*) is Allâh, may He be exalted, as is mentioned dozens of times in the Qur'ân. In *Sûrat At-Tawbah*, Allâh says:

﴿لَقَدْ جَآءَكُمْ رَسُولٌ مِّنْ أَنفُسِكُمْ عَزِيزٌ عَلَيْهِ مَا عَنِتُّمْ حَرِيصٌ عَلَيْكُم بِالْمُؤْمِنِينَ رَءُوفٌ رَّحِيمٌ ۝﴾

"Verily, there has come unto you a Messenger (Muhammad ﷺ) from amongst yourselves. It grieves him that you should receive any injury or difficulty. He (Muhammad ﷺ) is anxious over you; for the believers (he ﷺ is) full of pity, kind, and merciful."

[Qur'ân 9:128]

So Allâh has given him two of His beautiful Names, namely *Ra'ûf* (Compassionate) and *Rahim* (merciful).

9   Swearing by the life of someone is indicative of the high esteem in which that person is held by the one who swears the oath. The life of the Prophet ﷺ is worthy of such an honour, for it was a blessing for the Arab nation and for the entire world:

﴿لَعَمْرُكَ إِنَّهُمْ لَفِى سَكْرَتِهِمْ يَعْمَهُونَ ۝﴾

"Verily, by your life (O Muhammad ﷺ), in their wild intoxication, they were wandering blindly." [Qur'ân 15:72]

10 The way in which the beloved Prophet is addressed in the Book of Allâh is *Ya ayyuhan' Nabi* (O Prophet), *Ya ayyuhar-Rasûl* (O Messenger), *Ya ayyuhal-Muzzammil* (O you wrapped in garments – cf. *Al-Muzzammil* 73:1), *Ya ayyuhal-Muddaththir* (O you (Muhammad) enveloped (in garments) – cf. *Al-Muddaththir* 74:1). He is addressed in the most liked of terms, whereas the other Prophets are addressed by name only: O Adam, O Mûsa, O Nûh, O Dawûd, O Zakariyya, O Lot, O Yahya, O 'Îsa...

11 The miracles of the previous Prophets were temporary and came to an end immediately after they happened, so they belong in

the past. But the miracle of Muhammad ibn 'Abdullâh ﷺ is lasting and eternal, namely the Qur'ân, in which new miraculous aspects will always be discovered. Its miracle is ongoing and Allâh has guaranteed to preserve it:

$$﴿ إِنَّا نَحْنُ نَزَّلْنَا ٱلذِّكْرَ وَإِنَّا لَهُ لَحَٰفِظُونَ ٩ ﴾$$

"Verily, We, it is We Who have sent down the *Dhikr* (i.e. the Qur'ân) and surely, We will guard it (from corruption)."

[Qur'ân 15:9]

12   Allâh praises the Prophet's character:

$$﴿ وَإِنَّكَ لَعَلَىٰ خُلُقٍ عَظِيمٍ ٤ ﴾$$

"And verily, you (O Muhammad ﷺ) are on an exalted (standard of) character."

[Qur'ân 68:4]

$$﴿ فَبِمَا رَحْمَةٍ مِّنَ ٱللَّهِ لِنتَ لَهُمْ وَلَوْ كُنتَ فَظًّا غَلِيظَ ٱلْقَلْبِ لَٱنفَضُّوا مِنْ حَوْلِكَ فَٱعْفُ عَنْهُمْ وَٱسْتَغْفِرْ لَهُمْ وَشَاوِرْهُمْ فِي ٱلْأَمْرِ فَإِذَا عَزَمْتَ فَتَوَكَّلْ عَلَى ٱللَّهِ إِنَّ ٱللَّهَ يُحِبُّ ٱلْمُتَوَكِّلِينَ ١٥٩ ﴾$$

"And by the Mercy of Allâh, you dealt with them gently. And had you been severe and harsh-hearted, they would have broken away from about you; so pass over (their faults), and ask (Allâh's) forgiveness for them; and consult them in the affairs. Then when you have taken a decision, put your trust in Allâh, certainly, Allâh loves those who put their trust (in Him)."

[Qur'ân 3:159]

$$﴿ فَتَوَلَّ عَنْهُمْ فَمَآ أَنتَ بِمَلُومٍ ٥٤ ﴾$$

"So turn away (O Muhammad ﷺ) from them (Quraish pagans), you are not blameworthy (as you have conveyed Allâh's Message)."

[Qur'ân 51:54]

These are just a few aspects of the greatness of the Prophet ﷺ, the atlas of whose biography we present here. He was the one to whom the Final Message was revealed, the features of which are:

17

1 - A divinely-revealed belief system ('Aqidah)

﴿وَبِٱلْحَقِّ أَنزَلْنَٰهُ وَبِٱلْحَقِّ نَزَلَ وَمَآ أَرْسَلْنَٰكَ إِلَّا مُبَشِّرًا وَنَذِيرًا ۝١٠٥﴾

"And with truth We have sent it down (i.e. the Qur'ân), and with truth it has descended. And We have sent you (O Muhammad ﷺ) as nothing but a bearer of glad tidings (of Paradise, for those who follow your Message of Islamic Monotheism), and a warner (of Hell-fire for those who refuse to follow your Message of Islamic Monotheism)."

[Qur'ân 17:105]

﴿وَإِنَّهُۥ لَتَنزِيلُ رَبِّ ٱلْعَٰلَمِينَ ۝١٩٢ نَزَلَ بِهِ ٱلرُّوحُ ٱلْأَمِينُ ۝١٩٣ عَلَىٰ قَلْبِكَ لِتَكُونَ مِنَ ٱلْمُنذِرِينَ ۝١٩٤ بِلِسَانٍ عَرَبِىٍّ مُّبِينٍ ۝١٩٥﴾

"And truly, this (the Qur'ân) is a revelation from the Lord of the *'Alamin* (mankind, jinn and all that exists), which the trustworthy *Rûh* [Jibril (Gabriel)] has brought down upon your heart (O Muhammad ﷺ) that you may be (one) of the warners, in the plain Arabic language."

[Qur'ân 26:192-195]

Earthly, man-made belief systems are bound to collapse sooner or later, but the divinely revealed belief-system of Islam abides and continues to spread.

2 - A belief system that is centred on the laws of Allâh

Although the one to whom Allâh sent down His Message was the Chosen Prophet ﷺ, the *'Aqidah* is centred on the laws of Allâh, with which he (the Prophet ﷺ) was entrusted. The beloved Prophet ﷺ remained human, a slave of Allâh:

﴿قُلْ إِنَّمَآ أَنَا۠ بَشَرٌ مِّثْلُكُمْ يُوحَىٰٓ إِلَىَّ أَنَّمَآ إِلَٰهُكُمْ إِلَٰهٌ وَٰحِدٌ﴾

"Say (O Muhammad ﷺ): I am only a man like you. It has been revealed to me that your *Ilâh* (God) is One *Ilâh* (God, i.e., Allâh)."

[Qur'ân 18:110]

﴿قُل لَّآ أَمْلِكُ لِنَفْسِى نَفْعًا وَلَا ضَرًّا إِلَّا مَا شَآءَ ٱللَّهُ وَلَوْ كُنتُ أَعْلَمُ ٱلْغَيْبَ لَٱسْتَكْثَرْتُ مِنَ ٱلْخَيْرِ وَمَا مَسَّنِىَ ٱلسُّوٓءُ إِنْ أَنَا۠ إِلَّا نَذِيرٌ وَبَشِيرٌ لِّقَوْمٍ يُؤْمِنُونَ ١٨٨﴾

"Say (O Muhammad ﷺ): 'I possess no power over benefit or hurt to myself except as Allâh wills. If I had the knowledge of the *Ghayb* (Unseen), I should have secured for myself an abundance of wealth, and no evil should have touched me. I am but a warner, and a bringer of glad tidings unto people who believe.'"

[Qur'ân 7:188]

Even in the highest and most sublime spiritual position, the Prophet ﷺ remained a slave of Allâh. That was during the *Isra'* and *Mi'râj* (Night Journey and Ascent into heaven):

﴿سُبْحَٰنَ ٱلَّذِىٓ أَسْرَىٰ بِعَبْدِهِۦ لَيْلًا مِّنَ ٱلْمَسْجِدِ ٱلْحَرَامِ إِلَى ٱلْمَسْجِدِ ٱلْأَقْصَا﴾

"Glorified (and Exalted) be He (Allâh) [above all that (evil) they associate with Him], Who took His slave (Muhammad ﷺ) for a journey by night from Al-Masjid Al-Harâm (at Makkah) to Al-Masjid Al-Aqsa (in Jerusalem)."

[Qur'ân 17:1]

It does not say in this Verse that He took His Messenger, or His Prophet, or His Beloved, or His Close Friend... rather it says 'His slave'.

So this *'Aqidah* is centred on Allâh, the Sustainer of the heavens and the earth, the Creator, the Protector, the One, the Unique, and on His laws which are contained in His Glorious Book, which the *Sunnah* came to explain in detail.

3 - A final message, whose miracle is ongoing and eternal

Its miracle is nothing other than the Noble Qur'ân. When the *Mushrikin* of Quraish demanded immediate miracles, the response came:

﴿وَقَالُوا۟ لَوْلَآ أُنزِلَ عَلَيْهِ ءَايَٰتٌ مِّن رَّبِّهِۦ قُلْ إِنَّمَا ٱلْأَيَٰتُ عِندَ ٱللَّهِ وَإِنَّمَآ أَنَا۠ نَذِيرٌ

19

مُبِينٌ ۝ أَوَلَمْ يَكْفِهِمْ أَنَّا أَنزَلْنَا عَلَيْكَ ٱلْكِتَبَ يُتْلَىٰ عَلَيْهِمْ إِنَّ فِى ذَٰلِكَ لَرَحْمَةً وَذِكْرَىٰ لِقَوْمٍ يُؤْمِنُونَ ۝

"And they say: 'Why are not signs sent down to him from his Lord?' Say: 'The signs are only with Allâh, and I am only a plain warner.' Is it not sufficient for them that We have sent down to you the Book (the Qur'ân) which is recited to them? Verily, herein is mercy and a reminder (or an admonition) for a people who believe."

[Qur'ân 29:50 - 51]

It is a lasting miracle which will abide until the onset of the Hour:

﴿سَنُرِيهِمْ ءَايَٰتِنَا فِى ٱلْأَفَاقِ وَفِىٓ أَنفُسِهِمْ حَتَّىٰ يَتَبَيَّنَ لَهُمْ أَنَّهُ ٱلْحَقُّ أَوَلَمْ يَكْفِ بِرَبِّكَ أَنَّهُ عَلَىٰ كُلِّ شَىْءٍ شَهِيدٌ ۝﴾

"We will show them Our Signs in the universe, and in their own selves, until it becomes manifest to them that this (the Qur'ân) is the truth. Is it not sufficient in regard to your Lord that He is a Witness over all things?"

[Qur'ân 41:53]

4 - A message which addresses reason, not emotion

It is far removed from fanaticism and compulsion, a clear message which avoids secrets and symbols. So it does not go against reason or undermine rational thought, for the true religion can only embrace reason, and reason is nourished by knowledge:

﴿إِنَّ فِى ذَٰلِكَ لَءَايَٰتٍ لِّقَوْمٍ يَعْقِلُونَ ۝﴾

"Verily, in these things there are *Ayat* (proofs, evidences, lessons, signs) for the people who understand."

[Qur'ân 13:4]

﴿نُفَصِّلُ ٱلْأَيَٰتِ لِقَوْمٍ يَعْقِلُونَ ۝﴾

"Thus do We explain the signs in detail to a people who have sense."

It is a belief that addresses sound reason, a belief for people who have sense, people who think, people who reflect, people who consider, people of understanding. "If the Qur'ân were to look for a judge to rule according to divine revelation, it could not find anything better than reason, and when the Qur'ân presents an argument, it is based on reason. When it expresses discontent it is with those who do not exercise reason and when it is pleased it is pleased with those who have reason.

﴿قُلْ إِنَّمَآ أَعِظُكُم بِوَٰحِدَةٍ أَن تَقُومُوا۟ لِلَّهِ مَثْنَىٰ وَفُرَٰدَىٰ ثُمَّ تَتَفَكَّرُوا۟ مَا بِصَاحِبِكُم مِّن جِنَّةٍ إِنْ هُوَ إِلَّا نَذِيرٌ لَّكُم بَيْنَ يَدَىْ عَذَابٍ شَدِيدٍ ﴿٤٦﴾﴾

"Say (to them O Muhammad ﷺ): 'I exhort you to one (thing) only, that you stand up for Allâh's sake in pairs and singly, and reflect (within yourselves the life history of the Prophet ﷺ), there is no madness in your companion (Muhammad ﷺ). He is only a warner to you in face of a severe torment.'"

[Qur'ân 34:46]

5 - A message to all of mankind

This message is not for any specific people. The words "O people" refer to all of mankind, and the criteria for differentiating between people is based on piety:

﴿يَٰٓأَيُّهَا ٱلنَّاسُ إِنَّا خَلَقْنَٰكُم مِّن ذَكَرٍ وَأُنثَىٰ وَجَعَلْنَٰكُمْ شُعُوبًا وَقَبَآئِلَ لِتَعَارَفُوٓا۟ إِنَّ أَكْرَمَكُمْ عِندَ ٱللَّهِ أَتْقَىٰكُمْ إِنَّ ٱللَّهَ عَلِيمٌ خَبِيرٌ ﴿١٣﴾﴾

"O mankind! We have created you from a male and a female, and made you into nations and tribes, that you may know one another. Verily, the most honourable of you with Allâh is that (believer) who has At-Taqwa [i.e., he is one of the Muttaqûn (the pious)]. Verily, Allâh is All-Knowing, All-Aware."

[Qur'ân 49:13]

21

$$\langle\!\langle \text{إِن هُوَ إِلَّا ذِكْرٌ لِّلْعَلَمِينَ} \ \text{(87)} \ \text{وَلَتَعْلَمُنَّ نَبَأَهُ بَعْدَ حِينٍ} \ \text{(88)} \ \rangle\!\rangle$$

"It (this Qur'ân) is only a Reminder for all the 'Ālamin (mankind and jinn). And you shall certainly know the truth of it after a while."

[Qur'ân 38:87-88]

$$\langle\!\langle \text{وَمَا أَرْسَلْنَاكَ إِلَّا رَحْمَةً لِّلْعَلَمِينَ} \ \text{(107)} \ \rangle\!\rangle$$

"And We have sent you (O Muhammad ﷺ) not but as a mercy for the 'Ālamin (mankind, jinn and all that exists)."

[Qur'ân 21:107]

$$\langle\!\langle \text{قُلْ يَا أَيُّهَا النَّاسُ إِنِّي رَسُولُ اللَّهِ إِلَيْكُمْ جَمِيعًا} \ \rangle\!\rangle$$

"Say (O Muhammad ﷺ): "O mankind! Verily, I am sent to you all as the Messenger of Allâh."

[Qur'ân 7:158]

It is a message for all of mankind, and one of its permanent features is tolerance. It does not seek to uproot other systems or laws. It presents dialogue as the alternative. The fact that Islam accepts a variety of belief systems in the Muslim society is an affirmation of the Will of Allâh:

$$\langle\!\langle \text{وَلَوْ شَاءَ رَبُّكَ لَجَعَلَ النَّاسَ أُمَّةً وَاحِدَةً وَلَا يَزَالُونَ مُخْتَلِفِينَ} \ \text{(118)} \ \rangle\!\rangle$$

"And if your Lord had so willed, He could surely, have made mankind one *Ummah* [nation or community (following one religion, i.e., Islam)], but they will not cease to disagree."

[Qur'ân 11:118]

The important Islamic principle,

$$\langle\!\langle \text{لَا إِكْرَاهَ فِي الدِّينِ} \ \rangle\!\rangle$$

"There is no compulsion in religion," [Qur'ân 2:256]

Abides as proof against every closed-minded fanatic who does not belief in freedom of belief. So there should be no violence, no bloodshed, no imposing of belief by force. The alternative is dialogue, not simply with nice words but with those that are best:

﴿ٱدْعُ إِلَىٰ سَبِيلِ رَبِّكَ بِٱلْحِكْمَةِ وَٱلْمَوْعِظَةِ ٱلْحَسَنَةِ وَجَٰدِلْهُم بِٱلَّتِي هِيَ أَحْسَنُ إِنَّ رَبَّكَ هُوَ أَعْلَمُ بِمَن ضَلَّ عَن سَبِيلِهِۦ وَهُوَ أَعْلَمُ بِٱلْمُهْتَدِينَ ١٢٥ ﴾

"Invite (mankind, O Muhammad ﷺ) to the way of your Lord (i.e., Islam) with wisdom (i.e., with the Divine Revelation and the Qur'ân) and fair preaching, and argue with them in a way that is better. Truly, your Lord knows best who has gone astray from His path, and He is the Best Aware of those who are guided."

[Qur'ân 16:125]

But there is a great difference between tolerance and weakness and helplessness, because many do not appreciate this noble attitude, and they may abuse the tolerance and easy-going nature of Islam to destroy the Islam that allows them to live under its shelter where dialogue is the right of all, and where everyone has the right to engage in dialogue with no violence and no denial of the other's opinion, but rather with ongoing tolerance, then the reckoning with be with Allâh:

﴿ فَٱللَّهُ يَحْكُمُ بَيْنَهُمْ يَوْمَ ٱلْقِيَٰمَةِ فِيمَا كَانُوا۟ فِيهِ يَخْتَلِفُونَ ١١٣ ﴾

"Allâh will judge between them on the Day of Resurrection about that wherein they have been differing."

[Qur'ân 2:113]

"The beliefs that are built on hatred will be destroyed by vengeance, but the beliefs that are built on love will be protected by kindness."

6 - A precise balance between the spiritual and the material

The spiritual – in Islam – does not negate the material, and the material does not overwhelm the spiritual:

﴿ وَٱبْتَغِ فِيمَآ ءَاتَىٰكَ ٱللَّهُ ٱلدَّارَ ٱلْأَخِرَةَ وَلَا تَنسَ نَصِيبَكَ مِنَ ٱلدُّنْيَا وَأَحْسِن كَمَآ أَحْسَنَ ٱللَّهُ إِلَيْكَ وَلَا تَبْغِ ٱلْفَسَادَ فِي ٱلْأَرْضِ إِنَّ ٱللَّهَ لَا يُحِبُّ ٱلْمُفْسِدِينَ ٧٧ ﴾

"But seek, with that (wealth) which Allâh has bestowed on you, the home of the Hereafter, and forget not your portion of lawful enjoyment in this world; and do good as Allâh has been good to you, and seek not mischief in the land. Verily, Allâh likes not the *Mufsidûn* (those who commit great crimes and sins, oppressors, tyrants, mischief-makers, corrupters)."

[Qur'ân 28:77]

There is no conflict between the spiritual and the material.

It is a religion in which there is a precise balance between the spiritual and the material; it is a religion in which life is balanced and tranquil, in which what is good is permitted and what is bad is forbidden:

﴿قُلْ مَنْ حَرَّمَ زِينَةَ ٱللَّهِ ٱلَّتِىٓ أَخْرَجَ لِعِبَادِهِۦ وَٱلطَّيِّبَٰتِ مِنَ ٱلرِّزْقِ قُلْ هِىَ لِلَّذِينَ ءَامَنُوا۟ فِى ٱلْحَيَوٰةِ ٱلدُّنْيَا خَالِصَةً يَوْمَ ٱلْقِيَٰمَةِ كَذَٰلِكَ نُفَصِّلُ ٱلْءَايَٰتِ لِقَوْمٍ يَعْلَمُونَ ٣٢﴾

"Say (O Muhammad ﷺ): Who has forbidden the adornment with clothes given by Allâh, which He has produced for His slaves, and *At-Tayyibât* [all kinds of *Halâl* (lawful) things] of food? Say: They are, in the life of this world, for those who believe, (and) exclusively for them (believers) on the Day of Resurrection (the disbelievers will not share them). Thus We explain the *Āyât* (Islamic laws) in detail for people who have knowledge."

[Qur'ân 7:32]

7- An eternal message for every time and place

Because this is the *Fitrah* of Allâh, the natural disposition which Allâh has instilled in man:

﴿فَأَقِمْ وَجْهَكَ لِلدِّينِ حَنِيفًا فِطْرَتَ ٱللَّهِ ٱلَّتِى فَطَرَ ٱلنَّاسَ عَلَيْهَا لَا تَبْدِيلَ لِخَلْقِ ٱللَّهِ ذَٰلِكَ ٱلدِّينُ ٱلْقَيِّمُ وَلَٰكِنَّ أَكْثَرَ ٱلنَّاسِ لَا يَعْلَمُونَ ٣٠﴾

"So set you (O Muhammad ﷺ) your face towards the religion (of pure Islamic Monotheism) *Hanif* (worship none but Allâh Alone). Allâh's *Fitrah* (i.e. Allâh's Islamic Monotheism) with

which He has created mankind. No change let there be in
Khalqillâh (i.e., the religion of Allâh – Islamic Monotheism), that
is the straight religion, but most of men know not."

[Qur'ân 30:30]

"The *Fitrah* of Allâh", the natural disposition which Allâh has
instilled in man, because it is what is suited to human urges and
inclinations; it changed the sexual relationship into a contractual
relationship, on which is based the institution of the family in its
moral and spiritual dimensions. So it satisfies desires, protects
lineages, and lays a solid foundation for society.

It is the religion of moderation, based on the best of options, so that
society will be established along parallel lines with no conflicts of
class, race, family or position, and where the standard of nobility
and human dignity is subject to moral considerations, so it will be
the best of human societies.

8 - A message that is protected by the One Who revealed it

Nothing has been altered or changed in it, and nothing has been
added or taken away. We recite the Qur'ân today as it was recited
on the day it was revealed:

$$﴾ ٩ ﴿ إِنَّا نَحْنُ نَزَّلْنَا ٱلذِّكْرَ وَإِنَّا لَهُۥ لَحَٰفِظُونَ ﴿$$

"Verily, We, it is We Who have sent down the *Dhikr* (i.e. the
Qur'ân) and surely, We will guard it (from corruption)."

[Qur'ân 15:9]

Many ideologies have collapsed, many laws have been forsaken and
many beliefs have been abandoned, but Islam is the fastest-
spreading religion today, the Islam of human brotherhood, of ease
not hardship, the Islam of dialogue which is indicative of the
Muslim's confidence in the principles that speak to reason,
encourage the pursuit of knowledge and accept and recognize
others.

Based on this preserved message, Islam will reach all nations, but
that is the Islam which is gentle in its preaching and pure in thought,

objective in dialogue and idealistic in action, realistic and integrated.

* * *

Then I said to my students: Do you know who we are going to talk about in our study of the Prophet's biography? Do you realize how great he is? Do you appreciate the characteristics of the Message that was revealed to him ﷺ?

Only a few days passed before a brilliant idea came to me, which was to take this *Seerah* that has been written in such a precise manner, and explain it with maps and explanatory diagrams showing the places, cities, locations and directions which were honoured by the Prophet's coming to them or heading towards them. I start with some discussion of the father of the Prophets Ibrâhim عليه السلام, then I will speak about the birth of the Prophet Muhammad ﷺ and the events that took place before and after his mission began, the *Hijrah*, and events until he passed away.

This Atlas is not only a book of *Seerah*, it also includes maps and illustrations covering the entire *Seerah*. If something like this has been done before, may Allâh bless the one who did that. But I do not think that anyone has presented the *Seerah* in maps presented in chronological order as is done here, with explanatory comments.

This Atlas is the fourth volume in the series of Islamic Atlases, which are, in order: *Atlas Al-Târikh Al-'Arabi Al-Islami* (Atlas of Islamic Arab History), *Atlas Duwal Al-'Aalam Al-Islami* (Atlas of the Muslim World) and *Atlas Al-Qur'ân* (Atlas of the Qur'ân).

Praise is to Allâh, first and last, the Best of Protectors and the Best Disposer of Affairs. I ask Him, may He be exalted, to make this work beneficial, for He is the One Whose pleasure is sought.

Damascus
1 Muharram 1423 AH
14 March 2002 CE
Dr Shawqi Abu Khalil

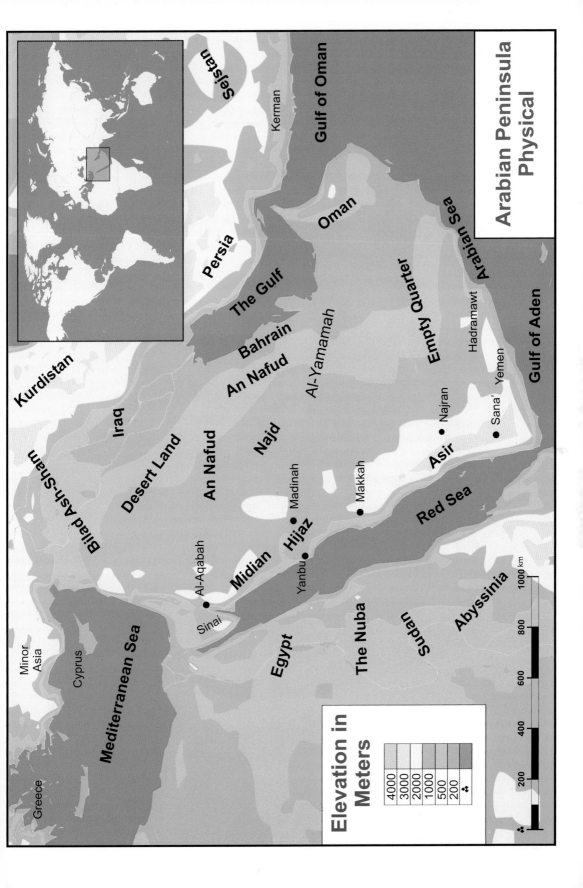

Arabian Peninsula
Physical

Selstan

Kerman

Gulf of Oman

Persia

Oman

The Gulf

Bahrain

An Nafud

Al-Yamamah

Empty Quarter

Arabian Sea

Hadramawt

Gulf of Aden

Yemen

Kurdistan

Iraq

Najd

An Nafud

Najran

Sana'

Asir

Bilad Ash-Sham

Desert Land

Madinah

Hijaz

Makkah

Red Sea

Midian

Yanbu

Al-Aqabah

Sinai

The Nuba

Egypt

Sudan

Abyssinia

Minor
Asia

Cyprus

Greece

Mediterranean Sea

Elevation in
Meters

4000	
3000	
2000	
1000	
500	
200	

1000 km

800

600

400

200

An-Nafud Great Desert

The Empty Quarter

The Eastern Region (Najd-Wadi Hanifah)

The Western Region (Mada'in Salih)

Hills in the Southwestern Region

Foothills of the Mountains of Southern Hijaz (Al-Baha)

The Arabian Peninsula

The Arabian Peninsula is the cradle of Islam, and the homeland of the ancient Arabs. It is situated in southwest Asia, surrounded by three seas: the Red Sea to the west, the Indian Ocean (the Arabian Sea and the Gulf of Aden) to the south, and the Arabian Gulf and the Gulf of Oman to the east. To the north is Bâdiyât Ash-Shâm which is mostly desert. The geographers have divided Arabia, according to climate, into five sections:

1 – **Tihâmah:** This refers to the coastal plains along the Red Sea, which extend from Yanbu' in the north to Najrân in the south. It is so called because of its severe heat and lack of wind, from the word *At-Taham* which refers to extreme heat and lack of wind.

2 – **The mountain range of As-Sarâh:** This is the western mountain range which runs parallel to the coast of the Red Sea, to the east of the plains of Tihâmah. Here there are a number of valleys that cut through the mountains. This range extends from the Gulf of 'Aqabah to Yemen. In the north it is called Jibâl Midian (the mountains of Madyan) and in the south it is called Jibâl 'Asir. In the center of this range is the Hijâz where Makkah Al-Mukarramah and Al-Madinah Al-Munawwarah are located. The Hijâz is so called because it is a barrier (*Hijâz*) between Tihâmah and Najd.

3 – **The Najd plateau:** It extends from Yemen in the south to southern Iraq in the north, where it is called Bâdiyat Al-Samâwah. Its eastern part is called Al-'Arud. It is called Najd because of its elevation (*Najd* = highland, plateau).

4 – **Yemen:** This is a mountainous area in the far southwest of Arabia, to the east of which are Hadramawt, Mahrah and Oman. Here is located the highest peak in the Arabian Peninsula, 3750 meters high, south west of San'a'.

5 – **Al-'Arud.** This region includes Al-Yamâmah, Oman and

31

Bahrain. It is called 'Arud because it stands in between (*A'tarada*) Yemen and Najd.

In the northern regions, the rains come in winter, and the amount of rainfall is very little. In Yemen, 'Asir and Oman, the monsoon rains come in summer, with a heavy rainfall of 500 mm in some regions of Yemen and 'Asir, and less than that in Oman.

The Arabian Peninsula is crossed by the Tropic of Cancer (23.5 degrees north of the Equator), hence high temperatures prevail in most regions, especially in summer.

Currently there are seven states within the Arabian Peninsula which are, in order of size from largest to smallest:

- The Kingdom of Saudi Arabia (2,248,000 sq km)

- The Republic of Yemen (472,099 sq km)

- The Sultanate of Oman (306,000 sq km)

- The United Arab Emirates (83,000 sq km)

- Kuwait (17,818 sq km)

- Qatar (11,437 sq km)

- Bahrain (694 sq km)

Total area: 3,139,048 sq km.

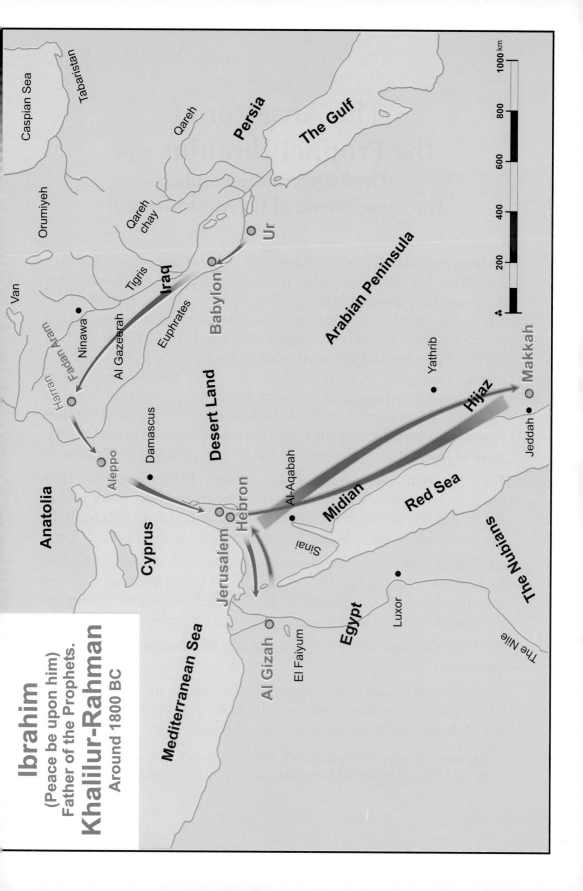

Ibrahim
(Peace be upon him)
Father of the Prophets.
Khalilur-Rahman
Around 1800 BC

Caspian Sea

Tabaristan

Qareh

Persia

The Gulf

Orumiyeh

Qareh chay

Van

Tigris

Ninawa

Iraq

Al Gazeerah

Euphrates

Babylon

Ur

Harran

Fadan Aram

Aram

Anatolia

Damascus

Desert Land

Aleppo

Arabian Peninsula

Yathrib

Hijaz

Makkah

Cyprus

Jerusalem

Hebron

Al-Aqabah

Midian

Red Sea

Jeddah

Mediterranean Sea

Sinai

Egypt

Al Gizah

El Faiyum

Luxor

The Nubians

The Nile

1000 km

800

600

400

200

The Ancestor of
the Prophet Ibrâhim ﷺ
–The Father of the Prophets
The Close Friend of the Most Merciful

Ibrâhim ﷺ was born in southern Iraq, and settled in the Chaldean city of Ur. His father was Azar ibn Nâhur; and it was also said that Azar was his paternal uncle, because according to the custom of the Arabs, the paternal uncle may also be called the father. He was of the people of Kutha which is a village in the vicinity of Al-Kufah. He was born in Kutha or Babylon or Al-Warka'. Kutha is the place where the people attempted to burn Ibrâhim ﷺ. After that attempt failed, Ibrâhim went to Harrân in northern Mesopotamia, then he went to Palestine, accompanied by his wife Sarah and his nephew Lot. Lot was also accompanied by his wife. Because of a famine in the land, he went to Egypt during the reign of the 'shepherd kings' or Hyksos.[1]

Then he went back with Lot to southern Palestine, where they separated so that each could find sufficient grazing and water for his flocks. Ibrâhim settled in B'ir Sheba and Lot settled in an area south of the Dead Sea, which was known as Buhayrat Lot (The Lake of Lot).

Ibrâhim traveled with his second wife Hâjir to Makkah, and she took Ismâ'il ﷺ with her. After he left them there, "in an uncultivable valley" [Ibrâhim 14:37], and after the spring of Zamzam began to flow, (the tribe of) Jurhum came via Kuda'.

Ibrâhim died and was buried in the city of Al-Khalil (Hebron), in Palestine.

Some historians said: The descendents of Ismâ'il are the 'Arabized' Arabs (Al-'Arab Al-Musta'ribah or Al-'Arab Al-Muta'rribah), who are the 'Adnâniyyin. They were so called because Ismâ'il spoke Syriac

---

[1] Hyksos (Egyptian, 'foreign rulers'), Semitic invaders who conquered Egypt in the 17th century BC and founded the 15th Dynasty. [Translator]

Al-Khalil (Hebron): One of the Two Minarets of Ibrahimi Mosque

or Hebrew. When Jurhum – who were from the Qahtaani branch – came to Makkah and settled with him and his mother, he married into their society and he and his children learned Arabic, so they were called the 'Arabized Arabs' (Al-'Arab Al-Musta'ribah), who formed the majority of the Arabs among both Bedouin and settled Arabs who lived in central Arabia and the Hijâz as far north as Bâdiyat Ash-Shâm. Arabs from Yemen also came and settled among them after the collapse of the Ma'rib Dam.

But this idea of the 'Arabized Arabs' is a myth that was mentioned by some historians and then became widespread, even though the time of Ibrâhim صلى الله عليه وسلم and his son Ismâ'il صلى الله عليه وسلم was a distinctly Arab era, with no connection to Aramaeans[1] or Jews. A clear distinction is now made between the people of Ibrâhim, the people of Ya'qub (Israel), the people of Mûsa, the Jews and the Hebrews.[2]

When the Jews compiled their Torah, after they were taken to Babylon as captives by Nebuchadnezzar in 586 BC, they sought to achieve two main goals:

1 – Glorifying their own history and establishing themselves as the 'chosen people' who were chosen by the Lord above all of mankind. In order to achieve that, they had to trace their origins to the holiest ancient character, namely Ibrâhim صلى الله عليه وسلم, whose fame was widespread throughout the earth at that time. So they skillfully narrated and recorded their history according to their whims and desires, adding religious connotations in order to make it acceptable to their followers. Similarly they traced their history back to Ibrâhim صلى الله عليه وسلم and his grandson Ya'qûb (Jacob) who was also known as Isrâ'il (Israel), and they called the people of Mûsa the 'Children of Israel' despite the fact that they appeared approximately 600 years after his time.

2 – Making Palestine their original homeland, despite the fact that the Torah itself confirms that Palestine was a foreign land to Ibrâhim (Abraham), Ishâq (Isaac), Ya'qûb (Jacob) and his sons who were born in Harrân and grew up there.

[1] Aramaeans – the original speakers of Aramaic or Syriac. [Translator]
[2] *Mufassal Al-'Arab wal-Yahud fi't-Târikh*, p. 86 ff; *Atlas Al-Qur'ân*, p. 41 ff.

Ibrahimi Mosque

Ibrâhim and his son Ismâ'il belonged to the Arab Aramaean tribes, which date back to several centuries before the appearance of the Israelites, the people of Moses and the Jews. Ibrâhim's era was a distinctly Arab era, which had no connection to the Jewish era. The Qur'ân itself mentions this:

﴿يَـٰٓأَهْلَ ٱلْكِتَـٰبِ لِمَ تُحَآجُّونَ فِىٓ إِبْرَٰهِيمَ وَمَآ أُنزِلَتِ ٱلتَّوْرَىٰةُ وَٱلْإِنجِيلُ إِلَّا مِنۢ بَعْدِهِۦٓ أَفَلَا تَعْقِلُونَ ٦٥ هَـٰٓأَنتُمْ هَـٰٓؤُلَآءِ حَـٰجَجْتُمْ فِيمَا لَكُم بِهِۦ عِلْمٌ فَلِمَ تُحَآجُّونَ فِيمَا لَيْسَ لَكُم بِهِۦ عِلْمٌۚ وَٱللَّهُ يَعْلَمُ وَأَنتُمْ لَا تَعْلَمُونَ ٦٦ مَا كَانَ إِبْرَٰهِيمُ يَهُودِيًّا وَلَا نَصْرَانِيًّا وَلَـٰكِن كَانَ حَنِيفًا مُّسْلِمًا وَمَا كَانَ مِنَ ٱلْمُشْرِكِينَ ٦٧﴾

"O people of the Scripture (Jews and Christians)! Why do you dispute about Ibrâhim (Abraham), while the *Tawrât* (Torah) and the *Injil* (Gospel) were not revealed till after him? Have you then no sense? Verily, you are those who have disputed about that of which you have knowledge. Why do you then dispute concerning that of which you have no knowledge? It is Allâh Who knows, and you know not. Ibrâhim (Abraham) was neither a Jew nor a Christian, but he was a true Muslim *Hanifa* (Islamic Monotheism — to worship none but Allâh Alone) and he was not of *Al-Mushrikun*."

[Qur'ân 3:65-67]

Muhammad ibn 'Abdullâh ﷺ was descended from Ibrâhim ﷺ, the father of the Prophets ﷺ, who was neither a Jew nor a Christian, but he was a *Hanif*, one who was true in faith, an upright man who had surrendered to Allâh, a Muslim.

* * *

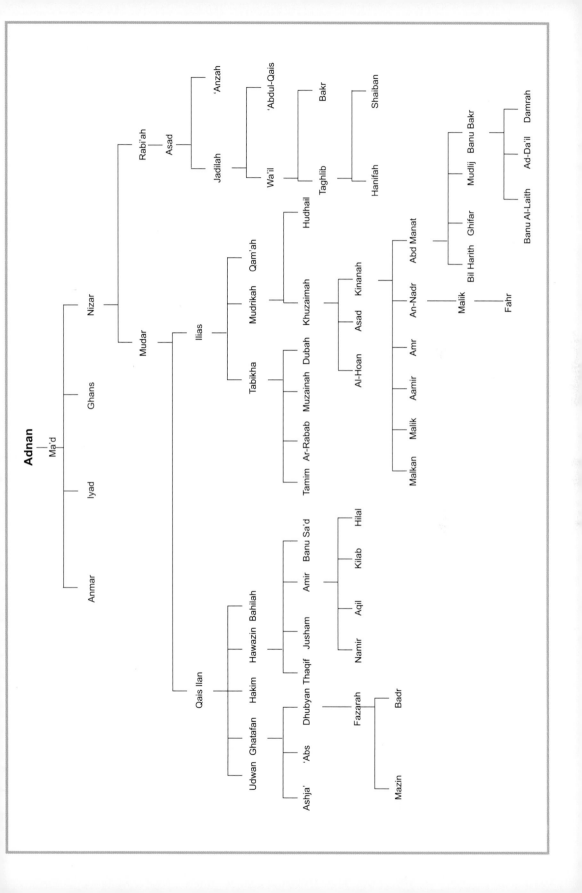

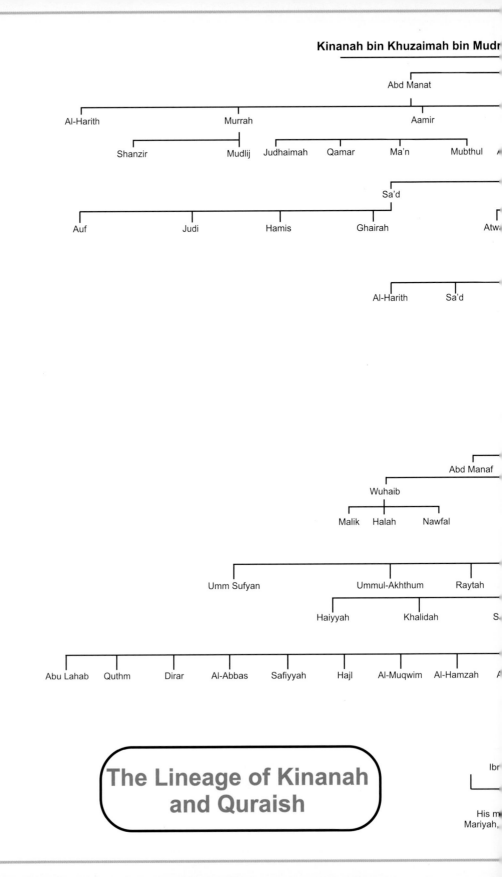

The Lineage of Kinanah and Quraish

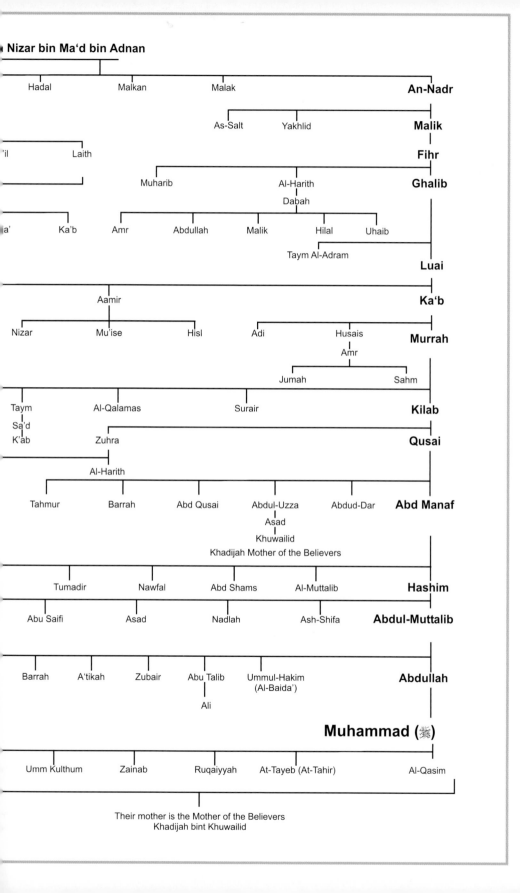

Nizar bin Ma'd bin Adnan

| Hadal | Malkan | Malak | **An-Nadr** |

| As-Salt | Yakhlid | **Malik** |

'il | Laith | **Fihr**

| Muharib | Al-Harith | **Ghalib**
Dabah

a' | Ka'b | Amr | Abdullah | Malik | Hilal | Uhaib

Taym Al-Adram

Luai

Aamir | **Ka'b**

Nizar | Mu'ise | Hisl | Adi | Husais | **Murrah**
Amr

Jumah | Sahm

Taym | Al-Qalamas | Surair | **Kilab**
Sa'd
K'ab | Zuhra | **Qusai**

Al-Harith

Tahmur | Barrah | Abd Qusai | Abdul-Uzza | Abdud-Dar | **Abd Manaf**
Asad
Khuwailid
Khadijah Mother of the Believers

Tumadir | Nawfal | Abd Shams | Al-Muttalib | **Hashim**

Abu Saifi | Asad | Nadlah | Ash-Shifa | **Abdul-Muttalib**

Barrah | A'tikah | Zubair | Abu Talib | Ummul-Hakim (Al-Baida') | **Abdullah**
Ali

Muhammad (ﷺ)

Umm Kulthum | Zainab | Ruqaiyyah | At-Tayeb (At-Tahir) | Al-Qasim

Their mother is the Mother of the Believers
Khadijah bint Khuwailid

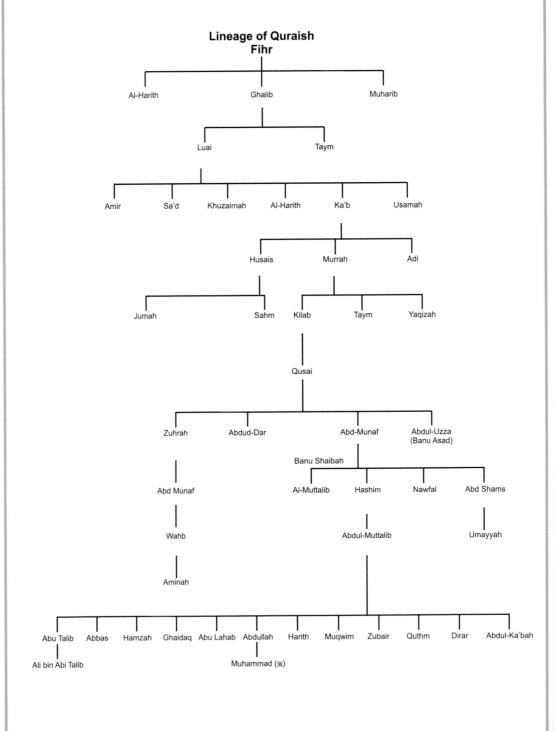

Lineage of Quraish
Fihr

- Al-Harith
- Ghalib
- Muharib

Ghalib:
- Luai
- Taym

Luai:
- Amir
- Sa'd
- Khuzaimah
- Al-Harith
- Ka'b
- Usamah

Ka'b:
- Husais
- Murrah
- Adi

Husais:
- Jumah
- Sahm

Murrah:
- Kilab
- Taym
- Yaqizah

Kilab:
- Qusai

Qusai:
- Zuhrah
- Abdud-Dar
- Abd-Munaf
- Abdul-Uzza (Banu Asad)

Abd-Munaf — Banu Shaibah:
- Al-Muttalib
- Hashim
- Nawfal
- Abd Shams

Zuhrah:
- Abd Munaf
  - Wahb
    - Aminah

Hashim:
- Abdul-Muttalib

Abd Shams:
- Umayyah

Abdul-Muttalib:
- Abu Talib
- Abbas
- Hamzah
- Ghaidaq
- Abu Lahab
- Abdullah
- Harith
- Muqwim
- Zubair
- Quthm
- Dirar
- Abdul-Ka'bah

Abu Talib:
- Ali bin Abi Talib

Abdullah:
- Muhammad (ﷺ)

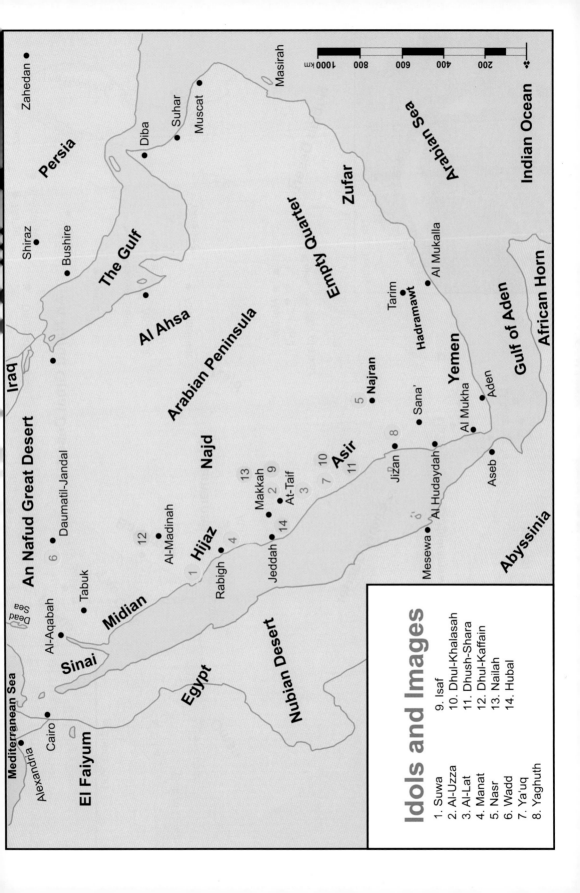

Idols and Images

1. Suwa
2. Al-Uzza
3. Al-Lat
4. Manat
5. Nasr
6. Wadd
7. Ya'uq
8. Yaghuth
9. Isaf
10. Dhul-Khalasah
11. Dhush-Shara
12. Dhul-Kaffain
13. Nailah
14. Hubal

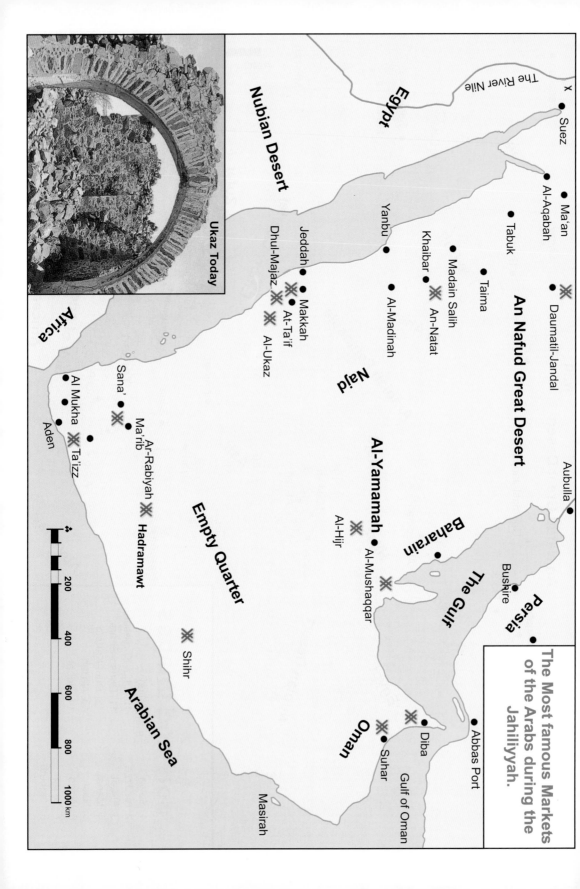

The Most famous Markets of the Arabs during the Jahiliyyah.

Ukaz Today

Nubian Desert

Egypt

The River Nile

x

Suez

Ma'an

Al-Aqabah

Tabuk

Daumatil-Jandal

An Nafud Great Desert

Taima

Khaibar

Madain Salih

An-Natat

Yanbu

Al-Madinah

Jeddah

Dhul-Majaz

Makkah

At-Ta'if

Al-Ukaz

Najd

Al-Yamamah

Al-Hijr

Al-Mushaqqar

Baharain

Aubulla

Bushire

Persia

Abbas Port

The Gulf

Africa

Sana'

Ma'rib

Al Mukha

Aden

Ta'izz

Ar-Rabiyah

Hadramawt

Empty Quarter

Shir

Oman

Suhar

Diba

Gulf of Oman

Masirah

Arabian Sea

200 400 600 800 1000 Km

The Most Famous Markets of the Arabs during the Jâhiliyyah

1. **Daumatil-Jandal:** which was held from the first day of Rabi' until the middle of the month, then it became less active but still continued until the beginning of the next month. Then the people would disperse until the following year. The tribes of Tay, Jadilah and Kalb were its closest neighbours.

2. **Al-Mushaqqar:** in Bahrain near Hajar. This was held from the first day of Jumâda Al-Akhirah until the end of the month. Persians used to come to this market from across the sea, bringing their goods with them. 'Abdul-Qais and Tamim were its closest neighbours.

3. **Suhâr:** which was held in Oman on the first day of Rajab and lasted for five days.

4. **Daba:** which was held on the last day of Rajab, and was attended by merchants from Sindh, India and China.

5. **Shihr or Shihr Mahrah:** which was held in the shade of the mountain on which was the grave of Hud صلى الله عليه وسلم. Banu Muhârib were its closest neighbours.

6. **Souq 'Aden:** which was held from the first day of Ramadân until the tenth.

7. **Souq San'a':** which was held from the middle of Ramadaan until the end.

8. **Al-Râbiyah:** in Hadramawt, among the tribe of Kindah. This was held on the same day as the Market of 'Ukâz, halfway through Dhul-Qa'dah until the end of the month.

9. **'Ukâz:** near 'Arafât. This was one of the greatest markets of the Arabs, attended by Quraish, Ghatafân, Hawâzin, Aslam and Al-Ahâbish. It ran from the middle to the end of Dhul-Qa'dah.

45

10. **Dhi'l-Majâz:** a market near 'Ukâz, which was held on the first day of Dhul-Hijjah and lasted until Yawmut-Tarwiyah (the 8th day of Dhul-Hijjah), after which they would go to Mina. To the north of Dhul-Majâz was Souq Mijannah.

11. **An-Natâh:** which was held in Khaibar from 'Āshura' until the end of Muharram.

12. **Al-Hijr:** which was held in Al-Yamâmah from 'Ashura until the end of Muharram also.

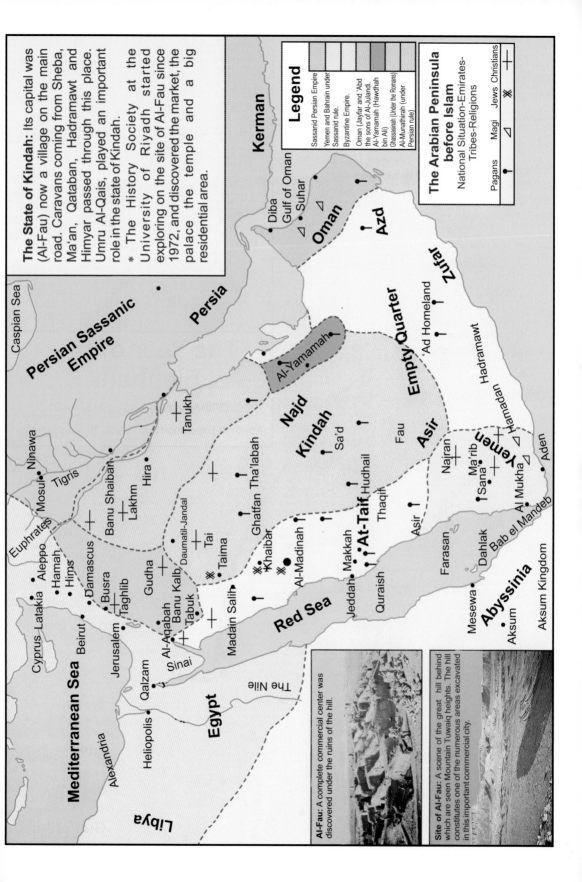

The State of Kindah: Its capital was (Al-Fau) now a village on the main road. Caravans coming from Sheba, Ma'an, Qataban, Hadramawt and Himyar passed through this place. Umru Al-Qais, played an important role in the state of Kindah.

* The History Society at the University of Riyadh started exploring on the site of Al-Fau since 1972, and discovered the market, the palace the temple and a big residential area.

Legend

	Sassanid Persian Empire
	Yemen and Bahrain under Sassanid rule.
	Byzantine Empire.
	Oman (Jayfar and 'Abd the sons of Al-Julandi.
	Al-Yamamah (Hawdhah bin Ali)
	Ghassassiah (Under the Romans)
	Al-Munathirah (under Persian rule)

The Arabian Peninsula before Islam
National Situation-Emirates-Tribes-Religions

Pagans • Magi ▽   Jews ※   Christians ✝

Caspian Sea

Persian Sassanic Empire

Kerman

Gulf of Oman

Diba

Suhar

Oman

Azd

Zufar

'Ad Homeland

Empty Quarter

Hadramawt

Hamadan

Aden

Persia

Al-Yamamah

Najd

Kindah

Sa'd

Fau

Asir

Tanukh

Mosul

Ninawa

Tigris

Hira

Lakhm

Banu Shaiban

Ghatfan Tha'labah

Khaibar

Daumatil-Jandal

Tai

Taima

Madain Salih

Tabuk

Banu Kalb

Al-Aqabah

Gudha

Taghlib

Busra

Damascus

Hims

Hamah

Aleppo

Latakia

Cyprus

Beirut

Jerusalem

Heliopolis

Alexandria

Mediterranean Sea

Euphrates

Libya

Qalzam

Sinai

The Nile

Egypt

Red Sea

Al-Madinah

Jeddah

Makkah

Quraish

Hudhail

Thaqif

At-Taif

Asir

Najran

Farasan

Dahlak

Ma'rib

Sana'

Al Mukha

Bab el Mandeb

Yemen

Abyssinia

Mesewa

Aksum

Aksum Kingdom

Al-Fau: A complete commercial center was discovered under the ruins of the hill.

Site of Al-Fau: A scene of the great hill behind which are seen Mountain Tuwaiq heights. The hill constitutes one of the numerous areas excavated in this important commercial city.

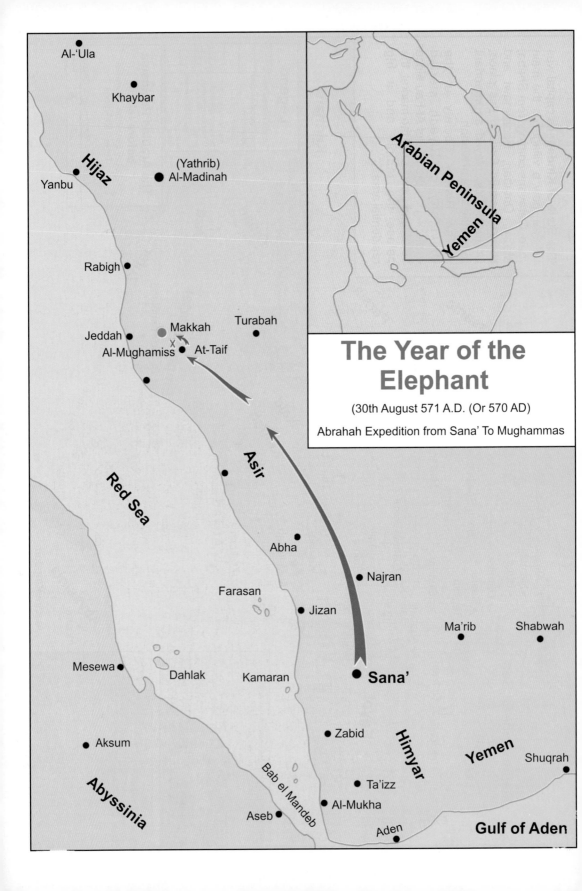

The Year of the Elephant
(30 August 571 or 570 CE)
The Birth of the Prophet ﷺ

The Abyssinians ruled Yemen after Himyar, and when Abrahah Al-Ashram became king, he built a huge church, called Al-Qullais, in San'a' beside Ghumdân, the like of which had never been seen at that time. He built it of marble and gold-plated wood. His aim was to divert the pilgrimage of the Arabs to this church and to abolish the Hajj to the Ka'bah. When news of that spread among the Arabs, a man from Kinânah got very angry. He went to Al-Qullais and defecated in it at night, then he fled home. When news of that reached Abrahah, he became angry and swore to go to the Ka'bah and destroy it. This year was called the Year of the Elephant.[1] Abrahah set out from San'a' to Khath'am, then to At-Tâ'if, from where he sent a man of his people to Makkah Al-Mukarramah, who confiscated the wealth of its people, including two hundred camels belonging to 'Abdul-Muttalib ibn Hâshim, and brought it to Abrahah. Then Abrahah sent another man to Makkah and told him: "Ask about the leader of the people of this city." So he asked, and he was told about 'Abdul-Muttalib[2] . He told him: "The king

---

[1] *As-Seerah An-Nabawiyyah*, 1/40; *Ar-Rawd Al-Unuf*, 1/63; *As-Seerah An-Nabawiyyah As-Sahihah* by Dr Akram Diya' Al-'Umari, 1/96; *Muhammad Rasul-Allâh* ﷺ , by Muhammad Rida, 17.

[2] 'Abdul-Muttalib: his mother was Salam bint Zayd An-Najjâriyyah. He was a man whose prayers were answered. He used to take some food from his table to feed the birds and animals on the mountaintops, hence he was known as *Mut'im At-Tayr* (Feeder of the Birds), and *Al-Fayyâd* (the Generous One). He was the one to whom Quraish turned at times of calamity or when there were important issues to decide, and he was the best among them in attitude and deeds. He lived for one hundred and twenty years. He used to tell his children to avoid wrongdoing, and towards the end of his life he refused to worship idols and he believed in Allâh alone. He is the one who uncovered Zamzam and prepared it to supply water to the

says that he has not come to wage war on you, he has only come to destroy this House." 'Abdul-Muttalib said to him: "By Allâh, we do not want to fight him and we do not have the power to do so. This is the Sacred House of Allâh, and the House of His Close Friend Ibrâhim. If He does not protect it, it is His House and sanctuary, and if He protects it, it will not be us who defended it." Then 'Abdul-Muttalib went with the envoy of Abrahah to meet the king. When permission was asked for 'Abdul-Muttalib to enter, they said to Abrahah: "This is the leader of Quraish," so he allowed him to enter. When Abrahah saw him he was impressed by him. He did not want to make him sit beneath him, but he also did not want the Abyssinians to see him sitting next to him on his throne. So Abrahah came down from his throne and sat on the carpet beside 'Abdul-Muttalib and asked him, "What do you want?" 'Abdul-Muttalib spoke about his camels which had been taken. Abrahah said: "I admired you when I first saw you, but now I have changed my mind. You speak to me about two hundred camels that I took from you, and you ignore the House that is the focal point of your religion and that of your forefathers which I have come to destroy, and you do not speak about it!" 'Abdul-Muttalib said: "I am the owner of the camels, and the House has an Owner Who will protect it." So Abrahah returned the camels to 'Abdul-Muttalib, and 'Abdul-Muttalib went back to Quraish and told them what had happened. He told them to go out of Makkah and seek refuge in the mountains and passes, fearing the attack of the army which outnumbered Quraish. Then 'Abdul-Muttalib took hold of the door-handle of the Ka'bah, and some of Quraish stood with him, praying to Allâh and seeking His help against Abrahah and his army. 'Abdul-Muttalib said, whilst holding on to the door-handle of the Ka'bah:

"O Allâh, any slave of Yours would protect his position, so protect Your House.

Do not let their cross or their power defeat Your power.

---

pilgrims. He used to honour the Prophet ﷺ when he was young, and he said: "This son of mine is destined for great things," because of what he had heard from the rabbis and priests before his birth and afterwards. 'Abdul-Muttalib died eight years after the Year of the Elephant. (At-Tabari, 2/277)

But if You are going to let them destroy our *Qiblah*, there must be a reason for that."

When Abrahah prepared to enter Makkah with his largest elephant, seeking to destroy the Ka'bah, every time they made the elephant face Makkah, it sat down and refused to move, but when they made it face any other direction it started to run. Whilst that was going on, Allâh sent against them birds in flocks, one after another, from the sea; birds like swifts or swallows, each of them carrying three stones, one in its beak and two in its feet, with which they pelted them. These stones were like chickpeas or lentils, and no sooner was any one of them struck with one but he died, but not all of them were struck. Then Allâh sent a flood which washed them into the sea. Those who were spared, turned and fled with Abrahah to Yemen. His body had started, to disintegrate, but he did not die in San'a' until his chest had fallen away from his heart. His son Yaksum succeeded him as king in 571 CE.

Based on the importance of this event, the Arabs started to date their history from this point. And Allâh says:

﴿أَلَمْ تَرَ كَيْفَ فَعَلَ رَبُّكَ بِأَصْحَابِ ٱلْفِيلِ ۝ أَلَمْ يَجْعَلْ كَيْدَهُمْ فِي تَضْلِيلٍ ۝ وَأَرْسَلَ عَلَيْهِمْ طَيْرًا أَبَابِيلَ ۝ تَرْمِيهِم بِحِجَارَةٍ مِّن سِجِّيلٍ ۝ فَجَعَلَهُمْ كَعَصْفٍ مَّأْكُولٍ ۝﴾

"Have you (O Muhammad ﷺ) not seen how your Lord dealt with the Owners of the Elephant? [The Elephant Army which came from Yemen under the command of Abrahah Al-Ashram intending to destroy the Ka'bah at Makkah. Did He not make their plot go astray? And He sent against them birds, in flocks, striking them with stones of *Sijjil* (baked clay). And He made them like (an empty field of) stalks (of which the corn has been eaten up by cattle)."

[Qur'ân 105: 1-5]

By means of the defeat of the Abyssinians, Allâh protected His sacred House from being destroyed, and it subsequently became the *Qiblah* for Muslims in all parts of the globe.

* * *

51

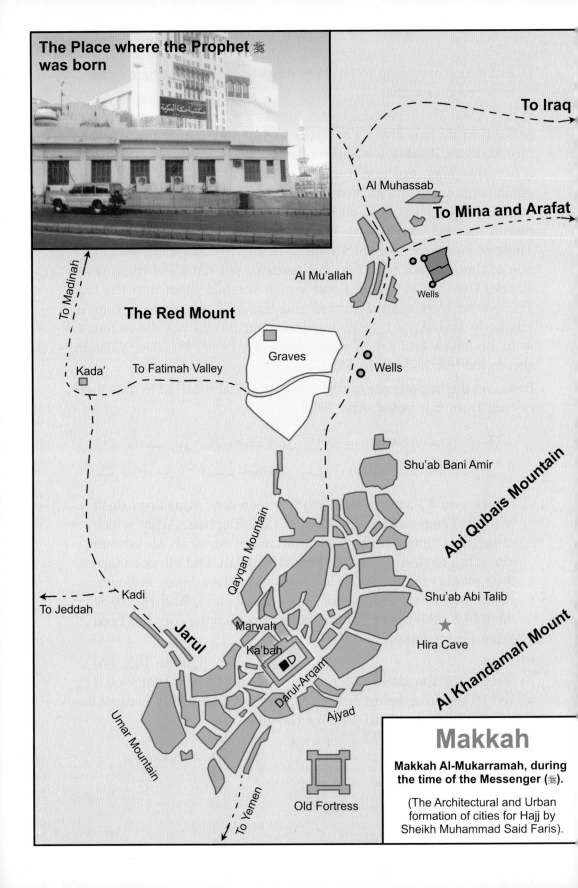

The Place where the Prophet ﷺ was born

To Iraq

Al Muhassab

To Mina and Arafat

Al Mu'allah

Wells

To Madinah

The Red Mount

Graves

Kada'

To Fatimah Valley

Wells

Shu'ab Bani Amir

Abi Qubais Mountain

Qayqan Mountain

Shu'ab Abi Talib

Kadi

To Jeddah

Hira Cave

Jarul

Marwah

Ka'bah

Darul-Arqam

Al Khandamah Mount

Umar Mountain

Ajyad

To Yemen

Old Fortress

Makkah

Makkah Al-Mukarramah, during the time of the Messenger (ﷺ).

(The Architectural and Urban formation of cities for Hajj by Sheikh Muhammad Said Faris).

The Lineage of the Prophet (ﷺ)

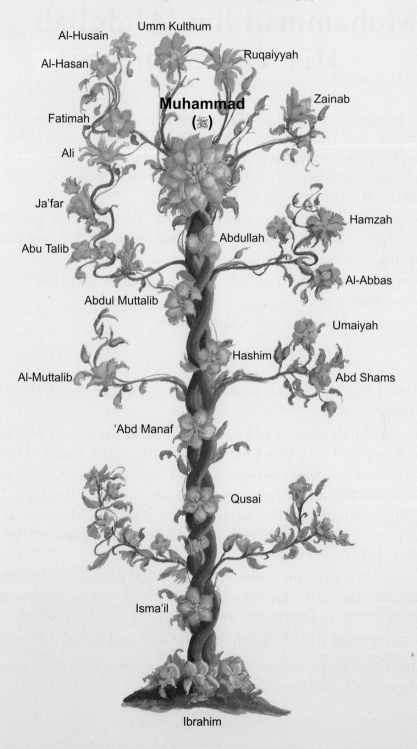

Umm Kulthum

Al-Husain

Ruqaiyyah

Al-Hasan

Muhammad
(ﷺ)

Zainab

Fatimah

Ali

Ja'far

Hamzah

Abdullah

Abu Talib

Al-Abbas

Abdul Muttalib

Umaiyah

Hashim

Al-Muttalib

Abd Shams

'Abd Manaf

Qusai

Isma'il

Ibrahim

Muhammad ibn 'Abdullâh ﷺ
His Noble Lineage

His lineage is as follows: Muhammad ibn 'Abdullâh ibn 'Abdul-Muttalib ibn Hâshim ibn 'Abd Manâf ibn Qusai ibn Kilâb ibn Murrah ibn Ka'b ibn Lu'ai ibn Ghâlib ibn Fihr ibn Mâlik[1] ibn An-Nadr ibn Kinânah ibn Khuzaimah ibn Mudrikah ibn Ilyâs ibn Mudar ibn Nizâr ibn Ma'ad ibn 'Adnân.

The genealogists differed concerning the details of his genealogy from 'Adnân back to Ismâ'il, but they are agreed that it goes back to Ismâ'il.

Umm Salamah (Hind bint Abi Umayyah), the wife of the Prophet ﷺ, narrated:

"I heard the Messenger of Allâh ﷺ say:

«مَعَدُّ بْنُ عَدْنَانَ بْنِ أُدَد بْنِ زَنْد بْنِ يَرَى بْنِ أَعْرَاق الثَّرَى»

'Ma'd ibn 'Adnân ibn Udad ibn Zand ibn Yara ibn A'râq At-Thara.'"

Umm Salamah said: "Zand was Al-Hamaisa', and Yara was Nabt, and A'râq At-Thara was Ismâ'il ibn Ibrâhim." (At-Tabari, 2/271)

In *As-Seerah An-Nabawiyyah*: " 'Adnân ibn Udad ibn Muqwim ibn Nâhur ibn Terah ibn Ya'rub ibn Yashjub ibn Nâbit ibn Ismâ'il ibn Ibrâhim al-Khalil ﷺ. This is how it was stated by Muhammad ibn Ishâq ibn Yasâr in *As-Seerah*." (*As-Seerah An-Nabawiyyah* by Ibn Kathir, 1/76).

His mother was Āminah bint Wahb ibn 'Abd Manâf ibn Zuhrah ibn Kilâb ibn Murrah ibn Ka'b ibn Lu'ai... So he ﷺ was the noblest of the sons of Adam in lineage on both his father's and his mother's side.

It was narrated that Wâthilah ibn Al-Asqa' said that the Messenger

---

[1] He is Quraish, so whoever is descended from him is Qurashi (of Quraish). *As-Seerah An-Nabawiyyah* by Ibn Kathir, 1/84.

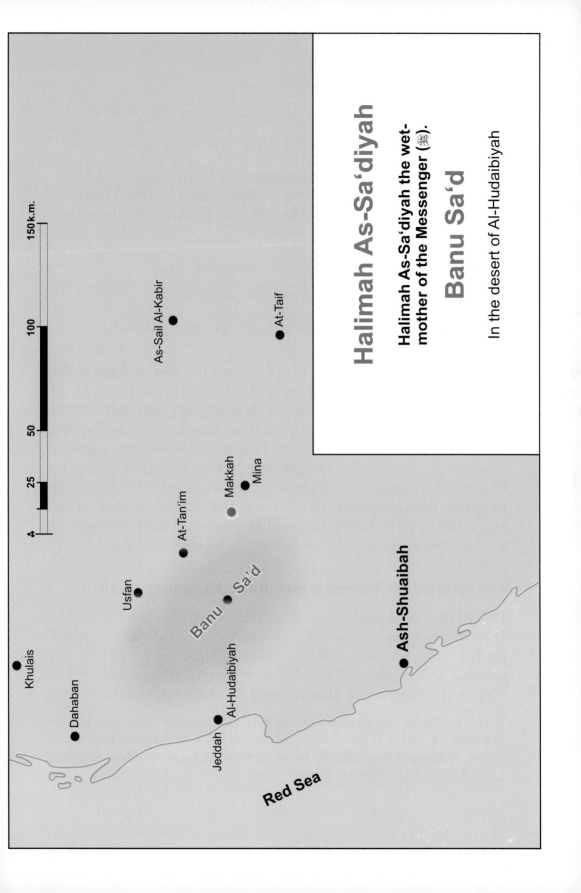

Halimah As-Saʻdiyah

Halimah As-Saʻdiyah the wet-mother of the Messenger (ﷺ).

Banu Saʻd

In the desert of Al-Hudaibiyah

of Allâh ﷺ said:

«إِنَّ اللهَ اصْطَفَى كِنَانَةَ مِنْ وَلَدِ إِسْمَاعِيلَ، وَاصْطَفَى قُرَيْشًا مِنْ كِنَانَةَ، وَاصْطَفَى هَاشِمًا مِنْ قُرَيْشٍ، وَاصْطَفَانِي مِنْ بَنِي هَاشِمٍ»

"Allâh chose Kinânah from among the children of Ismâ'il, and He chose Quraish from among Kinânah, and He chose Hâshim from among Quraish, and He chose me from among the tribe of Hâshim." (Reported by Muslim).

Allâh says:

﴿ٱللَّهُ أَعْلَمُ حَيْثُ يَجْعَلُ رِسَالَتَهُ﴾

"Allâh knows best with whom to place His Message."

[Qur'ân 6:124]

He is the Leader of the sons of Adam and the best of them in this world and in the Hereafter; he is Abul-Qâsim (the father of Al-Qâsim) and the father of Ibrâhim; Muhammad, Ahmad; *Al-Mâhi* (the eraser) by means of whom *Kufr* is erased; *Al-'Âqib* (the final Messenger) after whom there is no Prophet; *Al-Hâshir* (the gatherer) at whose feet people will be gathered;[1] the Prophet of Mercy; the Prophet of repentance; the Prophet of decisive battles; the Seal of the Prophets; the Conqueror; the Witness; the bringer of glad tidings and warnings; the shining lamp; Allâh made him kind and merciful towards the believers, and a reminder, a blessing and a guide...[2]

The paternal uncles and aunts of the Messenger of Allâh ﷺ

The children of 'Abdul-Muttalib included ten males: 'Abdullâh, Abu Tâlib (whose name was 'Abd Manâf) and Az-Zubair – whose mother was Fâtimah bint 'Amr Al-Makhzumi; Al-'Abbâs (the ancestor of the Abbasid caliphs) and Dirâr – whose mother was Natilah Al-'Umariyyah; Hamzah and Al-Muqwim – whose mother

---

[1] i.e., on the Day of Resurrection, as they will be resurrected after him; or during the period of his Message (which will last until the Hour begins).

[2] See: *Muhammad Rasul-Allâh* ﷺ by Muhammad Rida, p. 22, where he quotes the *Ahâdith* which mention the names and titles of the Prophet ﷺ.

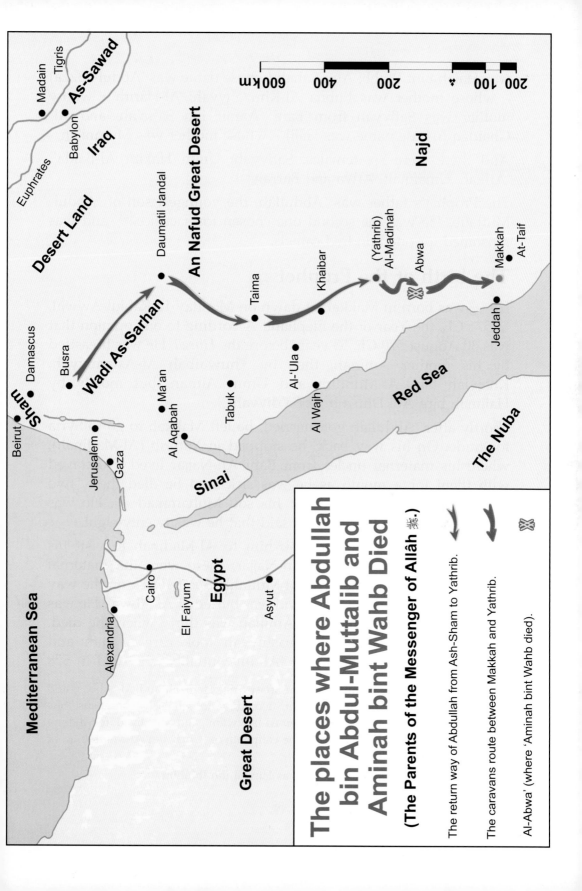

The places where Abdullah bin Abdul-Muttalib and Aminah bint Wahb Died

(The Parents of the Messenger of Allâh ﷺ.)

The return way of Abdullah from Ash-Sham to Yathrib.

The caravans route between Makkah and Yathrib.

Al-Abwa' (where 'Aminah bint Wahb died).

was Hâlah bint Wahb; Abu Lahab (whose name was 'Abdul-'Uzza) – whose mother was Lubna Al-Khuzâ'iyyah; Al-Hârith – whose mother was Safiyyah from Bani 'Aamir ibn Sa'sa'ah; and Al-Ghaidâq (whose name was Hajl) – whose mother was Mumni'ah.

And there were six females: Safiyyah, Umm Hakim Al-Baida', 'Ātikah, Umaimah, Arwa and Barrah.[1]

The Prophet's father was 'Abdullâh, the youngest son of 'Abdul-Muttalib. He was the second one chosen for sacrifice,[2] and was ransomed for one hundred camels.

The birth of the Prophet ﷺ

He ﷺ was born in Makkah at dawn on Monday 12 Rabiul-Awwal, in 571 CE, the Year of the Elephant. According to one opinion that was 30 August 570 CE, 53 years before the *Hijrah*. He was breastfed by his mother Āminah, then by Thuwaibah Al-Aslamiyyah, Khawlah bint Al-Mundhir and Umm Aiman, but mostly by Halimah bint Abi Dhu'aib As-Sa'diyyah.

Shortly after 'Abdullâh got married, he left Makkah to go to Syria for trade. On his way back, he stopped in Yathrib (Al-Madinah), where his maternal uncles from Bani An-Najjâr lived. He stayed with them for a month as he was sick, and he died there, two months after the conception of his son Muhammad ﷺ. He was twenty-five years old, or it was said that he was twenty-eight.

In 575-576 CE, his mother took him to Al-Madinah to visit his maternal uncles from Banu An-Najjâr; these were the maternal uncles of his grandfather 'Abdul-Muttalib. She fell sick on the way back to Makkah, and she died and was buried at Al-Abwa'. He was six years old at the time, and Āminah was thirty when she died. Umm Aiman Barakah Al-Habashiyyah took care of him and brought him to his grandfather 'Abdul-Muttalib, who died in 578

---

[1] None of his uncles became Muslim apart from Hamzah and Al-'Abbâs, and his aunt Safiyyah became Muslim, according to scholarly consensus. She was the mother of Az-Zubair ibn Al-'Awwâm, and she lived for a long time. She died in 20 AH, during the caliphate of 'Umar ibn Al-Khattâb ؓ, at the age of seventy-three.

[2] The first one chosen for sacrifice was Ismâ'il ibn Ibrâhim.

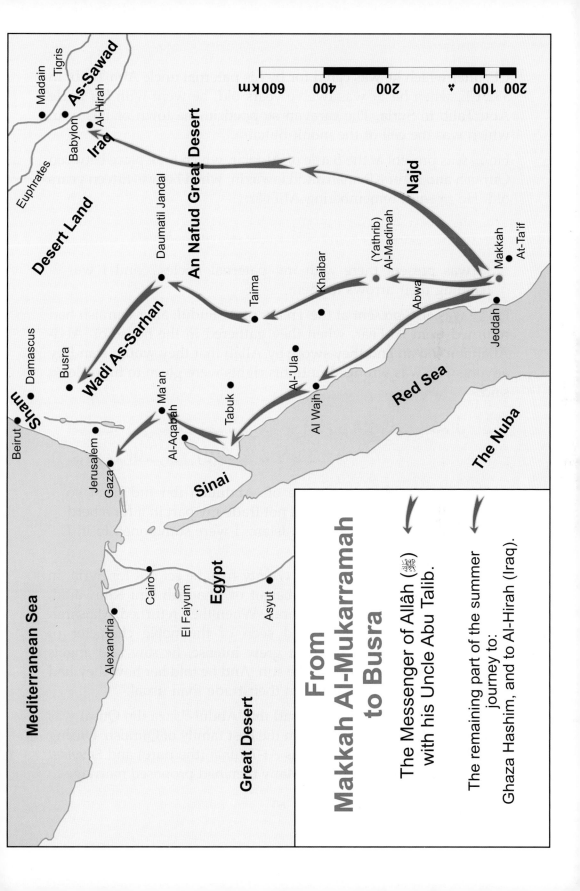

From
Makkah Al-Mukarramah
to Busra

The Messenger of Allâh (ﷺ)
with his Uncle Abu Talib.

The remaining part of the summer
journey to:
Ghaza Hashim, and to Al-Hirah (Iraq).

CE, after which he was cared for by his paternal uncle Abu Tâlib. In 582 CE, when he ﷺ was twelve years old, he went with his uncle Abu Tâlib to Syria. The caravan stopped in the town of Busra, in which was the cell of the monk Buhaira.

He ﷺ was present at the Battle of Al-Fijâr, which took place between Quraish and all of Kinânah and Hawâzin, when he was fifteen years old. He ﷺ said, remembering Al-Fijâr:

«قَدْ حَضَرْتُهُ مَعَ عُمُومَتِي. . كُنْتُ أَنْبُلُ عَلَى أَعْمَامِي»

"I was present there with my paternal uncles... and I was handing their arrows to them."

He ﷺ was also present at the Treaty of Al-Fudul, after Quraish had returned from Al-Fijâr, when they gathered in the house of 'Abd-Allâh ibn Jud'ân and they swore by Allâh that they would stand by anyone who was wronged until his rights were given to him. He ﷺ said:

«مَا أُحِبُّ أَنَّ لِي بِحَلْفٍ حَضَرْتُهُ فِي دَارِ ابْنِ جُدْعَانَ حُمْرَ النَّعَمِ. . تَحَالَفُوا أَنْ يَكُونُوا مَعَ الْمَظْلُومِ. . وَلَوْ دُعِيتُ بِهِ لَأَجَبْتُ. .»

"I was present in the house of 'Abdullâh ibn Jud'ân at so excellent a treaty that I would not trade my part in it for a herd of red camels; and if now, in Islam, I were summoned to it, I would gladly respond."

When he ﷺ reached the age of twenty-five, he set out for Syria, in 595 CE, to engage in trade on behalf of Khadijah bint Khuwailid, accompanied by her slave Maisarah. When they returned, Maisarah told Khadijah of what he had seen of the noble character of Muhammad ﷺ. When the heat grew intense, he saw two angels shading Muhammad ﷺ from the sun. And he told her how they had made many more times profit in their trade than usual.

Khadijah bint Khuwailid ibn Asad ibn 'Abdul-'Uzza ibn Qusai was an intelligent, noble woman from the best family of Quraish. During the Jâhiliyyah she was known as *At-Tâhirah* (the pure) and *Sayyidat Quraish* (the Lady of Quraish). Many men had proposed marriage to

The Monastery of the Monk Buhaira from the inside

The Monastery of the Monk Buhaira from the outside

The Mosque of the Kneeding Place of the Camel from the inside

↑ The Mosque of the Kneeling Place of the Camel from inside.

her but she did not accept. When Muhammad ﷺ came back from his journey to Syria, and she heard what she heard from Maisarah, she sent someone to him to suggest marriage, and the Messenger of Allâh ﷺ married her when he was twenty-five and Khadijah ؓ was forty.

Khadijah ؓ bore all the children of the Messenger of Allâh ﷺ apart from Ibrâhim, who was born to Mâriyah At-Qibtiyyah. The oldest of his children was Al-Qâsim, then Al-Tayyib (*Al-Tahir*), then Ruqaiyyah, then Zainab, then Umm Kulthum, then Fâtimah.

He ﷺ was given the nickname of *Al-Ameen* (the Trustworthy), by consensus of the people of Makkah, because of his good character. They used to entrust things to him for safekeeping, until he migrated to Al- Madinah, when he left 'Ali ؓ behind in his place. 'Ali remained in Makkah until he had returned all entrusted items to their owners, then he migrated to Al-Madinah.

When the time of the *Wahy* (Revelation) was approaching, seclusion was made dear to him, so he would go and seclude himself in the Cave of Hira', where he would worship for many nights. His worship was in accordance with the religion of Ibrâhim ﷺ. When he reached the age of forty, Jibril came to him in the cave of Hira', on the seventeenth of Ramadân in his forty-first year. At that time his age according to the lunar calendar was 40 years, 6 months and 8 days. That date was equivalent to 6 August 610 CE.

The first free man to believe in him was Abu Bakr, the first boy was 'Ali, the first woman was Khadijah, the first freed slave was Zaid ibn Hârithah, and the first slave was Bilâl ibn Rabâh Al-Habashi.

ount Hira'

"Read!" The light of guidance shone from the cave of Hira' and revived a nation who alongside the people whose lands they conquered produced a new civilization that represented the pinnacle of human achievements.

The Cave of Hira'

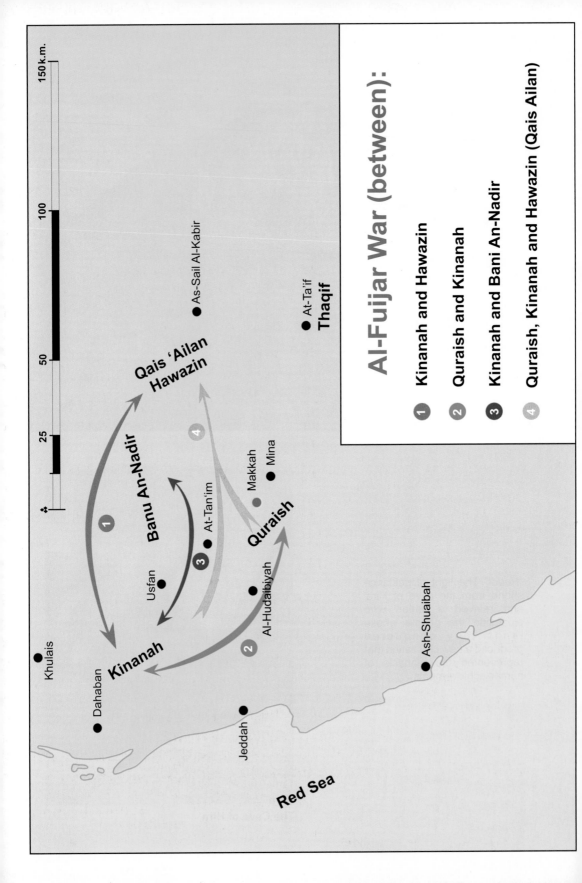

The War of Al-Fijâr
(the Sacrilegious War)
(580-90 CE)

Al-Fijâr means sacrilege. This war was so called because the fighting took place during the Sacred Month, so they committed an act of sacrilege by violating the sanctity of that month. In *Lisân Al-'Arab* [a famous Arabic-language dictionary] it says, under the heading *Fajara: Ayyâmul-Fijâr* (the days of sacrilege) refers to battles that took place among the Arabs in which they violated the sacred limits in 'Ukâz. There were four such incidents:

The first took place between Kinânah and Hawâzin (Qais 'Ailân).

The second took place between Quraish and Kinânah.

The third took place between Kinânah and Bani Nadr ibn Mu'âwiyah.

The fourth took place between Quraish and all of Kinânah and Hawâzin (Qais 'Ailân).

The Prophet ﷺ was present at the last war of *Fijâr*, when he was fifteen years old.

The cause of the last war of Al-Fijâr:

An-Nu'mân ibn Al-Mundhir, the ruler of Al-Hirah, sent some camels carrying trade goods of his to the market of 'Ukâz, and 'Urwatur-Rijâl from Banu Hawâzin gave protection to the caravan. They stopped at an oasis called Awârah, where Al-Barrâd, who was from Banu Kinânah, attacked 'Urwah and killed him, then fled to Khaibar where he hid. He met Bishr ibn Abi Khâzim Al-Asadi, the poet, and told him what had happened, and told him to tell 'Abdullâh ibn Jud'ân, Hishâm ibn Al-Mughirah, Harb ibn Umayyah, Nawfal ibn Mu'âwiyah Al-Dailami and Bal'a' ibn Qais about it. So he came to 'Ukâz and told them, and they went out

65

seeking sanctuary in the *Haram*. News of that reached Qais that day, so Abu Bara' the leader of Hawâzin said: "Quraish have deceived us." So they set out in pursuit of them, and caught up with them after they had entered the *Haram*. A man from Banu 'Aamir whose name was Al-Adram ibn Shu'aib called out to them at the top of his voice: "We shall meet at the same time next year (to fight), and we will not go back on our word."

The market of 'Ukâz was not held that year. Quraish and others – Kinânah, Asad ibn Khuzaimah and the Ahâbesh (black troops) who had ties with them – spent that year preparing for this war. Qais 'Ailân also prepared for war. When the time came, the leaders of Quraish – 'Abdullâh ibn Jud'ân, Hishâm ibn Al-Mughirah, Harb ibn Umayyah, Abu Uhaihah Sa'eed ibn Al-'Aas, 'Utbah ibn Rabi'ah, Al-'Aas ibn Wâ'il, Mu'ammar ibn Habib Al-Jumahi, 'Ikrimah ibn 'Aamir ibn Hâshim ibn 'Abd Manâf ibn 'Abdud-Dâr – all went out separately. They did not have a single leader to unite them, or it was said that they were led by 'Abdullâh ibn Jud'ân.

Among Qais 'Ailân there were Abu Bara' 'Aamir ibn Mâlik ibn Ja'far, Subay' and Rabi'ah the two sons of Mu'âwiyah An-Nadri, Duraid ibn As-Simmah, Mas'ud ibn Ma'tab, Abu Ma'tab, Abu 'Urwah ibn Mas'ud, 'Awf ibn Abi Hârithah al-Murri and 'Abbâs ibn Ri'l As-Sulami. These were the leaders and chiefs.

And it was said that rather they were led by Abu Bara', in whose hand was the banner and he was the one who organized their ranks for battle. They met in battle and initially Qais and Kinânah defeated Hawâzin and those who had joined them, then the battle turned and at the end of the day Quraish and Kinânah defeated Qais and killed many of them, until 'Utbah ibn Rabee'ah called out for reconciliation. So they reconciled on the basis that the number of dead would be counted, and Quraish paid restitution to Qais for those who had been killed above the number of their own slain. So they lay down their weapons and Quraish and Qais departed.

The Prophet ﷺ was present with his paternal uncles at the battle of Al-Fijâr, and he said: "I used to hand arrows to my uncles."

The Treaty of Al-Fudul
(the Treaty of the Scented Ones)

This took place after Quraish came back from the Sacrilegious wars and it was the most noble of treaties, advocated by Az-Zubair ibn 'Abdul-Muttalib. Banu Hâshim, Zuhrah and Taim gathered in the house of 'Abdullâh ibn Jud'ân, who prepared food for them, and they swore by Allâh that they would stand by the one who was wronged until he was given his rights.

The Prophet ﷺ said:

> "I was present in the house of 'Abdullâh ibn Jud'ân, with Hâshim, Zuhrah and Taim bin Murrah, at so excellent a treaty that I would not trade my part in it for a herd of red camels; and if now, in Islam, I were summoned to it, I would gladly respond."

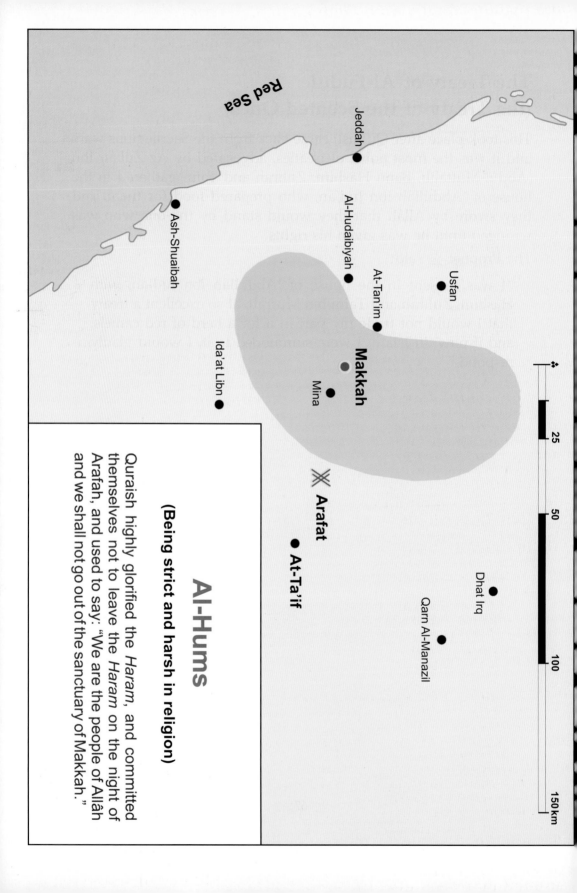

Red Sea

Jeddah

Ash-Shuaibah

Al-Hudaibiyah

At-Tan'im

Usfan

Ida'at Libn

Makkah

Mina

✕ **Arafat**

● At-Ta'if

Dhat Irq

Qarn Al-Manazil

25   50   100   150km

Al-Hums
(Being strict and harsh in religion)

Quraish highly glorified the *Haram*, and committed themselves not to leave the *Haram* on the night of Arafah, and used to say: "We are the people of Allâh and we shall not go out of the sanctuary of Makkah."

The Hums

Hums is a word which denotes extremism, including in the matters of religion. (*Lisânul-'Arab*: *Hamasa*).

Quraish introduced the idea of the Hums

Ibn Ishâq said:

I do not know whether it was before or after the Year of the Elephant that Quraish invented the idea of the *Hums* and put it into practice. They said: "We are the sons of Ibrâhim, the people of the holy sanctuary, the guardians of the House and the citizens of Makkah. No one else among the Arabs has rights like ours or a position like ours. The Arabs recognize none as they recognize us, so do not attach the same importance to land outside the sanctuary as you do to the sanctuary, for if you do, the Arabs will lose respect for your sacred position and they will say, 'They have given the same importance to the land outside the sanctuary as to the sanctuary.'" So they gave up stopping at 'Arafa and the departure therefrom, even though they recognized that these were part of the rituals of *Hajj* and the religion of Ibrâhim. They believed that the other Arabs should stop there and depart from there, but they said: "We are the people of the sanctuary and it is not appropriate that we should leave the sanctuary and venerate any other place as we, the *Hums*, honour it, for the *Hums* are the people of the sanctuary." They then proceeded to apply the same rules on other Arabs who were descended from them, whether they were born within or outside the sanctuary.[1]

The tribes who believed in the Hums along with Quraish

Kinânah and Khuzâ'ah joined Quraish in that. Ibn Hishâm said: Abu 'Ubaidah An-Nahwi told me that Banu 'Aamir ibn Sa'sa'ah ibn

---

[1] Ibn Hishâm, 1/184

69

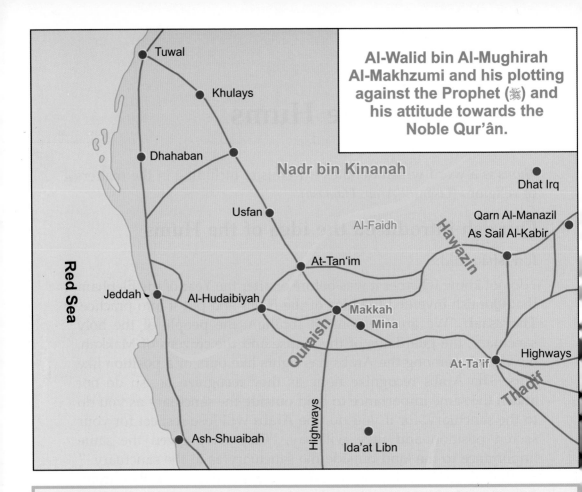

Al-Walid bin Al-Mughirah Al-Makhzumi and his plotting against the Prophet (ﷺ) and his attitude towards the Noble Qur'ân.

Al-Walid ibn Al-Mughirah came to attend the Hajj, and he said: "O Quraish, this season has come and the delegations of the Arabs will come to you. They have heard about your companion, so you should agree on what you will say to them and not contradict one another lest you appear to be liars." They said: "O Abu 'Abd Shams, tell us what to say and we will say it." He said, "No, tell me what you think and I will listen." They said: "We will say that he is a soothsayer." He said: "No, by Allâh, he is not a soothsayer. We know about soothsayers and what he says is not like the muttering of a soothsayer." They said: "We will say that he is insane." He said: "He is not insane. We have seen insanity and we know what it is. He does not have spasms or whispers like the insane." They said: "We will say that he is a poet." He said: "He is not a poet. We know all about poetry and its various types. This is not poetry." They said: "We will say that he is a sorcerer." He said: "He is not a sorcerer. We have seen the sorcerers and their magic and tying knots and blowing on them." They said: "Then what should we say, O Abu 'Abd Shams?" He said: "By Allâh, his words are sweet. Whatever you say will be known to be false. The best you can do is to say that he is a sorcerer who creates division between a man and his father or brother or wife or clan."

After agreeing on that, they went away, and they started to wait on the routes by which people came to Hajj. No one passed by them but they warned him about him (the Prophet ﷺ). Then Allâh revealed concerning Al-Walid ibn Al-Mughirah the words:

"Leave Me Alone (to deal) with whom I created lonely (without any wealth and children, i.e., Al-Walid bin Al-Mughirah Al-Makhzumi). And then granted him resources in abundance. And children to be by his side. And made life smooth and comfortable for him. After all that he desires that I should give more. Nay! Verily, he has been opposing Our *Ayât* (proofs, evidences, verses, lessons, signs, revelations, etc.)." [Qur'ân 74:11-16]

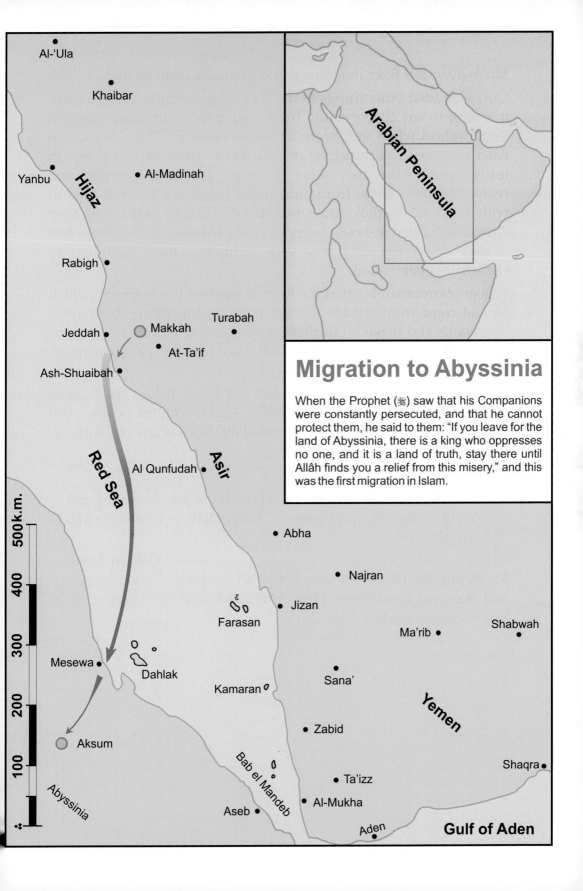

Al-'Ula

Khaibar

Yanbu

Hijaz

Al-Madinah

Rabigh

Turabah

Jeddah

Makkah

At-Ta'if

Ash-Shuaibah

Red Sea

Asir

Al Qunfudah

Arabian Peninsula

Migration to Abyssinia

When the Prophet (ﷺ) saw that his Companions were constantly persecuted, and that he cannot protect them, he said to them: "If you leave for the land of Abyssinia, there is a king who oppresses no one, and it is a land of truth, stay there until Allâh finds you a relief from this misery," and this was the first migration in Islam.

Abha

Najran

Jizan

Farasan

Ma'rib

Shabwah

500 k.m.

400

300

Mesewa

Dahlak

Sana'

200

Kamaran

Yemen

100

Aksum

Zabid

Shaqra

Bab el Mandeb

Ta'izz

Abyssinia

Aseb

Al-Mukha

Aden

Gulf of Aden

Mu'âwiyah ibn Bakr ibn Hawâzin also joined them in that.

Quraish added other things to the *Hums*, for example: they thought it wrong to eat cheese made from sour milk or to make clarified butter (ghee) when they were in a state of *Ihrâm*. They would not enter tents made of camelhair or seek shelter from the sun except in leather tents when they were in *Ihrâm*. They went further and refused to allow those from outside the sanctuary to bring food in with them when they came for *Hajj* or *'Umrah*, nor could they circumambulate the house except in the garments of the *Hums*, and if they could not find any such garments, then they had to circumambulate naked.

Whoever circumambulated the Ka'bah wearing the clothes in which he had come from outside the sanctuary had to throw them away afterwards and make no further use of them; neither he nor anyone else could ever touch them. The Arabs used to call these garments *al-Luqa* (thrown away).

The Messenger of Allâh ﷺ opposed the *Hums* before his mission began. He stopped on a camel of his in 'Arafât with the people. And after his mission began Islam abolished all the customs of the *Hums*:

﴿ثُمَّ أَفِيضُوا۟ مِنْ حَيْثُ أَفَاضَ ٱلنَّاسُ وَٱسْتَغْفِرُوا۟ ٱللَّهَ إِنَّ ٱللَّهَ غَفُورٌ رَّحِيمٌ ۝١٩٩﴾

"Then depart from the place whence all the people depart and ask Allâh for His forgiveness. Truly, Allâh is Oft-Forgiving, Most-Merciful."

[Qur'ân 2:199]

So, during the *Hajj* of the Prophet ﷺ all the people stood in 'Arafat and departed from there. Thus Allâh abolished the *Hums* and the innovations introduced by Quraish.

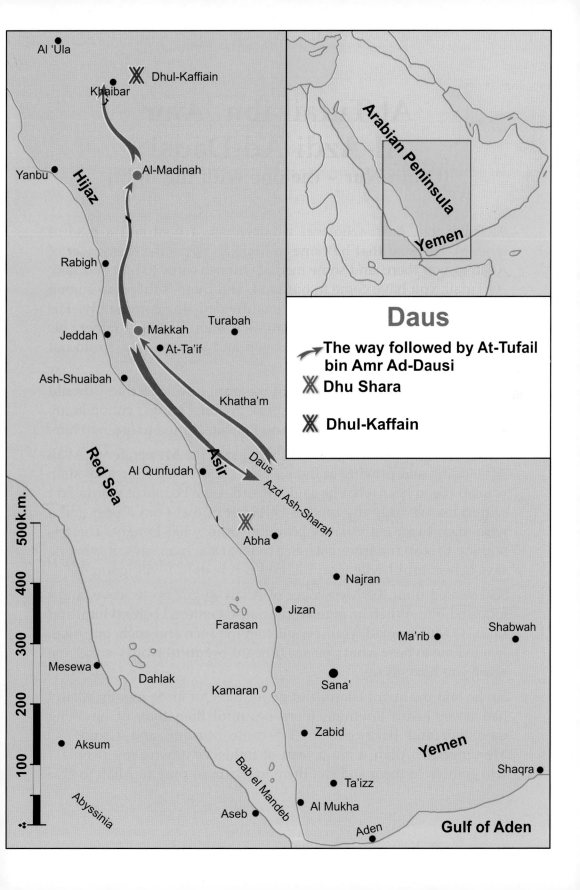

Al 'Ula

Dhul-Kaffiain

Khaibar

Yanbu

Hijaz

Al-Madinah

Rabigh

Turabah

Jeddah

Makkah

At-Ta'if

Ash-Shuaibah

Khatha'm

Asir

Daus

Red Sea

Al Qunfudah

Azd Ash-Sharah

Abha

Najran

Jizan

Farasan

Ma'rib

Shabwah

Mesewa

Dahlak

Kamaran

Sana'

200

Zabid

Yemen

100

Aksum

Shaqra

Bab el Mandeb

Ta'izz

Abyssinia

Aseb

Al Mukha

Aden

Gulf of Aden

Arabian Peninsula

Yemen

Daus

➤ The way followed by At-Tufail bin Amr Ad-Dausi

✖ Dhu Shara

✖ Dhul-Kaffain

500 k.m.

400

300

At-Tufail ibn 'Amr
Al-Azdi Ad-Dausi
(Dhun-Nur – the one with the light)

At-Tufail ibn 'Amr, who was a nobleman, a poet and a man of wisdom, narrated that he came to Makkah when the Messenger of Allâh ﷺ was there, and some men of Quraish came to him and said: "O Tufail, you have come to our land, and there is this man among us who is getting stronger. He has divided our community. His words are like sorcery; he separates a man from his father, his brother and his wife. We fear for you and your people, so do not speak to him or listen to him."

He said: By Allâh, they kept on at me until I decided that I should not listen to anything he said, or speak to him. I stuffed cotton in my ears lest I hear anything he said, and I never wanted to listen to him.

Then I went to the mosque, and there I saw the Messenger of Allâh ﷺ standing and praying at the Ka'bah. I stood near him, and Allâh wanted me to hear what he said. I heard some beautiful words, so I said to myself: May my mother be bereft of me! I am a poet and a wise man; I can tell what is beautiful from what is ugly. There is nothing to stop me from listening to what the man says. If what he says is beautiful I will accept it, and if it is ugly I will ignore it.

So I waited until the Messenger of Allâh ﷺ got up to leave, and I followed him. When he entered his house I entered behind him, and said: "O Muhammad, your people told me such and such, but Allâh wanted me to hear what you say. I heard beautiful words, so tell me what you have to say."

So, he told me about Islam, and he recited Qur'ân to me. By Allâh I had never heard anything more beautiful than that, or anything more fair and balanced. So, I became Muslim, and I said: "O Messenger of Allâh, I am a man of influence among my people. I will go back to them and call them to Islam, so pray to Allâh to give me a sign that will help me to call them." He said: "O Allâh, give him a sign."

He said: So I went back to my people and when I was in the mountain pass that overlooks the land of Daus, a light appeared between my eyes like a lamp. I said: "O Allâh, not in my face, for I fear that they will think I have been mutilated for leaving my religion." So it moved to the end of my whip. The people started looking at this light like a hanging lamp in my whip, as I was coming down to them from the pass. When I had come down, my father, who was an old man, came to me. I said: "Keep away from me, O my father. I do not belong to you and you do not belong to me." He said, "Why is that, O my son?" I said: "Because I have become Muslim." He said: "O my son, my religion is your religion." So he became Muslim. Then I went to my wife and said something similar to her, and she became Muslim and said: "Is there anything to fear from Dhu-Shara (an idol of theirs)?" I said: "No, I guarantee it."

Then I called Daus but they were slow to embrace Islam, so I went back to the Messenger of Allâh ﷺ in Makkah and said: "O Messenger of Allâh, I have not succeeded because Daus are too fond of Zina. Pray to Allâh against them." He said: "O Allâh, guide Daus. Go back to your people and call them, and be kind to them."

So I went back, and I stayed in the land of my people Daus, calling them to Islam, until the Prophet ﷺ migrated to Al-Madinah, and Badr, Uhud and Al-Khandaq all came and went. Then I came to the Messenger of Allâh ﷺ with those among my people who had become Muslim, when the Messenger of Allâh ﷺ was in Khaybar. I came to Madinah with seventy or eighty families of Daus, then we joined the Messenger of Allâh ﷺ in Khaibar, and he gave us a share of the booty along with the other Muslims.

Then I stayed with the Messenger of Allâh ﷺ until Allâh enabled him to conquer Makkah. I said: "O Messenger of Allâh, send me to Dhul-Kaffain – the idol of 'Amr ibn Humamah – so that I can burn it."

So he went out to it and burned it, then At-Tufail came back to the Messenger of Allâh ﷺ and stayed with him in Al-Madinah until the

Messenger of Allâh ﷺ passed away.

When the Arabs apostatized, At-Tufail went out with the Muslims to fight the apostates. He went to Al-Yamâmah with the Muslims and was killed there as a martyr.[1]

---

[1] *Usdul-Ghâbah*, 3/78; Ibn Hishâm, 1/198

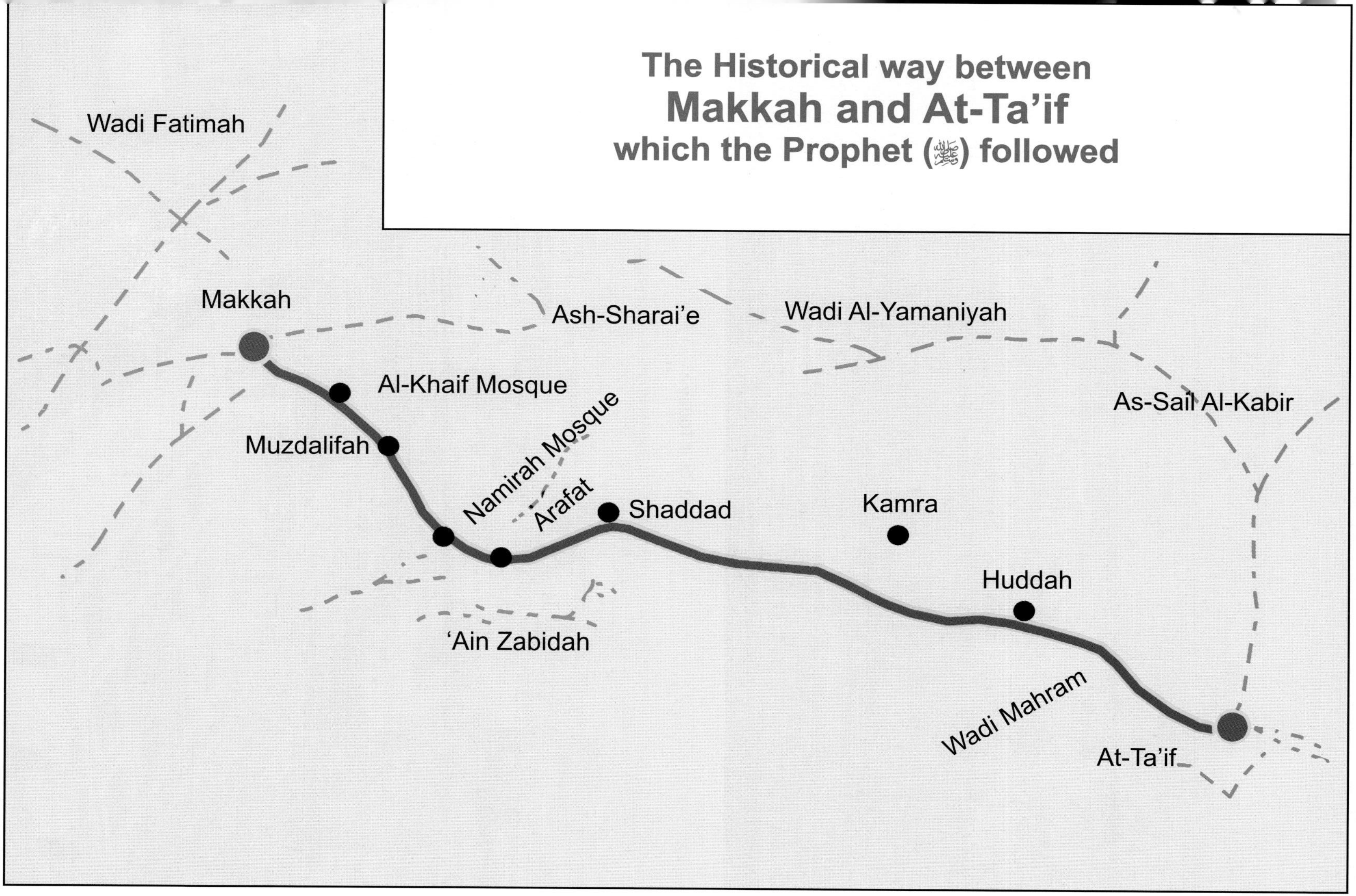

The Historical way between
Makkah and At-Ta'if
which the Prophet (ﷺ) followed

Wadi Fatimah

Ash-Sharai'e

Wadi Al-Yamaniyah

As-Sail Al-Kabir

Makkah

Al-Khaif Mosque

Muzdalifah

Namirah Mosque

Arafat

'Ain Zabidah

Shaddad

Kamra

Huddah

Wadi Mahram

At-Ta'if

At-Ta'if Today

Addas Mosque on the way to At-Ta'if

Minaret of the mosque of Ibn Abbas in At-Ta'if

The Jinn of Nasibin

(The Island)

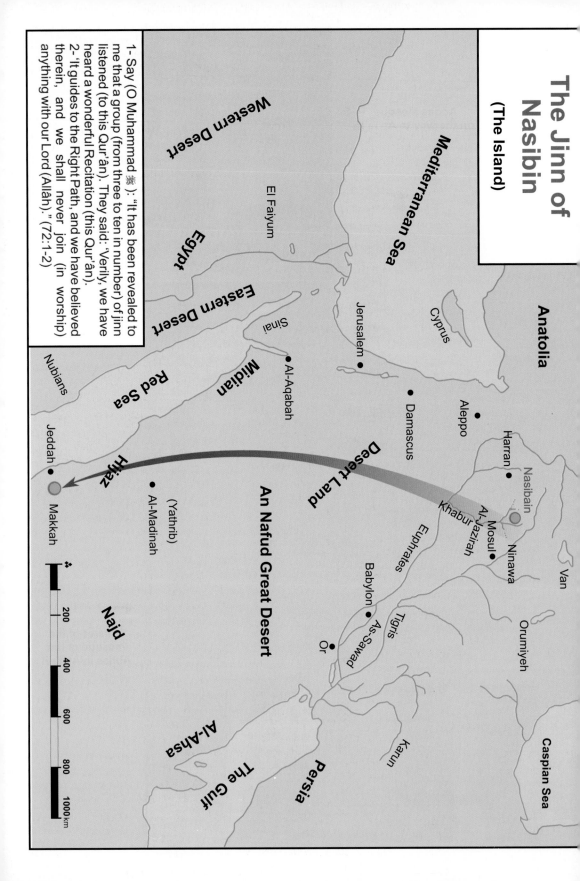

Anatolia

Mediterranean Sea

Western Desert

Egypt

Eastern Desert

Red Sea

Nubians

El Faiyum

Jerusalem

Cyprus

Sinai

Midian

Al-Aqabah

Damascus

Aleppo

Harran

Nasibain

Al-Jazirah

Mosul

Ninawa

Van

Orumiyeh

Caspian Sea

Khabur

Desert Land

Euphrates

Babylon

As-Sawad

Tigris

Ur

Karun

Persia

An Nafud Great Desert

(Yathrib)
Al-Madinah

Hijaz

Jeddah

Makkah

Najd

Al-Ahsa

The Gulf

200 400 600 800 1000 km

1- Say (O Muhammad ﷺ): "It has been revealed to me that a group (from three to ten in number) of jinn listened (to this Qur'ân). They said: 'Verily, we have heard a wonderful Recitation (this Qur'ân).
2- 'It guides to the Right Path, and we have believed therein, and we shall never join (in worship) anything with our Lord (Allâh)." (72:1-2)

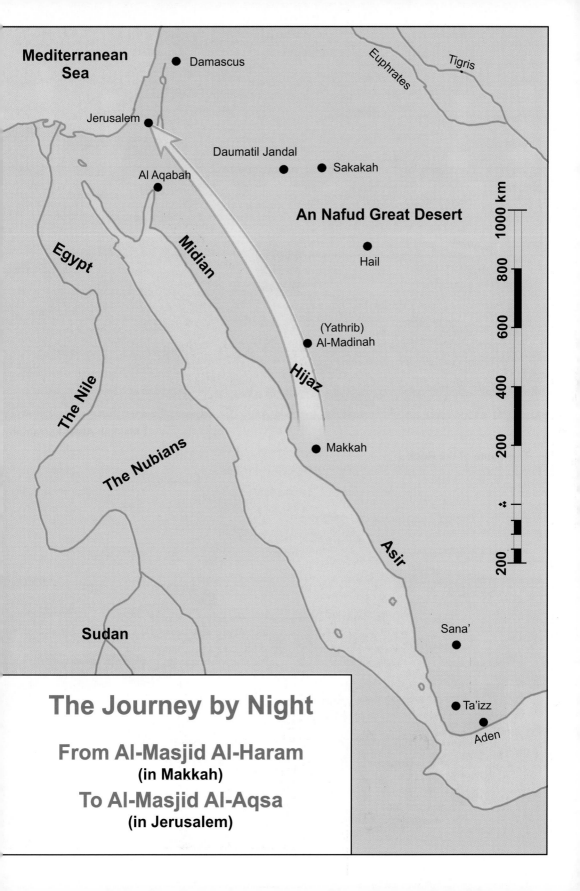

↑ Makkah Al-Mukarramah

The Dome of the Rock ↓

Shortly before the Hijrah
The first and second Pledges at Al-'Aqabah

Banu Hâshim came out from Shi'b Abi Tâlib (the place where they had gone during the boycott) and Allâh decreed that Khadijah and Abu Tâlib should both die in the same year, which the Messenger of Allâh ﷺ called the Year of Sorrow. This was the tenth year of his mission, three years before the *Hijrah*. Quraish started to persecute the Messenger of Allâh ﷺ mercilessly after the death of his uncle, so he went out to Al-Tâ'if, accompanied by Zaid ibn Hârithah, seeking help from Thaqif, but they did not respond. During this journey and on the way back, a slave of 'Utbah and Shaibah – the sons of Rabi'ah, whose name was 'Addâs, became a believer.

The Prophet ﷺ returned to Makkah and started to present himself to the Arab tribes on special occasions, especially on the occasion of *Hajj*. At Al-'Aqabah – which is between Makkah and Mina – he met twelve men of the Ansâr, and presented himself to them. That was the first Pledge of Al-'Aqabah.

'Ubâdah ibn As-Sâmit Al-Ansâri Al-Khazraji said: I was among those who were present at Al-'Aqabah. We were twelve men who took an oath of allegiance to the Messenger of Allâh ﷺ in the Pledge of Al-'Aqabah, which was called *Bai'at An-Nisa'* (the Pledge of the Women).[1] This was before fighting was enjoined, so we pledged not to associate anything with Allâh, not to steal, not to commit adultery, not to kill our children, not to intentionally forge falsehood (cf. *Al-Mumtahanah* 60:12), and not to disobey him in any just matter. "If you fulfil that then Paradise will be yours, but if you commit any of these sins, it is for Allâh to forgive or punish as He wills."

---

[1] It was called the Pledge of the Women because of the presence of 'Afra' bint 'Ubaid ibn Tha'labah, who was the first women to swear an oath of allegiance. For more information on the first and second Pledges, see: Ibn Hishâm, 2/54; At-Tabari, 2/355; *Al-Kâmil fit-Târikh*, 2/67; *Al-Bidâyah wan-Nihâyah*, 2/67; *'Uyun Al-Athar*, 2/155.

The Mosque of the Pledge (Masjid Al-Bai'ah) at Al-Aqabah

Those who had sworn the first Pledge of Al-'Aqabah returned to Yathrib (Al-Madinah), accompanied by Mus'ab ibn 'Uma'ir, who was to teach them the Qur'ân and Islam. He came back the following year, with seventy-three men and two women. The two women were Nusaibah bint Ka'b (Umm 'Amârah) and Asma' bint 'Amr ibn 'Adi (Umm Mani'). The second Pledge of Al-'Aqabah (the pledge of war) was:

"Blood is blood and blood not to be paid for is blood not to be paid for.[1]   I am of you and you are of me. I will war against them that war against you, and be at peace with those at peace with you."

Among the first to make this pledge and give their hand in allegiance to the Messenger of Allâh ﷺ were As'ad ibn Zurârah, Abul-Haitham ibn At-Tihân and Al-Bara' ibn Ma'rur... then the rest of them followed suit.

The Prophet ﷺ said:

«أَخْرِجُوا إِلَيَّ مِنْكُمْ اثْنَي عَشَرَ نَقِيبًا لِيَكُونُوا عَلَى قَوْمِهِمْ بِمَا فِيهِمْ، فَأَخْرَجُوا مِنْهُمْ تِسْعَةً مِنَ الْخَزْرَجِ، وَثَلَاثَةً مِنَ الْأَوْسِ»

"Send to me twelve men to look after your people's affairs." So they sent nine from Al-Khazraj and three from Al-Aws."

When Al-Aws and Al-Khazraj went back to Al-Madinah, they professed their Islam openly. Thus their society was prepared for the migration of the Companions and of the Messenger of Allâh ﷺ.

---

[1] i.e., he would treat blood revenge and its obligations as common to both parties.

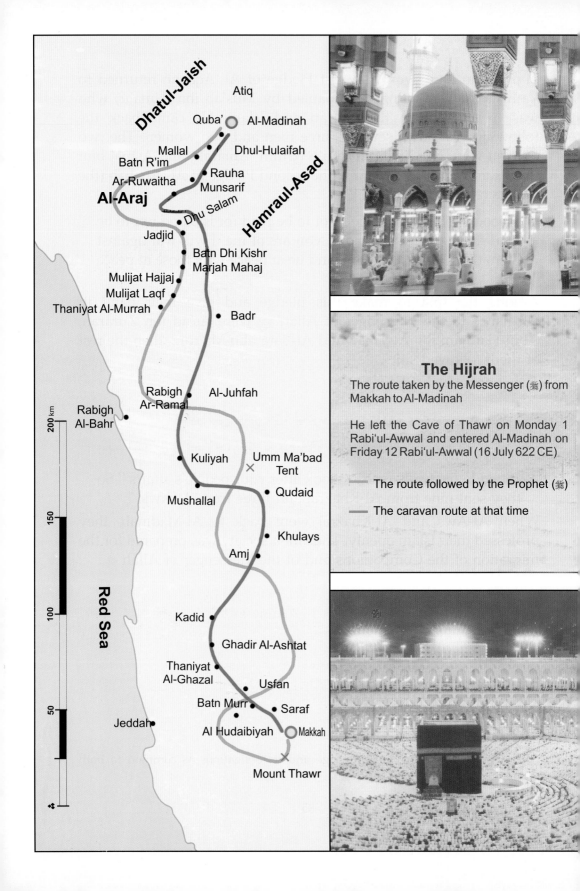

Dhatul-Jaish

Atiq

Quba'   Al-Madinah

Mallal   Dhul-Hulaifah

Batn R'im

Ar-Ruwaitha   Rauha
Munsarif

Al-Araj

Dhu Salam

Hamraul-Asad

Jadjid

Batn Dhi Kishr
Marjah Mahaj

Mulijat Hajjaj

Mulijat Laqf

Thaniyat Al-Murrah   •   Badr

Rabigh   Al-Juhfah
Ar-Ramal

Rabigh
Al-Bahr

Kuliyah   Umm Ma'bad
Tent

Mushallal   Qudaid

Khulays

Amj

Kadid

Ghadir Al-Ashtat

Thaniyat
Al-Ghazal   Usfan

Batn Murr   Saraf

Jeddah

Al Hudaibiyah   Makkah

Mount Thawr

Red Sea

200 km

150

100

50

The Hijrah

The route taken by the Messenger (ﷺ) from
Makkah to Al-Madinah

He left the Cave of Thawr on Monday 1
Rabi'ul-Awwal and entered Al-Madinah on
Friday 12 Rabi'ul-Awwal (16 July 622 CE)

— The route followed by the Prophet (ﷺ)

— The caravan route at that time

The *Hijrah*

Quraish understood the seriousness of the situation, and realized that the reins of power were slipping from their hands. The Messenger of Allâh ﷺ had gained followers who were not of Quraish and not of their land; they were there in Yathrib (Al-Madinah). They saw the *Muhâjirun* going there and growing stronger with the help and protection of the *Ansâr*. They realized that they were coming together in order to oppose them (Quraish). So the leaders of Quraish gathered in Dar An-Nadwah and decided to move from persecution to extermination. They drew up a plan to kill the Messenger of Allâh ﷺ at the hands of a number of young men, representing all the tribes, so that the responsibility for killing him would be shared by all the tribes.

﴿وَإِذْ يَمْكُرُ بِكَ الَّذِينَ كَفَرُوا لِيُثْبِتُوكَ أَوْ يَقْتُلُوكَ أَوْ يُخْرِجُوكَ وَيَمْكُرُونَ وَيَمْكُرُ اللَّهُ وَاللَّهُ خَيْرُ الْمَاكِرِينَ ﴿٣٠﴾﴾

"And (remember) when the disbelievers plotted against you (O Muhammad ﷺ) to imprison you, or to kill you, or to get you out (from your home, i.e., Makkah); they were plotting and Allâh too was plotting; and Allâh is the Best of those who plot."

[Qur'ân 8:30]

So, Jibril came down by Allâh's command and told the Messenger of Allâh ﷺ what they were plotting, and gave him permission to migrate.

After three nights in the cave of Thawr, they set off for Al-Madinah in the Name of Allâh and under His care, at the beginning of Rabi'ul-Awwal. The Prophet ﷺ looked back at Makkah, bidding it a heartfelt farewell, then he said:

«إِنِّي لَأُخْرَجُ مِنْكِ، وَإِنِّي لَأَعْلَمُ أَنَّكِ أَحَبُّ بِلَادِ اللهِ إِلَى اللهِ، وَأَكْرَمُهَا عَلَى اللهِ

87

The Mountain of Thawr

تَعَالَى، وَلَوْلَا أَنَّ أَهْلَكِ أَخْرَجُونِي مِنْكِ مَا خَرَجْتُ مِنْكِ، اللَّهُمَّ إِنَّكَ تَعْلَمُ أَنَّهُمْ أَخْرَجُونِي مِنْ أَحَبِّ الْبِلَادِ إِلَيَّ، فَأَسْكِنِّي أَحَبَّ الْبِلَادِ إِلَيْكَ»

"I am leaving you, but I know that you are the most beloved of the land of Allâh to Allâh, and the dearest to Allâh. Were it not that your people expelled me from you, I would not have left. O Allâh, You know that they drove me out from the land that is most beloved to me, so cause me to dwell in the land that is most beloved to You."

On 12 Rabi'ul-Awwal, he reached Quba', where he stayed from Monday to Thursday, and established the first mosque to be built in Islam.[1]

Then he ﷺ entered Al-Madinah, and stopped at the house of Abu Ayyub Al-Ansâri (Khâlid ibn Zaid Al-Khazraji), where he stayed until he built his apartment and his mosque, then he moved there. (*Usd Al-Ghâbah*, 2/94).

One of the outcomes of the *Hijrah* was that the Muslims now had a place where they could gather and defend themselves, call others to their religion and practise it openly. Thus the first Islamic state was established, and the merchants of Quraish were now faced with a threat to their route to and from Syria.

---

[1] Ibn Hishâm, 2/89; At-Tabari, 2/369; *Al-Bidâyah Wan-Nihâyah*, 3/170; *Al-Tabaqât Al-Kubra*, 1/227; *Al-Kâmil fit-Târikh*, 2/71; *Muruh Adh-Dhahb*, 2/285; *'Uyun Al-Athar*, 2/81; *Al-Wafa' bi Ahwâl Al-Mustafa*, 1/235.

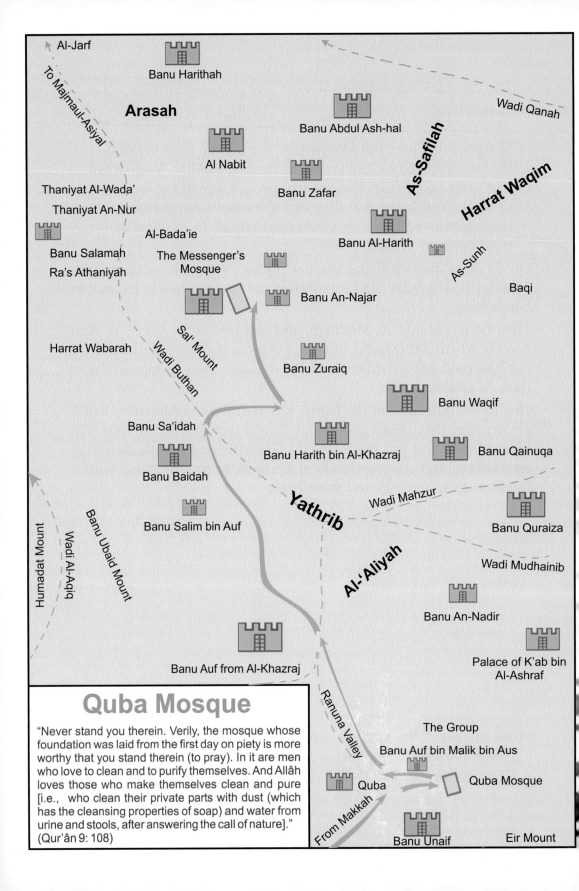

Al-Jarf

Banu Harithah

To Majmaul-Asiyal

Arasah

Banu Abdul Ash-hal

Wadi Qanah

Al Nabit

As-Safilah

Harrat Waqim

Banu Zafar

Thaniyat Al-Wada'

Thaniyat An-Nur

Al-Bada'ie

Banu Al-Harith

As-Sunh

Banu Salamah

The Messenger's
Mosque

Baqi

Ra's Athaniyah

Banu An-Najar

Harrat Wabarah

Sal' Mount

Banu Zuraiq

Wadi Buthan

Banu Waqif

Banu Sa'idah

Banu Harith bin Al-Khazraj

Banu Baidah

Banu Qainuqa

Wadi Mahzur

Banu Salim bin Auf

Yathrib

Banu Quraiza

Humadat Mount

Wadi Al-Aqiq

Banu Ubaid Mount

Al-'Aliyah

Wadi Mudhainib

Banu An-Nadir

Banu Auf from Al-Khazraj

Ranuna Valley

Palace of K'ab bin
Al-Ashraf

From Makkah

The Group

Banu Auf bin Malik bin Aus

Quba Mosque

"Never stand you therein. Verily, the mosque whose
foundation was laid from the first day on piety is more
worthy that you stand therein (to pray). In it are men
who love to clean and to purify themselves. And Allâh
loves those who make themselves clean and pure
[i.e., who clean their private parts with dust (which
has the cleansing properties of soap) and water from
urine and stools, after answering the call of nature]."
(Qur'ân 9: 108)

Quba

Quba Mosque

Banu Unaif

Eir Mount

↑ **The Mosque of Quba'** ↓

Friday Prayer Mosque

The House of Abu Ayyub Al-Ansari (in Al-Madinah)

The Grave of Abu Ayyub Al-Ansari in Istanbul.

Al Madinah Al-Munawwarah

An Archeological Representation.

The Forest

Majmaul-Asiyal ✗

Orchards

Uhud Mount

Harrah Waqim

Zaghabah ✗

'Ain Ash-Shuhada ●

Wadi Qanah

Roumah Well ●

Thaniyatul-Wada'

The Trench

The Trench

Bani Harithah Houses ✗

Al-Fath Mosque

To Uhud

Mosque

Harratul-Wabrah

Sal' Mount

Abi Ayub Well ●

As-Sunh

Bani Muawiyah Houses

Sa'eed bin Al 'As Palace ✗

Al-'Aqiq Valley

Quest House

Al-Ijabah Mosque ✗

Al-Manakh Market

The Green Dome

The Haram

Al-Jum'a Gate

Way to Najd

Al-Ghamamah Mosque

Baqi

To Yanbu

Al-Awali Door

Palm Trees

Drinking Well ●

Quba Door

Bani Zafar Mosque

Bani Qainuqa' Houses ✗

Bani Zafar Houses ✗

Wadi Mahzur

To Quba

Wadi Buthan

Bani Quraizah Houses ✗

Ghars Well ●

Al Juma' Mosque

Urwa Well ●

Aris Well ●

Orchards

Al-Aliyah

Quba Mosque

Bani An-Nadir Houses

Sa'd bin Khaithamah House ✗

Kulthum bin Al-Hadm House ✗

✗

Ka'b bin Al-Ashraf fortress

Harrah

Dhul-Hulaifah ✗

Eer Mount

Illustration by Abdul-Quddus Al-Ansari

Al-Madinah Today

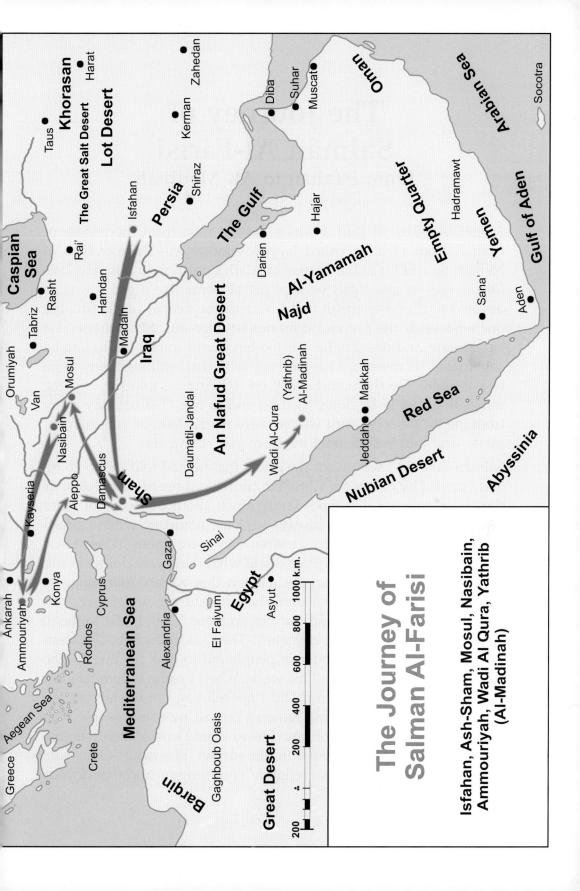

The Journey of
Salman Al-Farisi

Isfahan, Ash-Sham, Mosul, Nasibain,
Ammouriyah, Wadi Al Qura, Yathrib
(Al-Madinah)

The Journey of
Salmân Al-Fârisi
From Isfahan to Al- Madinah

Salmân Al-Fârisi ☙ said: I was a Persian man from the people of Isfahan, from a village called Jayy. My father was the merchant of his village, and I was the dearest of Allâh's creation to him. His love for me was so great that he kept me at home like a girl. I was so devoted to Zoroastrianism that I became the keeper of the fire, the one who tends the fire and does not let it go out. My father had a large estate, and one day he was too busy with some building, so he said to me: "O my son, I am too busy with this building today to go to my estate. Go there and check on it." And he told me of some things that had to be done, then he said to me: "Do not stay away from me for too long, for I will be more worried about you than my estate, and that will distract me from everything else."

Salmân said: So I set out for the estate that he had told me to go to, and I passed by one of the Christian churches. I heard their voices as they were praying. I did not know much about the ways of other people because my father always kept me home, so when I heard their voices I went inside to see what they were doing. When I saw them, I liked the way they prayed and what they were doing. I said: By Allâh, this is better than the religion that we are following. By Allâh, I did not leave them until the sun had set, and I forgot all about my father's estate and did not go there. Then I said to them: "Where did this religion originate?" They said: "In Syria." I went back to my father, who had sent people out to look for me, and he had been distracted from all his work. When I came to him he said: "O my son, where were you? Did I not tell you not to stay out too long?" I said to him: "O my father, I passed by some people who were praying in their church, and I liked what I saw of their religion. By Allâh, I stayed with them until the sun set." He said: "O my son, there is nothing good in that religion. Your religion and that of your

Isfahan (The Mosque & the courtyard of the Imam) from the period of Shah Abbas As-Safawi

forefathers is better than that." I said to him: "No, by Allâh, it is better than our religion." Then he got worried about me, and he put fetters on my feet and detained me in his house.

Salmân flees to Syria

Salmân said: I sent word to the Christians and told them: "If any travelers come to you from Syria, tell me about them." Then some travelers came from Syria, Christian merchants, so they told me about them. I said to them: "When they have finished their business and want to go back to their country, tell me." So when they wanted to go back to their country, they told me. I took the irons from my feet and went out with them to Syria. When we reached there I said: "Who is the most knowledgeable man of this religion?" They said: "The bishop in the church."

Salmân stayed with the Christian bishop, who was a bad man. When he died, he went to a righteous bishop. When the latter was on his deathbed, Salmân said: "The decree of Allâh (death) has come to you. To whom do you advise me to go? What do you command me to do?" He said: "O my son, by Allâh I do not know of anyone now who follows the same path as I was following. The people are doomed; they have changed and abandoned most of what they used to follow, except for a man in Mosul, who follows the same path as I was following, so go and join him."

Salmân joins the Bishop of Mosul

Salmân said: When he died and was buried, I went to the man in Mosul and said to him: "So-and-so told me, as he was dying, to come to you, and he told me that you are following the same path as he followed." He said to me: "Stay with me." So I stayed with him and I found him to be a good man, following the same path as his companion. But soon he died. When he was on his deathbed I said to him: "Your companion told me about you and advised me to join you. Now the Decree of Allâh has come to you. To whom do you advise me to go? What do you command me to do?" He said: "O my son, by Allâh I do not know of anyone who follows the same path as us, except for a man in Nasibain, so go and join him."

100

Fire Temple near Baku ↑

↓ Fire worshipper sitting

↓ Fire worshipper standing

Salmân joins the Bishop of Nasibain

Salmân said: When he died and was buried, I went to the man in Nasibain and told him my story, and what my companion had advised me to do. He said: "Stay with me." So I stayed with him and I found him to be a follower of the same path as his two companions. I was staying with a good man. But soon death came to him, and when he was dying I said: "To whom do you advise me to go? What do you command me to do?" He said: "O my son, by Allâh, I do not know that there is anyone left to whom I can tell you to go, except for a man in 'Ammuriyah in the land of the Byzantines. He follows the same path as us, so if you like you can go to him."

Salmân joins the man in 'Ammuriyah

Salmân said: When he died and was buried, I went to the man in 'Ammuriyah and told him my story. He said: "Stay with me." ... When he was dying, I said to him: "To whom do you advise me to go? What do you command me to do?" He said: "O my son, by Allâh, I do not know of anyone today who is following the same path as us to whom I can tell you to go. But the time of a new Prophet is fast approaching. He will be sent with the religion of Ibrâhim ﷺ and will emerge in the land of the Arabs, and will migrate to a land between two lava fields between which are date palms. On him will be signs which cannot be hidden. He will accept gifts but will not accept charity. Between his shoulders will be the Seal of Prophecy. If you can go to that land, then do so.

Salmân goes to Wadi Al-Qura

Salmân said: Then he died and was buried, and I stayed in 'Ammûriyah for as long as Allâh willed I should stay. Then a group of merchants from Kalb passed by me, and I said to them: "Take me to the land of the Arabs, and I will give you these cows of mine and this little sheep of mine." They agreed, so I gave those (animals) to them and they took me with them. But when we reached Wadi Al-Qura, they wronged me and sold me to a Jewish man as a slave. While I was with him I saw some palm trees and I hoped that this was

Jawatha Mosque (The First Mosque in which Friday Prayer was held after the Mosque of the Prophet ﷺ)

The Citadel and City of Darain

the land that my companion had described to me, but I was not sure.

Salmân goes to Al-Madinah

Salmân said: Whilst I was with him, a cousin of his from Banu Quraizah came to him from Al-Madinah and bought me from him, and took me back with him to Al-Madinah. By Allâh, as soon as I saw it, I recognized it from the description my companion had given. So I stayed there, and the Messenger of Allâh ﷺ was sent and stayed in Makkah for a while, but I did not hear anything about him because I was preoccupied with the work of a slave. Then he migrated to Al-Madinah.

Salmân hears of the migration of the Prophet ﷺ

Salmân said: By Allâh, I was at the top of my master's palm tree, doing some work for him, and my master was sitting beneath me, when a cousin of his came to him and said: "O so-and-so, may Allâh destroy Bani Qailah;[1] by Allâh, right now they are gathering in Quba' to meet a man who has come to them from Makkah today, and they claim that he is a Prophet."

Salmân said: When I heard that I began to shiver, until I thought that I would fall on top of my master. I climbed down from the tree and starting saying to that cousin of his: "What did you say?" My master got angry and punched me, then he said: "What is it to do with you? Go back to your work!" I said, "It is nothing, I just wanted to check what he said."

Salmân checks on the authenticity of the Prophethood of Muhammad ﷺ

Salmân said: I had been saving something, so when evening came I took it and went to the Messenger of Allâh ﷺ in Quba'. I entered upon him and said: "I have heard that you are a righteous man, and you have

---

[1] Qailah was the mother of Al-Aws and Al-Khazraj; this is the name of their ancient female ancestor, whose full name was Qailah bint Kâhil.

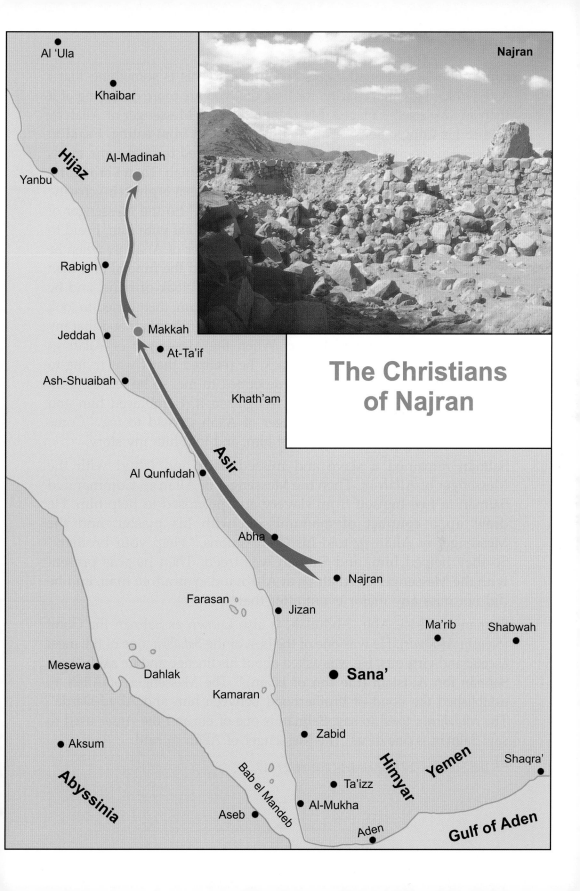

Najran

The Christians of Najran

Al 'Ula

Khaibar

Hijaz

Al-Madinah

Yanbu

Rabigh

Jeddah

Makkah

At-Ta'if

Ash-Shuaibah

Khath'am

Asir

Al Qunfudah

Abha

Najran

Farasan

Jizan

Ma'rib

Shabwah

Mesewa

Dahlak

Sana'

Kamaran

Zabid

Aksum

Himyar

Yemen

Shaqra'

Abyssinia

Bab el Mandeb

Ta'izz

Al-Mukha

Aseb

Aden

Gulf of Aden

companions who are strangers and in need. This is something that I had, (which I give) in charity, for I see that you are more deserving of it than anyone else." I placed it near him, then the Messenger of Allâh ﷺ said to his Companions: "Eat," but he refrained from eating. I said to myself: This is one. Then I went away and started to save some more, and the Messenger of Allâh ﷺ moved to Al-Madinah. Then I brought it and said to him: "I noticed that you do not eat (what is given in) charity; this is a gift with which I wish to honour you." So the Messenger of Allâh ﷺ ate from it and told his Companions to eat with him. I said to myself: this is two. Then I came to the Messenger of Allâh ﷺ when he was in Baqi' Al-Gharqad, when he had attended the funeral of a man from among his Companions. I was wearing a cloak of mine, and he was sitting amongst his Companions. I greeted him, then I tried to look at his back, to see whether I could spot the Seal of Prophethood that my companion had described to me. When the Messenger of Allâh ﷺ noticed me trying to look at his back, he realized that I was trying to confirm something that had been described to me, so he let his cloak drop, and I look at the Seal and recognized it. I embraced him and kissed him, weeping. The Messenger of Allâh ﷺ said to me, "Come here." So I came and sat in front of him, and told him my story.

Salmân remained a slave and missed Badr and Uhud with the Messenger of Allâh ﷺ. Then the Messenger of Allâh ﷺ Commanded Salmân to free himself from slavery and promised to help him. He drew up a contract of manumission with his master, and the Messenger of Allâh ﷺ told his Companions, "Help your brother." So they helped him, and Salmân was freed. Then he was present with the Messenger of Allâh ﷺ at Al-Khandaq as a free man, and he did not miss any major event after that.[1]

Salmân Al-Fârisi, Abu 'Abdullâh, is also known as Salmân the Good (Salmân Al-Khair). He was one of the best of the Sahâbah, one of the most ascetic and virtuous. He was asked about his lineage and he said: "I am Salmân ibn Al-Islam (the son of Islam)." The Messenger of Allâh ﷺ established the bond of brotherhood between him and Abud-Darda'. The Muhâjirun used to say: Salmân is one of us; and the Ansâr used to say: Salmân is one of us. The Messenger of Allâh ﷺ said:

---

[1] Ibn Hishâm, 1/198; Usdul-Ghâbah, 2/417

The Mosque of the Two Qiblahs
(Masjid Al-Qiblatain)

«سَلْمَانُ مِنَّا أَهْلَ الْبَيْتِ»

"Salmân is one of us, *Ahlul-Bait* (the people of his household)."
He died in 35 AH after living a long life.

* * *

The change of the *Qiblah* from Baitul-Maqdis (Jerusalem) to the Holy Ka'bah

In Makkah, the Prophet ﷺ used to pray towards Jerusalem, with the Ka'bah in front of him. When he migrated to Al-Madinah, he prayed towards Jerusalem for sixteen months, but he hoped that it would be changed to the Ka'bah:

﴿قَدْ نَرَىٰ تَقَلُّبَ وَجْهِكَ فِى ٱلسَّمَآءِ فَلَنُوَلِّيَنَّكَ قِبْلَةً تَرْضَىٰهَا فَوَلِّ وَجْهَكَ شَطْرَ ٱلْمَسْجِدِ ٱلْحَرَامِ وَحَيْثُ مَا كُنتُمْ فَوَلُّوا وُجُوهَكُمْ شَطْرَهُۥ﴾

"Verily, We have seen the turning of your (Muhammad's) face towards the heaven. Surely, We shall turn you to a *Qiblah* (prayer direction) that shall please you, so turn your face in the direction of *Al-Masjid Al-Harâm* (at Makkah). And wheresoever you people are, turn your faces (in prayer) in that direction."

[Qur'ân 2:144]

During *Zuhr* prayer – or it was said that it was *'Asr* – the Prophet ﷺ had led his Companions in praying two *Rak'ahs*, then he was commanded to face towards the Ka'bah, so he turned around towards the Ka'bah. The mosque where he offered this prayer became known as the mosque of the Two *Qiblahs* (Masjid Al-Qiblatain). That took place on a Monday half way through the month of Rajab in 2 AH, two months before the great battle of Badr. [Ibn Sa'd 1/242]

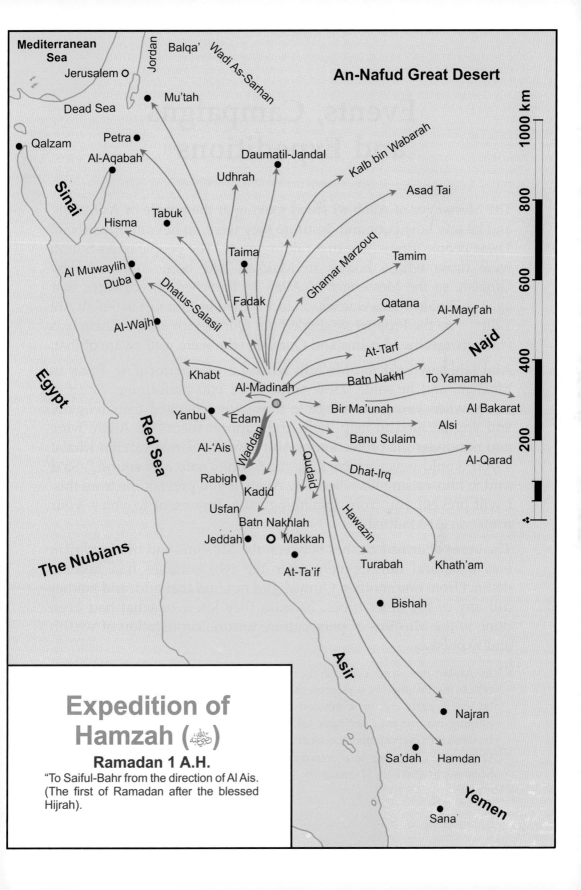

Mediterranean Sea

Jordan

Balqa'

Wadi As-Sarhan

An-Nafud Great Desert

Jerusalem O

Mu'tah

Dead Sea

Petra

Qalzam

Al-Aqabah

Sinai

Daumatil-Jandal

Udhrah

Kalb bin Wabarah

Asad Tai

Hisma

Tabuk

Taima

Ghamar Marzouq

Tamim

Al Muwaylih

Duba

Dhatus-Salasil

Fadak

Qatana

Al-Mayf'ah

Al-Wajh

Najd

At-Tarf

Khabt

Al-Madinah

Batn Nakhl

To Yamamah

Bir Ma'unah

Al Bakarat

Yanbu

Edam

Alsi

Al-'Ais

Waddan

Banu Sulaim

Al-Qarad

Egypt

Red Sea

Rabigh

Kadid

Qudaid

Dhat-Irq

Usfan

Batn Nakhlah

Hawazin

Jeddah

Makkah

The Nubians

At-Ta'if

Turabah

Khath'am

Bishah

Asir

Najran

Sa'dah

Hamdan

Expedition of Hamzah (ﷺ)

Ramadan 1 A.H.

"To Saiful-Bahr from the direction of Al Ais. (The first of Ramadan after the blessed Hijrah).

Yemen

Sana'

1000 km

800

600

400

200

Events, Campaigns and Expeditions[1]

The Messenger of Allâh ﷺ stood looking at the people of As-Suffah, and he saw how poor and destitute they were, so he comforted them. These people formed the first raiding party. The people of As-Suffah were those whose homes in Makkah had been confiscated by Quraish, so the Messenger of Allâh ﷺ launched an economic war against Quraish. This war was in fact started by Quraish in Shi'ab Abi Tâlib[2] , so the Prophet ﷺ singled out Quraish for attack. There was war between the Muslims and Quraish, who were well aware of that.

Abu Jahl saw Sa'd ibn Mu'âdh when he was performing *Tawâf* in Makkah, and he said: "How come I see you performing *Tawâf* in safety when you gave refuge to those who changed their religion, and you decided to help them and support them? By Allâh, were you not under the protection of Abu Safwân – Umayyah ibn Khalaf – you would never go back to your family safe and sound." Sa'd said to him, raising his voice: "By Allâh, if you prevent me from this, I will prevent you from something more important to you – your route via Al-Madinah."

The onset of armed clashes between the Muslims and the *Mushrikin* was a natural development after the two societies had become distinct from one another. Quraish did not find that odd, and neither did any of the other tribes, because they knew of what had been done to the Muslims of persecution, torture, confiscation of wealth and expulsion.

---

[1] In Arabic the word *Ghazwah* is used to refer to a battle or campaign in which the Prophet ﷺ was present, and *Sariyyah* is used for occasions when he sent a party out on a mission but did not go with them; in either case, fighting may or may not have taken place. Here the word "campaign" will be used for *Ghazwah* and the word "expedition" for *Sariyyah*. [Translator]

[2] Shi'b Abi Tâlib: this is a reference to the boycott of Quraish against the Muslims in Makkah. [Translator]

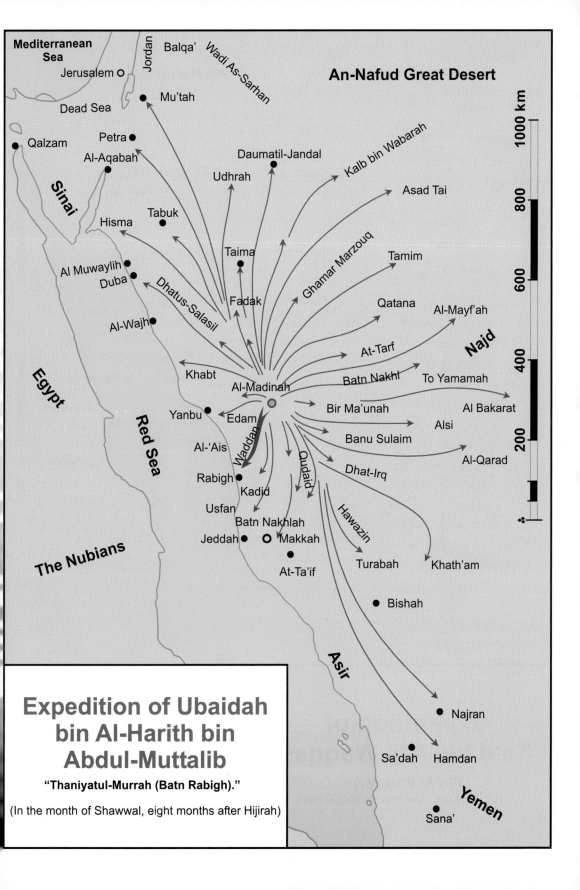

Expedition of Ubaidah bin Al-Harith bin Abdul-Muttalib

"Thaniyatul-Murrah (Batn Rabigh)."

(In the month of Shawwal, eight months after Hijirah)

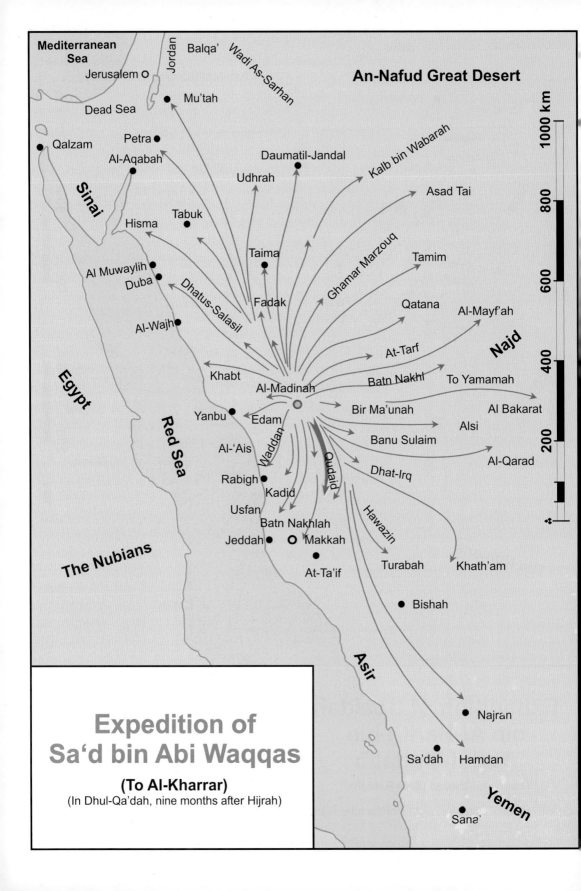

Expedition of Sa'd bin Abi Waqqas

(To Al-Kharrar)
(In Dhul-Qa'dah, nine months after Hijrah)

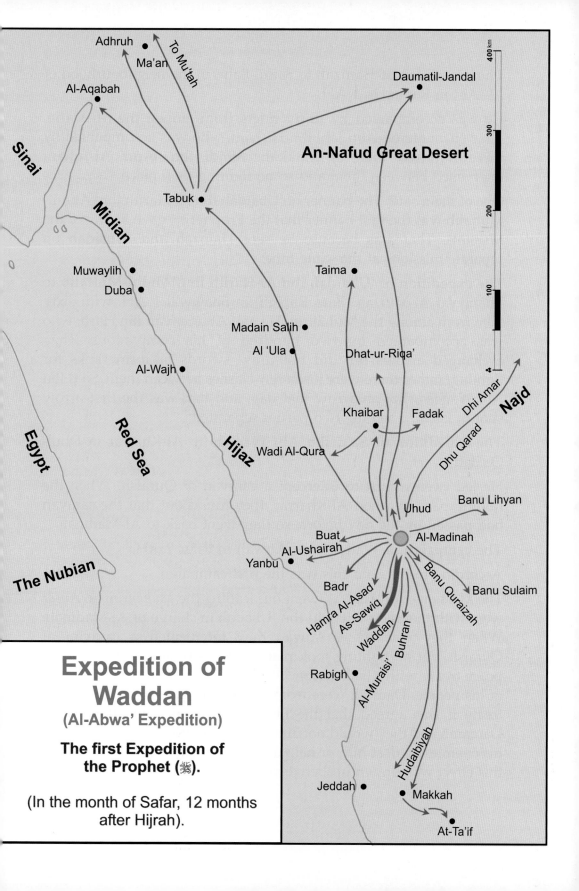

Adhruh

Ma'an

To Mu'tah

Al-Aqabah

Sinai

Midian

Daumatil-Jandal

An-Nafud Great Desert

Tabuk

Muwaylih

Duba

Taima

Madain Salih

Al 'Ula

Dhat-ur-Riqa'

Al-Wajh

Najd

Dhi Amar

Egypt

Red Sea

Hijaz

Khaibar

Fadak

Dhu Qarad

Wadi Al-Qura

Banu Lihyan

Uhud

Buat

Al-Madinah

Al-Ushairah

Banu Quraizah

The Nubian

Yanbu

Banu Sulaim

Badr

Hamra Al-Asad

As-Sawiq

Waddan

Buhran

Rabigh

Al-Muraisi'

Hudaibiyah

Jeddah

Makkah

At-Ta'if

400 km

300

200

100

0

Expedition of Waddan

(Al-Abwa' Expedition)

The first Expedition of the Prophet (ﷺ).

(In the month of Safar, 12 months after Hijrah).

The expedition of Hamzah to Saiful-Bahr, in the neighbourhood of Al-'Ais, in Ramadân 1 AH.

He was accompanied by thirty riders from among the *Muhâjirin*. They encountered Abu Jahl ibn Hishâm, who was accompanied by three hundred men of Makkah. Majdi ibn 'Amr Al-Juhani intervened between them and so no fighting took place.

One of them said: The banner of 'Ubaidah ibn Al-Hârith ibn 'Abdul-Muttalib was the first banner that the Prophet ﷺ gave to any of the Muslims. That was because he sent Hamzah and 'Ubaidah on separate missions at the same time.

The expedition of 'Ubaidah ibn Al-Hârith ibn 'Abdul-Muttalib to Thaniyyat Al-Murrah (Batn Râbigh) in Shawwâl 1 AH, with sixty men from among the Muhâjirin. He met Abu Sufyân ibn Harb, who was accompanied by two hundred of his companions. They exchanged arrows but did not draw swords or form ranks for fighting, rather there were just a few clashes between them. Sa'd ibn Abi Waqqâs shot an arrow that day, and that was the first arrow shot in Islam. Then the two parties separated.

The expedition of Sa'd ibn Abi Waqqâs to Al-Kharrâr in Dhul-Qa'dah 1 AH.

He led twenty men to intercept a caravan of Quraish. When the raiding party reached Al-Kharrâr, they found out that the caravan had passed by the day before, so they went back to Al-Madinah.

The campaign of Waddân (Al-Abwa') in Safar 2 AH.

According to Ibn Sa'd this was the first campaign.

The Messenger of Allâh ﷺ went out leading the *Muhâjirin*; no *Ansâr* were with them. He left Sa'd ibn 'Ubâdah in charge of Al-Madinah. When they reached Al-Abwa', they intercepted a caravan of Quraish, but no fighting took place. On this occasion they made a peace treaty with Makhshi ibn 'Amr Al-Damri, who was the leader of his people. Damrah were from the tribe of Bani Kinânah. In this treaty it was agreed that the Prophet ﷺ would not attack Banu Damarah and they would not attack him, nor would they join any of his enemies against him or help any of his enemies. A document to this effect was drawn up between them.

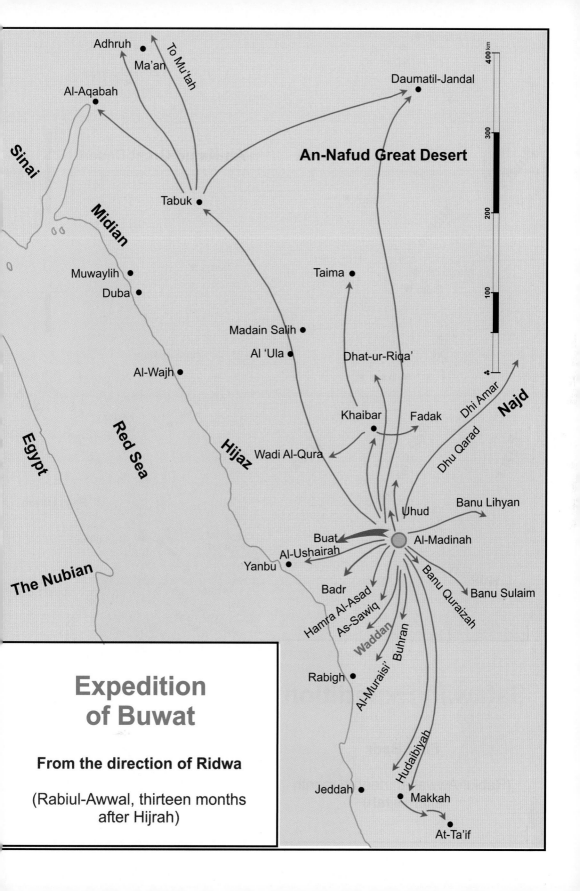

Adhruh

Ma'an

To Mu'tah

Al-Aqabah

Daumatil-Jandal

Sinai

An-Nafud Great Desert

Midian

Tabuk

Muwaylih

Duba

Taima

Madain Salih

Al 'Ula

Dhat-ur-Riqa'

Al-Wajh

Dhi Amar

Najd

Egypt

Red Sea

Hijaz

Khaibar

Fadak

Dhu Qarad

Wadi Al-Qura

Banu Lihyan

Uhud

Al-Madinah

Buat

Al-Ushairah

Yanbu

Banu Quraizah

Banu Sulaim

Badr

The Nubian

Hamra Al-Asad

As-Sawiq

Waddan

Buhran

Al-Muraisi'

Rabigh

Expedition
of Buwat

From the direction of Ridwa

(Rabiul-Awwal, thirteen months
after Hijrah)

Hudaibiyah

Jeddah

Makkah

At-Ta'if

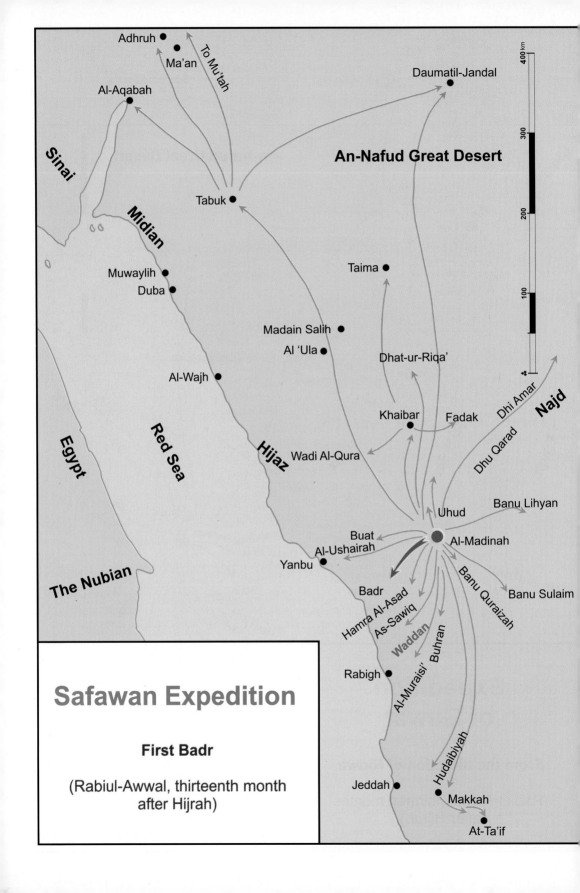

Adhruh •
• Ma'an
To Mu'tah
Al-Aqabah •

Sinai

Midian

Muwaylih •
Duba •

Al-Wajh •

Egypt

Red Sea

Hijaz

The Nubian

Daumatil-Jandal •

An-Nafud Great Desert

Tabuk •

Taima •

Madain Salih •
Al 'Ula •

Dhat-ur-Riqa'

Khaibar •   Fadak   Dhi Amar   Najd

Wadi Al-Qura   Dhu Qarad

Uhud   Banu Lihyan

Buat
Al-Ushairah •   Al-Madinah
Yanbu •

Badr
Hamra Al-Asad   Banu Quraizah
As-Sawiq   Banu Sulaim
Waddan
Rabigh •   Al-Muraisi'   Buhran

Hudaibiyah

Jeddah •   • Makkah
At-Ta'if •

Safawan Expedition

First Badr

(Rabiul-Awwal, thirteenth month
after Hijrah)

400 km
300
200
100

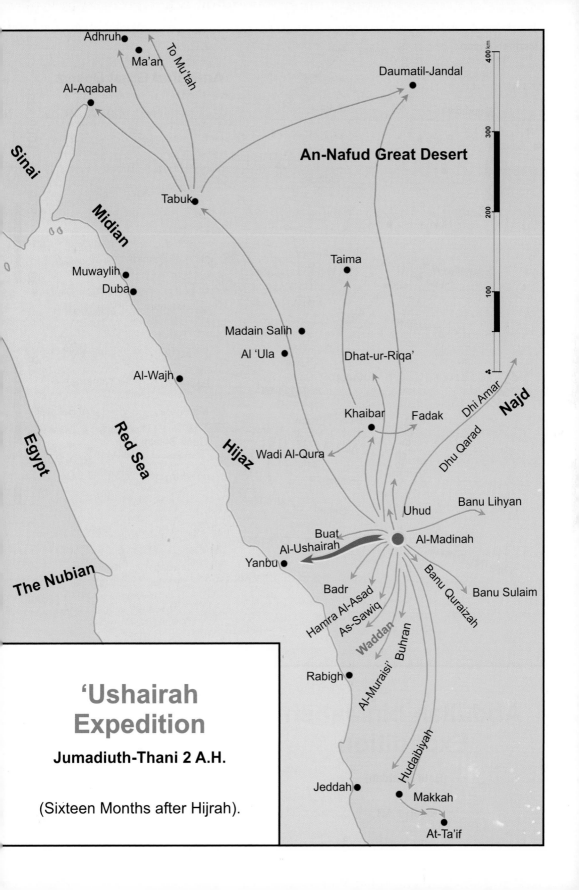

'Ushairah Expedition

Jumadiuth-Thani 2 A.H.

(Sixteen Months after Hijrah).

Adhruh

Ma'an

To Mu'tah

Al-Aqabah

Daumatil-Jandal

An-Nafud Great Desert

Sinai

Midian

Tabuk

400 km

300

200

100

Taima

Muwaylih

Duba

Madain Salih

Al 'Ula

Dhat-ur-Riqa'

Al-Wajh

Khaibar

Fadak

Dhi Amar

Najd

Hijaz

Wadi Al-Qura

Dhu Qarad

Egypt

Red Sea

Uhud

Banu Lihyan

Buat

Al-Ushairah

Al-Madinah

Yanbu

Banu Quraizah

Banu Sulaim

The Nubian

Badr

Hamra Al-Asad

As-Sawiq

Waddan

Buhran

Rabigh

Al-Muraisi'

Hudaibiyah

Jeddah

Makkah

At-Ta'if

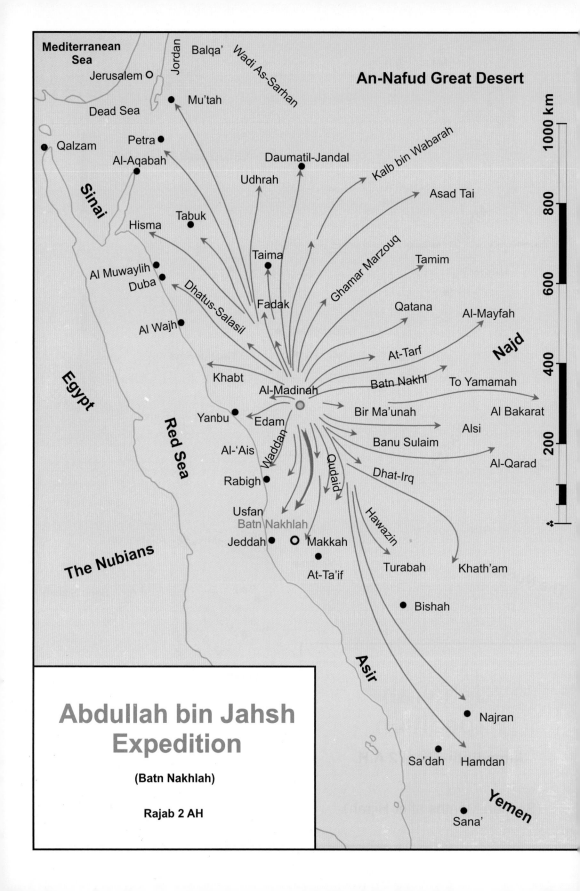

Mediterranean Sea

An-Nafud Great Desert

Jordan
Balqa'
Wadi As-Sarhan

Jerusalem O

Dead Sea
Mu'tah

Qalzam
Petra
Daumatil-Jandal
Kalb bin Wabarah

Al-Aqabah
Udhrah
Asad Tai

Sinai
Tabuk
Taima
Ghamar Marzouq
Tamim

Hisma
Al Muwaylih
Duba
Dhatus-Salasil
Fadak
Qatana
Al-Mayfah

Al Wajh
At-Tarf
Najd

Egypt
Khabt
Batn Nakhl
To Yamamah

Al-Madinah
Bir Ma'unah
Al Bakarat

Red Sea
Yanbu
Edam
Banu Sulaim
Alsi

Al-'Ais
Waddan
Al-Qarad

Rabigh
Qudaid
Dhat-Irq

Usfan
Batn Nakhlah
Hawazin

The Nubians
Jeddah
O Makkah

At-Ta'if
Turabah
Khath'am

Bishah

Asir

Najran

Sa'dah
Hamdan

Yemen
Sana'

1000 km
800
600
400
200

Abdullah bin Jahsh Expedition

(Batn Nakhlah)

Rajab 2 AH

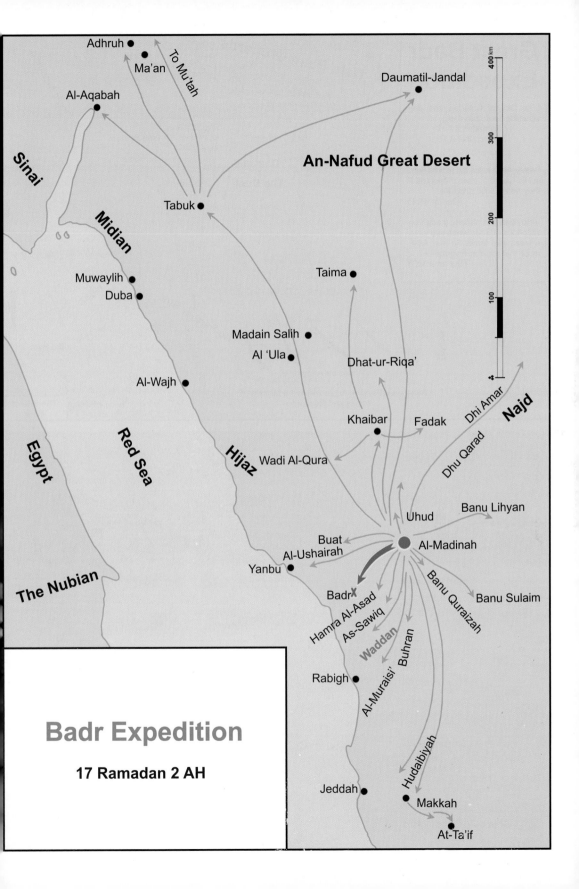

Badr Expedition

17 Ramadan 2 AH

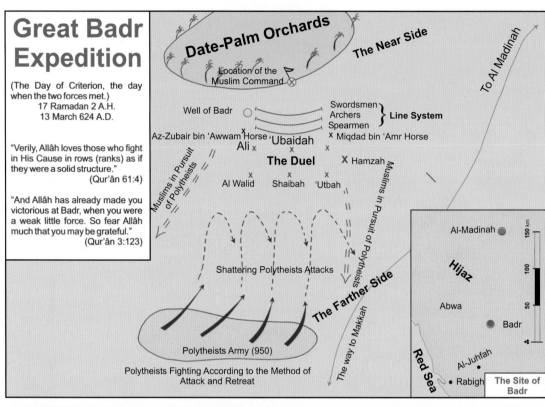

Great Badr Expedition

(The Day of Criterion, the day when the two forces met.)
17 Ramadan 2 A.H.
13 March 624 A.D.

"Verily, Allâh loves those who fight in His Cause in rows (ranks) as if they were a solid structure."
(Qur'ân 61:4)

"And Allâh has already made you victorious at Badr, when you were a weak little force. So fear Allâh much that you may be grateful."
(Qur'ân 3:123)

Date-Palm Orchards

The Near Side

To Al Madinah

Location of the Muslim Command ⊗

Well of Badr ○

Swordsmen
Archers   } Line System
Spearmen

Az-Zubair bin 'Awwam Horse ×   'Ubaidah
Ali ×

× Miqdad bin 'Amr Horse

Muslims in Pursuit of Polytheists

× Ubaidah

The Duel

× Hamzah

× Al Walid   × Shaibah   × 'Utbah

Muslims in Pursuit of Polytheists

Shattering Polytheists Attacks

The Farther Side

Polytheists Army (950)

Polytheists Fighting According to the Method of Attack and Retreat

The way to Makkah

The Site of Badr

Al-Madinah ●

Hijaz

Abwa

● Badr

Al-Juhfah ●

Red Sea

● Rabigh

150 km
100
50

Graves of Badr Martyrs

The Spring of Badr and the Mosque of Al-Arish

The campaign of Buwât, in the neighbourhood of Radwa, in Rabi'ul-Awwal, 2 AH.

The Messenger of Allâh ﷺ went out with two hundred of his Companions to intercept a caravan of Quraish which included Umayyah ibn Khalaf Al-Juhani and a hundred men of Quraish, and 2500 camels. The Prophet ﷺ reached Buwât but no fighting took place, then he returned to Al-Madinah.

The campaign of Safawân (the first campaign of Badr) in Rabi'ul-Awwal 2 AH.

The Messenger of Allâh ﷺ went out in pursuit of Kurz ibn Jabir Al-Fihri, who had raided the pasturing camels of Al-Madinah. He pursued him until he reached a valley called Safawân, in the vicinity of Badr, but Kurz got away from him and he could not catch him, so he went back to Al-Madinah.

The campaign of Dhul-'Ushairah in Jumâda Al-Ākhirah 2 AH.

The Messenger of Allâh ﷺ went out with one hundred and fifty – or two hundred – men to intercept a caravan of Quraish. He reached Dhul-'Ushairah which belonged to Bani Mudlij, in the vicinity of Yanbu', where he found out that the caravan had passed by a few days before, heading for Syria. So he went back to Al-Madinah.

The expedition of 'Abdullâh ibn Jahsh Al-Asadi to Batn Al-Nakhlah (near Makkah) in Rajab 2 AH.

The Messenger of Allâh ﷺ sent him with twelve men of the *Muhâjirin* to lie in wait for a caravan of Quraish. He and his men clashed with the traders of Quraish who were coming from Al-Tâ'if. This took place on the last day of Rajab. They captured the caravan and killed 'Amr ibn Al-Hadrami, and took two men captive. During this expedition 'Abdullâh ibn Jahsh was named *Amirul-Mu'minin* (Commander of the Faithful).

The great campaign of Badr in Ramadan 2 AH

The Prophet ﷺ went out with 313 men to intercept a caravan of Quraish that was led by Abu Sufyân. The caravan of Abu Sufyân managed to escape, but Quraish had set out from Makkah for Badr, under the leadership of Abu Jahl, who had nine hundred and fifty

Death of Usma' Bint Marwan (The poetess)

Harrat Waqim

Banu Abdul Ash-hal and Za'wara

An-Nabit

Banu Al-Harith from Al-Khazraj

The Messenger's Mosque

As-Sanh Baqi

Sala' Mount

Wadi Buthan

Banu Waqif

Banu Al Harith

Wadi Mahzour

Houses of Bani Qainuqa'

Bani Quraiza

Wadi Mudhainib

Wadi Al-'Aqiq

Expedition of Umair bin Adi
Rural areas of Al-Madinah
Ramadan 2 A.H.

Banu Auf from Al-Khazraj

Houses of Bani An-Nadir

Quba Mosque

Banu Auf bin Malik from Al-Aws

This area is considered to be the border line between the Orchards of the Ansar and the Orchards of the Jews in Yathrib.

Banu An-Nadir

The Killing of Abi Afak

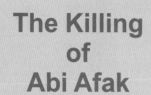 An-Nabit

  Banu Abdul Ash-hal and Za'wara

Harrat Waqim

 Banu Zafar

 Banu Al-Harith from Al-Khazraj

Sala' Mount

The Messenger's Mosque

As-Sanh

Baqi

Wadi Buthan

Banu Waqif

Banu Wuraiq

Banu Al-Harith

Houses of Bani Qainuqa'

Wadi Mahzour

Bani Quraizah

Wadi Al-'Aqiq

Wadi Mudhainib

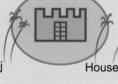

Banu Auf from Al-Khazraj

Houses of Bani An-Nadir

Expedition of Salim bin Umair

Shawwal 2 A.H.

 Quba Mosque

Banu Auf bin Malik from Al-Aws

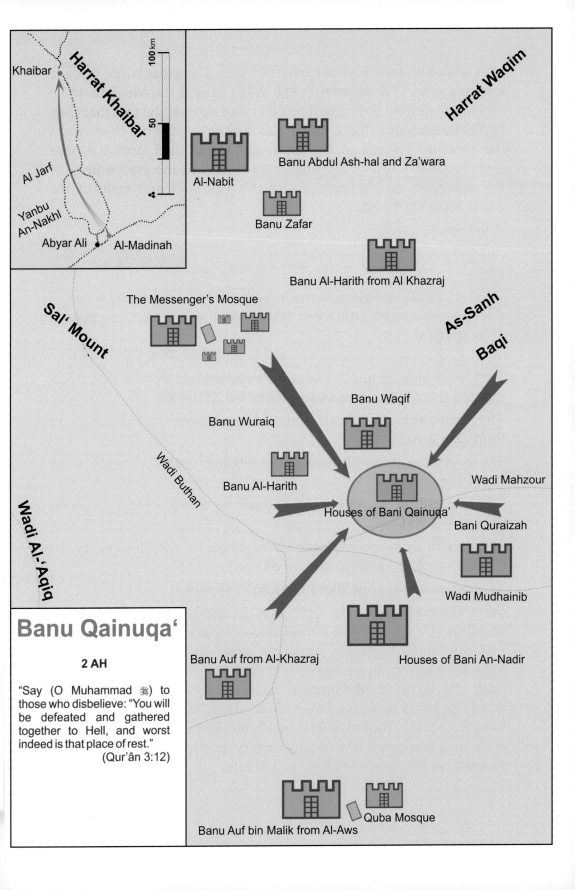

Khaibar

Harrat Khaibar

100 km

50

Al Jarf

Yanbu An-Nakhl

Abyar Ali   Al-Madinah

Harrat Waqim

Al-Nabit

Banu Abdul Ash-hal and Za'wara

Banu Zafar

Banu Al-Harith from Al Khazraj

The Messenger's Mosque

Sal' Mount

As-Sanh

Baqi

Banu Waqif

Banu Wuraiq

Wadi Buthan

Banu Al-Harith

Wadi Al-'Aqiq

Houses of Bani Qainuqa'

Wadi Mahzour

Bani Quraizah

Wadi Mudhainib

Banu Qainuqa'

2 AH

"Say (O Muhammad ﷺ) to those who disbelieve: "You will be defeated and gathered together to Hell, and worst indeed is that place of rest."
(Qur'ân 3:12)

Banu Auf from Al-Khazraj

Houses of Bani An-Nadir

Banu Auf bin Malik from Al-Aws

Quba Mosque

men with him who had prepared for war. The great battle of Badr took place on 17 Ramadân 2 AH. Allâh caused the Muslims to be victorious despite their small number and despite the fact that they had not come out to fight, rather they had only come out to intercept the caravan. Seventy of the *Mushrikin* were killed, and a further seventy taken captive, and the Prophet ﷺ sent the glad tidings of the victory to Al-Madinah. Six of the *Muhâjirin* and eight of the *Ansâr* were martyred.

Allâh said:

﴿وَلَقَدْ نَصَرَكُمُ ٱللَّهُ بِبَدْرٍ وَأَنتُمْ أَذِلَّةٌ فَٱتَّقُوا۟ ٱللَّهَ لَعَلَّكُمْ تَشْكُرُونَ ﴿١٢٣﴾﴾

"And Allâh has already made you victorious at Badr, when you were a weak little force. So fear Allâh much that you may be grateful."

[Qur'â 3:123]

They were lacking in numbers and weapons, yet despite that Allâh granted them a manifest victory over the *Mushrikin*.

The expedition of 'Umair ibn 'Adi to 'Asma' bint Marwân in Ramadân 2 AH.

She used to incite people against the Muslims with her poetry, so he killed her.

The expedition of Sâlim ibn 'Umair to the Jew Abu 'Afak in Shawwâl 2 AH.

He used to incite people against the Muslims with his poetry, so Sâlim vowed to kill him, and he did so.

The campaign against Banu Qainuqa', Shawwâl 2 AH.

Banu Qaynuqa' were the first Jews to break the treaty with the Muslims. They expressed hatred and envy after the Muslims were victorious at Badr, so they broke the treaty and showed themselves to be treacherous, to such an extent that the Jew Ka'b ibn Al-Ashraf said: "By Allâh, if Muhammad has indeed slain these people, it would be better to be dead than alive." Then he went out to Makkah weeping for the *Mushrikin* who had been slain at Badr, then he came back and composed insulting amatory poems about the Muslim women, so the *Ansâr* resolved to kill him.

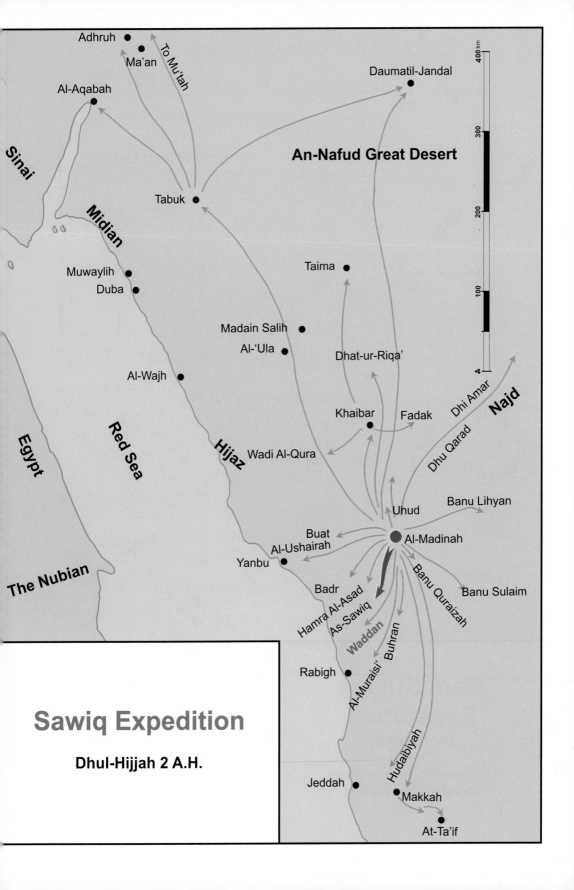

Sawiq Expedition

Dhul-Hijjah 2 A.H.

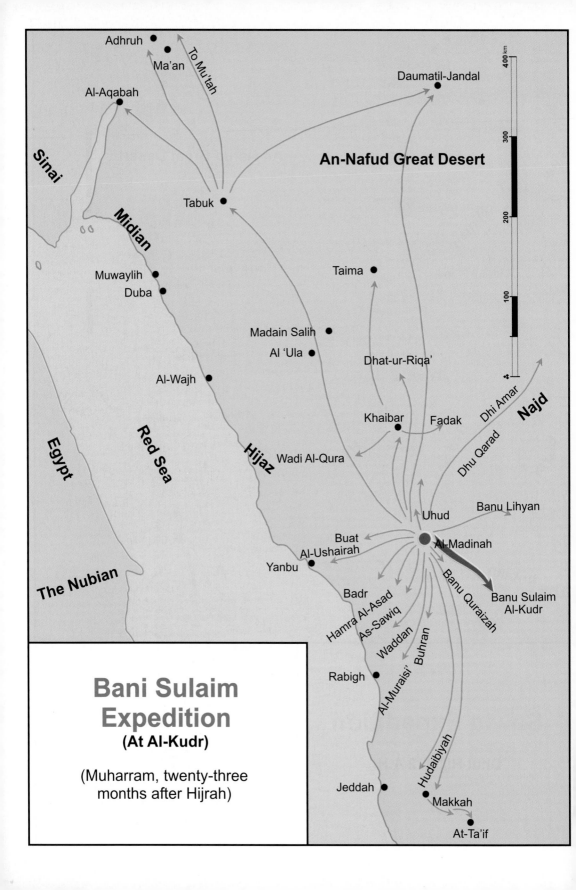

Adhruh

Ma'an

To Mu'tah

Al-Aqabah

Daumatil-Jandal

Sinai

An-Nafud Great Desert

400 km

300

Tabuk

Midian

200

Muwaylih

Taima

100

Duba

Madain Salih

Al 'Ula

Dhat-ur-Riqa'

Al-Wajh

Khaibar

Fadak

Dhi Amar

Najd

Red Sea

Hijaz

Wadi Al-Qura

Dhu Qarad

Egypt

Banu Lihyan

Uhud

The Nubian

Buat

Al-Ushairah

Al-Madinah

Yanbu

Badr

Banu Quraizah

Banu Sulaim
Al-Kudr

Hamra Al-Asad

As-Sawiq

Waddan

Buhran

Rabigh

Al-Muraisi'

Hudaibiyah

Jeddah

Makkah

At-Ta'if

Bani Sulaim
Expedition
(At Al-Kudr)

(Muharram, twenty-three
months after Hijrah)

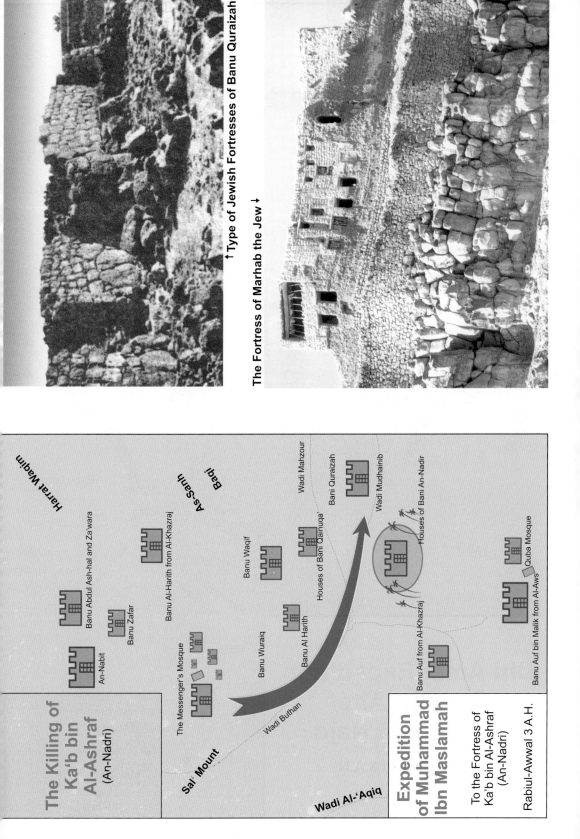

↑ Type of Jewish Fortresses of Banu Quraizah

The Fortress of Marhab the Jew ↓

The Killing of Ka'b bin Al-Ashraf (An-Nadri)

Harrat Waqim

Banu Abdul Ash-hal and Za'wara

An-Nabit

Banu Zafar

Banu Al-Harith from Al-Khazraj

As-Sanh

Baqi'

The Messenger's Mosque

Banu Waqif

Wadi Mahzour

Bani Quraizah

Wadi Mudhainib

Houses of Bani Qainuqa'

Houses of Bani An-Nadir

Banu Wuraiq

Banu Al Harith

Sal' Mount

Wadi Buthan

Banu Auf from Al-Khazraj

Quba Mosque

Banu Auf bin Malik from Al-Aws

Expedition of Muhammad Ibn Maslamah

To the Fortress of Ka'b bin Al-Ashraf (An-Nadri)

Rabiul-Awwal 3 A.H.

Wadi Al-'Aqiq

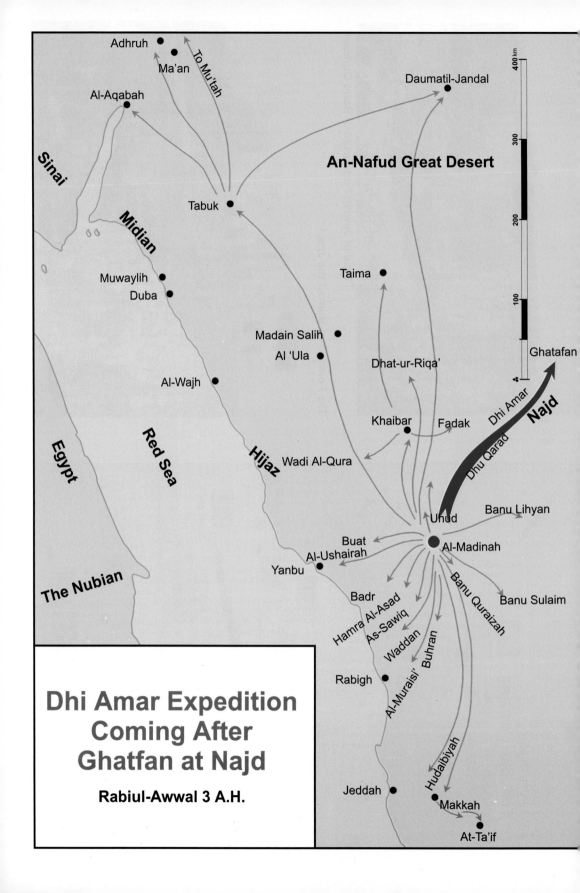

Dhi Amar Expedition Coming After Ghatfan at Najd

Rabiul-Awwal 3 A.H.

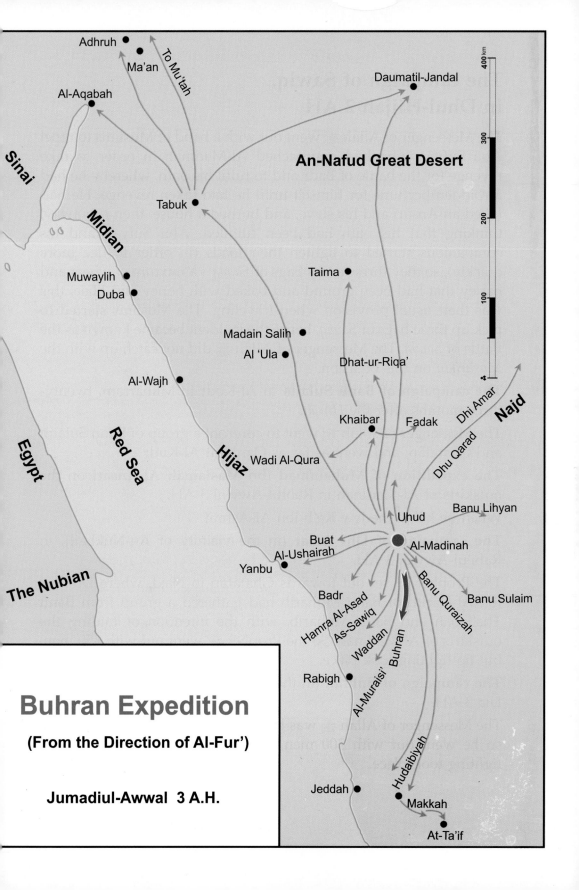

Adhruh
Ma'an
To Mutah
Al-Aqabah
Daumatil-Jandal
Sinai
Midian
An-Nafud Great Desert
Tabuk
Muwaylih
Duba
Taima
Madain Salih
Al 'Ula
Dhat-ur-Riqa'
Al-Wajh
Red Sea
Hijaz
Egypt
Wadi Al-Qura
Khaibar
Fadak
Dhi Amar
Dhu Qarad
Najd
The Nubian
Uhud
Banu Lihyan
Buat
Al-Ushairah
Al-Madinah
Yanbu
Badr
Hamra Al-Asad
As-Sawiq
Waddan
Buhran
Al-Muraisi'
Banu Quraizah
Banu Sulaim
Rabigh
Hudaibiyah
Jeddah
Makkah
At-Ta'if

400 km
300
200
100

Buhran Expedition

(From the Direction of Al-Fur')

Jumadiul-Awwal 3 A.H.

The campaign of Sawiq, in Dhul-Hijjah 2 AH

The Messenger of Allâh ﷺ went out with a band of Muslims to repel Abu Sufyân who had approached Al-Madinah in order to take revenge for the battle of Badr and to fulfil his oath, whereby he had forbidden perfume for himself until he had taken revenge. He had killed an Ansâri and his slave, and burned a house, then run away, thinking that his oath had been fulfilled. Abu Sufyân and his companions started to lighten their loads (in order to flee more quickly), so they threw away bags of *Sawiq* – a mixture of wheat and barley that had been ground and baked with honey and ghee; this was their usual provision when traveling. The Muslims started to pick up these bags of *Sawiq*, hence the incident became known as the Battle of *Sawiq*. The Messenger of Allâh ﷺ did not catch up with the *Mushrikin* on this occasion.

The campaign of Banu Sulaim in Al-Kudr in Muharram, twenty-three months after the *Hijrah*.

The Messenger of Allâh ﷺ went to confront a group of Banu Sulaim and Ghatafân, and went as far as Qarqarat Al-Kudr

The expedition of Muhammad ibn Maslamah Al-Ansâri on the outskirts of Al-Madinah in Rabiul-Awwal 3 AH.

When he killed the Jew Ka'b ibn Al-Ashraf.

The campaign of Dhi Amar (in the vicinity of An-Nukhail), in Rabi'ul-Awwal 3 AH.

The Prophet ﷺ set out towards Ghatafân in Najd, where Du'thur ibn Al-Hârith of Banu Muhârib had gathered a group from Banu Tha'labah and Banu Muhârib, with the intention of raiding the outskirts of Al-Madinah. So the Prophet ﷺ went out with 450 men, but no fighting took place.

The campaign of Buhrân (in the vicinity of Al-Fur') in Jumâda Al-Ula 3 AH.

The Messenger of Allâh ﷺ was looking for a group of Banu Sulaim, so he went out with 300 men, but the group dispersed and no fighting took place.

132

Northern side of the Fortress of Ka'b bin Al-Ashraf ↑

Entrance to the Fortress of Ka'b bin Al-Ashraf from the inside ↓

The killing of
Ka'b ibn Al-Ashraf

When the *Mushrikin* were defeated at Badr in 2 AH, Zaid ibn Hârithah came to the people of the lower quarter and 'Abdullâh ibn Rawâhah came to the people of the upper quarter, sent by the Messenger of Allâh ﷺ to the Muslims in Al-Madinah to bring them the good news of the victory that Allâh had granted him, and of the *Mushrikin* who had been killed. When this news reached Ka'b ibn Al-Ashraf, he said: "Is this true? Do you believe that Muhammad really killed the people named by these two men (meaning Zaid and 'Abdullâh ibn Rawâhah)? These are the nobles of the Arabs and kingly men. By Allâh, if Muhammad has really slain these people then it is better to be dead than alive."

When the news was confirmed, Ka'b went out to Makkah and incited the people against the Messenger of Allâh ﷺ, composing poetry and weeping for the *Mushrikin* who had been slain at Badr. Thus he broke the treaty that had been agreed between the Muslims and the Jews of Al-Madinah.

Then Ka'b went back to Al-Madinah, where he composed insulting amatory verses about the Muslim woman, which offended them. The Messenger of Allâh ﷺ said: "Who will deal with the son of Al-Ashraf for me?" Muhammad ibn Maslamah Al-Ansâri, from the tribe of Banu 'Abdul-Ashhal, said to him: "I will deal with him for you, O Messenger of Allâh." So Ibn Maslamah went, accompanied by Salkân ibn Salâmah ibn Waqsh (Abu Nâ'ilah) and 'Abbâd ibn Bishr ibn Waqsh. The Messenger of Allâh ﷺ went with them as far as Baqi' Al-Gharqad, then they went on to the fortress of Ka'b, where Abu Nâ'ilah called out to him; he came down to meet them and they killed him. Then they returned via Banu Quraizah and Harratul-'Arid. Al-Hârith ibn Aws had stayed behind because of an injury to his head or his leg, and they continued on their way after Al-Hârith joined them. They came to the Messenger of Allâh ﷺ at the end of the night, when he was standing in prayer, and told him that Ka'b ibn Al-Ashraf had been killed, then they went back to their families. Then the Jews became worried about their breaking the treaty with the Muslims and their inciting Quraish and their composing offensive amatory verses about the Muslim women.[1]

---

[1] Ibn Hishâm, 3/7

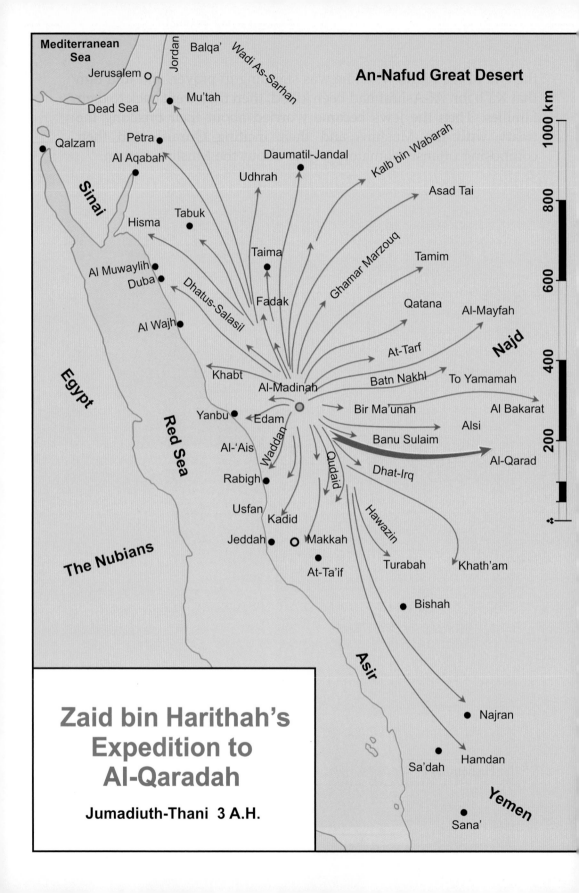

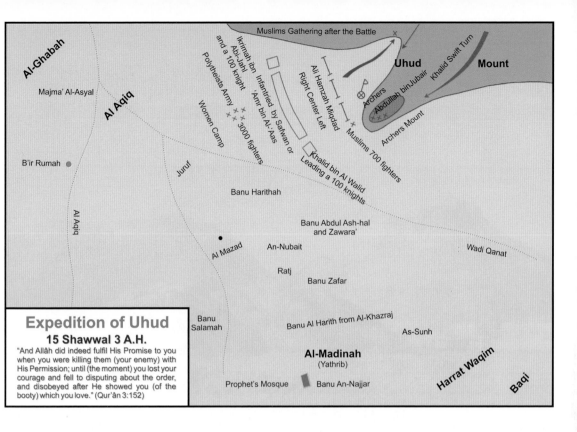

Muslims Gathering after the Battle

Uhud   Mount

Ikrimah ibn Abi-Jahl and a 100 knight

Infantried by Safwan or 'Amr bin Al-'Aas

Polytheists Army

3000 fighters

Women Camp

Ali Hamzah Miqdad
Right Center Left

Khalid Swift Turn

Archers

Abdullah binJubair

Archers Mount

Muslims 700 fighters

Khalid bin Al Walid
Leading a 100 knights

Al-Ghabah

Majma' Al-Asyal

Al Aqiq

B'ir Rumah

Al Aqiq

Juruf

Banu Harithah

Al Mazad   An-Nubait

Ratj

Banu Zafar

Banu Abdul Ash-hal
and Zawara'

Wadi Qanat

Banu
Salamah

Banu Al Harith from Al-Khazraj

As-Sunh

Al-Madinah
(Yathrib)

Harrat Waqim

Baqi

Prophet's Mosque   Banu An-Najjar

Expedition of Uhud
15 Shawwal 3 A.H.
"And Allâh did indeed fulfil His Promise to you
when you were killing them (your enemy) with
His Permission; until (the moment) you lost your
courage and fell to disputing about the order,
and disobeyed after He showed you (of the
booty) which you love." (Qur'ân 3:152)

The Grave of Hamzah (Master of the Martyrs)
Mount Uhud can be seen in the background

The Mount of the Archers, with Mount Uhud in the background ↑

Mount Uhud ↓

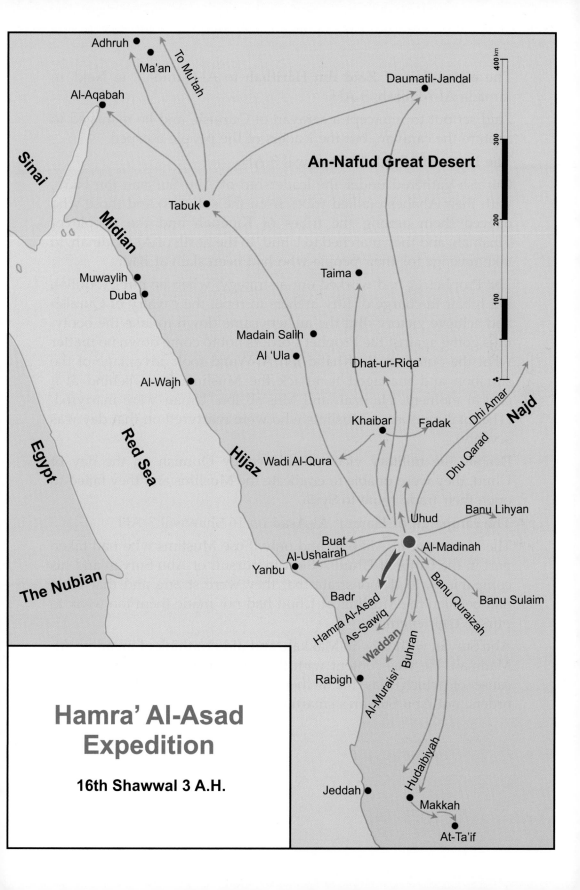

Adhruh
Ma'an
To Mu'tah
Al-Aqabah
Sinai
Midian
Daumatil-Jandal
An-Nafud Great Desert
Tabuk
Muwaylih
Duba
Taima
Madain Salih
Al 'Ula
Dhat-ur-Riqa'
Al-Wajh
Red Sea
Hijaz
Wadi Al-Qura
Khaibar
Fadak
Dhi Amar
Dhu Qarad
Najd
Egypt
Uhud
Banu Lihyan
Buat
Al-Ushairah
Al-Madinah
The Nubian
Yanbu
Badr
Banu Quraizah
Banu Sulaim
Hamra Al-Asad
As-Sawiq
Waddan
Buhran
Rabigh
Al-Muraisi'
Jeddah
Hudaibiyah
Makkah
At-Ta'if

400 km
300
200
100

Hamra' Al-Asad Expedition

16th Shawwal 3 A.H.

The expedition of Zaid ibn Hârithah to Al-Qaradah, in Najd, in Jumâda Al-Akhirah, 3 AH.

Zaid set out to intercept a caravan of Quraish, and he managed to capture the caravan, but the leaders of the people escaped.

The battle of Uhud, 15 Shawwâl 3 AH.

Quraish gathered under the leadership of Abu Sufyaan ibn Harb, with their Ahâbesh (allied tribes from the suburbs) and those who obeyed them among the tribes of Kinânah and the people of Tihâmah, and they marched to Uhud, to the north of Al-Madinah, to take revenge for their people who had been slain at Badr.

The Prophet ﷺ had worked out a strategy, when he put 'Abdullâh ibn Jubair in charge of fifty archers to repel the cavalry of Quraish and achieve victory. But the archers came down to take the booty, thus going against the Prophet's orders not to come down no matter what the outcome. So Khâlid ibn Al-Walid took advantage of the situation and managed to attack the Muslims from behind at a critical moment. Hamzah and Mus'ab ibn 'Umair were martyred. (The total number of Muslims who were martyred on that day was seventy).

Despite the military victory achieved by Quraish on the day of Uhud, they were unable to eradicate the Muslims and they failed to open their trade route to Syria.

The campaign of Hamra' Al-Asad on 16 Shawwâl 3 AH.

The Messenger of Allâh ﷺ and only those Muslims who had taken part in the battle of Uhud set out in pursuit of Abu Sufyân and his companions, to demonstrate that they were strong and that what had befallen the Muslims at Uhud had not made them too weak to pursue their enemies.

Abu Sufyân withdrew to Makkah, and did not think of invading Al-Madinah. He was content with the apparent victory at Uhud, the cause of which was the archers' disobedience of the Prophet's orders, not Abu Sufyan's smartness or capabilities.

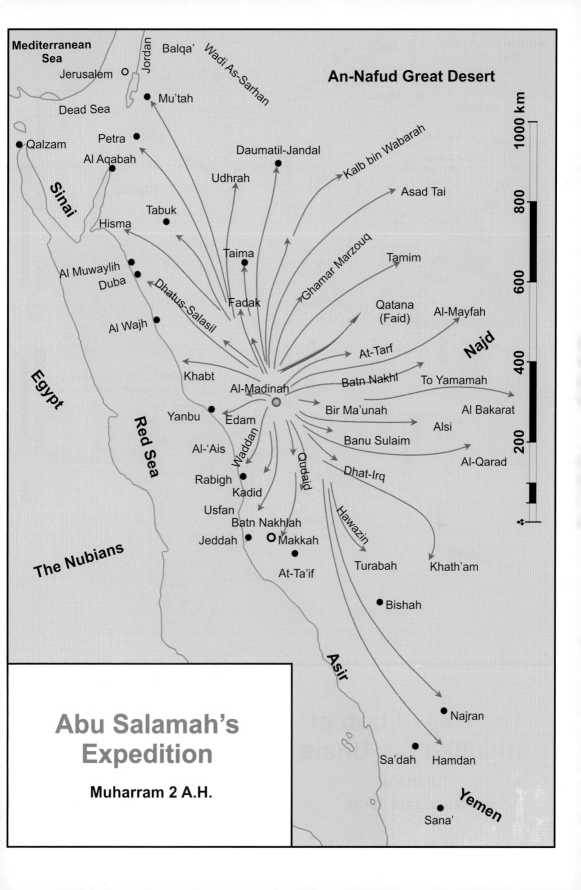

Abu Salamah's Expedition

Muharram 2 A.H.

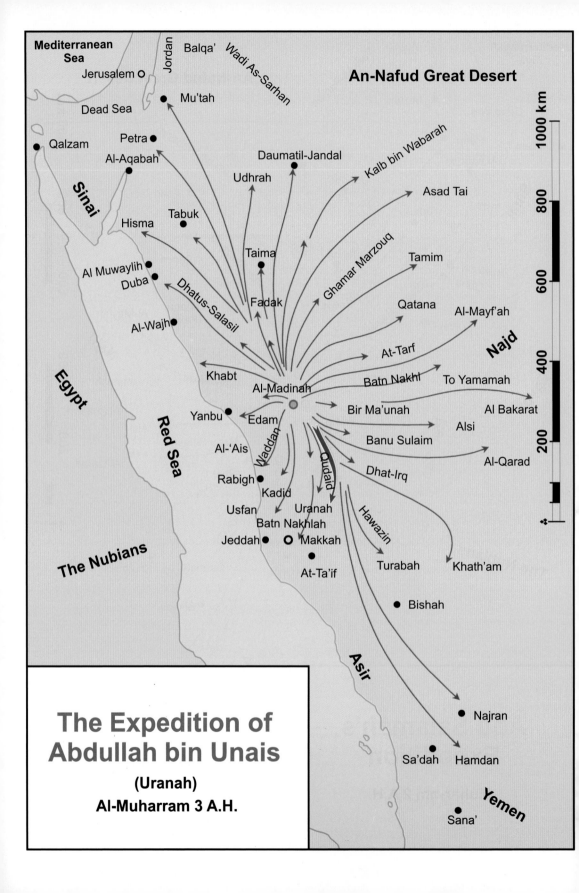

The Expedition of
Abdullah bin Unais

(Uranah)
Al-Muharram 3 A.H.

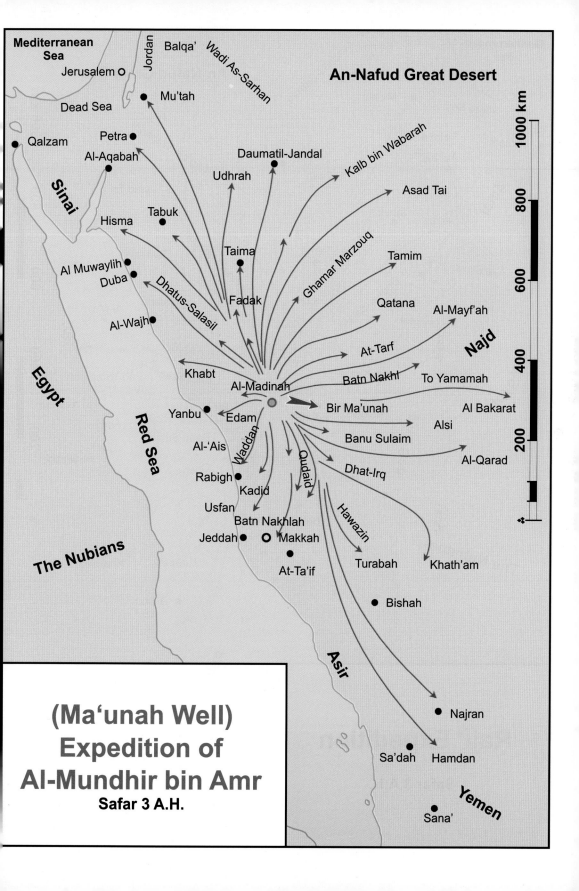

(Ma'unah Well)
Expedition of
Al-Mundhir bin Amr
Safar 3 A.H.

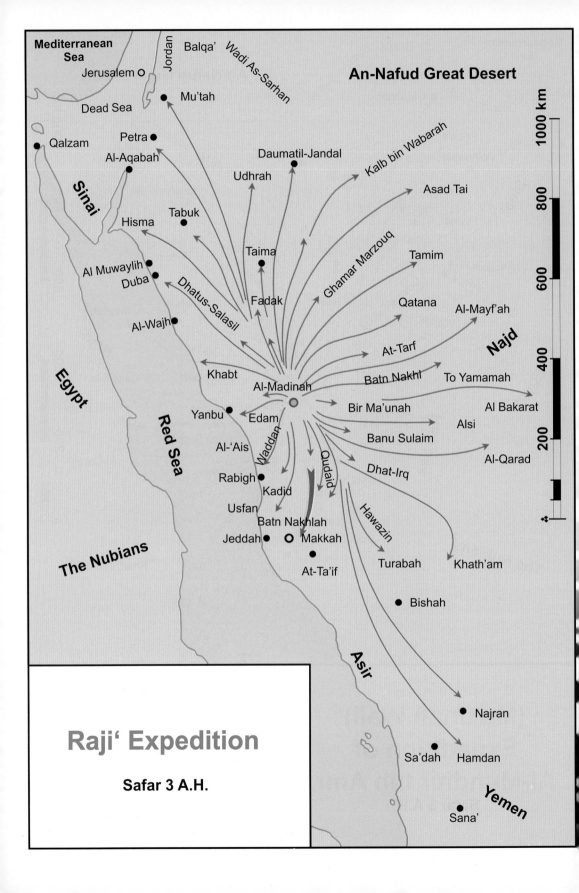

Raji' Expedition

Safar 3 A.H.

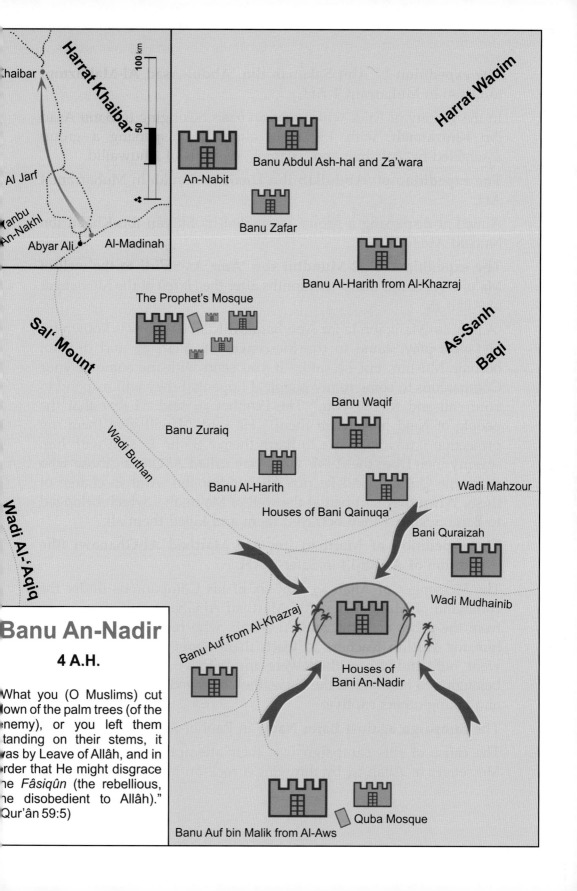

Khaibar

Harrat Khaibar

100 km

50

Al Jarf

Yanbu
An-Nakhl

Abyar Ali

Al-Madinah

Harrat Waqim

An-Nabit

Banu Abdul Ash-hal and Za'wara

Banu Zafar

Banu Al-Harith from Al-Khazraj

The Prophet's Mosque

Sal' Mount

Wadi Buthan

Wadi Al-'Aqiq

As-Sanh

Baqi

Banu Waqif

Banu Zuraiq

Banu Al-Harith

Houses of Bani Qainuqa'

Wadi Mahzour

Bani Quraizah

Wadi Mudhainib

Banu Auf from Al-Khazraj

Houses of
Bani An-Nadir

Banu An-Nadir

4 A.H.

What you (O Muslims) cut down of the palm trees (of the enemy), or you left them standing on their stems, it was by Leave of Allâh, and in order that He might disgrace the *Fâsiqûn* (the rebellious, the disobedient to Allâh)." (Qur'ân 59:5)

Banu Auf bin Malik from Al-Aws

Quba Mosque

The expedition of Abu Salamah ibn 'Abdul-Asad Al-Makhzumi to Qatan in Muharram 4 AH.

In the vicinity of Faid, which was an oasis belonging to Banu Asad ibn Khuzaimah, with 150 men, aimed at dispersing a group assembled by Tulaihah and Salamah, the sons of Khuwailid.

The expedition of 'Abdullâh ibn Unais to 'Urnah in Muharram 4 AH.

Aimed at dispersing a group assembled by Sufyân ibn Khâlid ibn Nubaih Al-Hudhali.

The expedition of Al-Mundhir ibn 'Amr As-Sâ'idi to the well of Ma'unah in Safar, thirty-six months after the *Hijrah* of the Messenger of Allâh ﷺ.

'Aamir ibn Mâlik ibn Ja'far Abu Bara' Al-Kilâbi, who was known for his spear-play, came to the Messenger of Allâh ﷺ and did not become Muslim, but he said: "If you send with me some of your Companions to come to my people, I hope that they will respond to your call and follow you." The Prophet ﷺ said: "I fear that the people of Najd may harm them." He said: "I will give them my protection if anyone seeks to harm them." So he ﷺ sent with him seventy men from the *Ansâr* who were called *Al-Qurra'* (those who recite the Qur'ân), and he put Al-Mundhir ibn 'Amr in charge of them. When they stopped at the well of Ma'unah – which belonged to Banu Sulaim – they betrayed them and killed them all.

The expedition of Marthad ibn Abi Marthad Al-Ghanawi (the expedition of Ar-Raji') in Safar 4 AH.

The Messenger of Allâh ﷺ sent six of his Companions under the command of Marthad ibn Abi Marthad Al-Ghanawi with a group from the tribes of 'Adal and Al-Qârah, who had come and asked him for Muslim teachers to teach them about Islam. The people went out, and when they were in Ar-Raji', which is an oasis belonging to Hudhail in the Hijâz, they betrayed them, killing some and taking others captive.

The campaign against Banu Nadir in Rabi'ul-Awwal 4 AH.

The cause of this campaign was their attempt to assassinate the Messenger of Allâh ﷺ by throwing a rock on him. The Prophet ﷺ

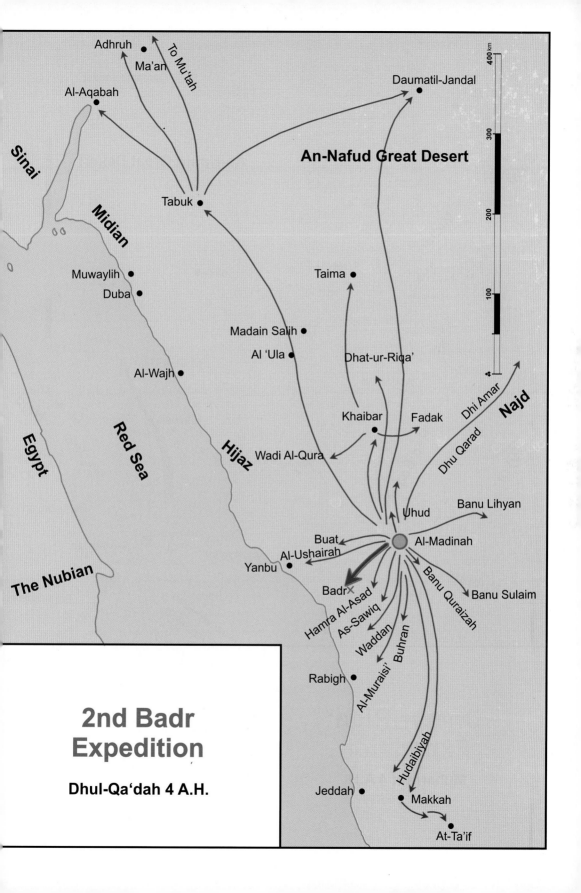

2nd Badr
Expedition

Dhul-Qa'dah 4 A.H.

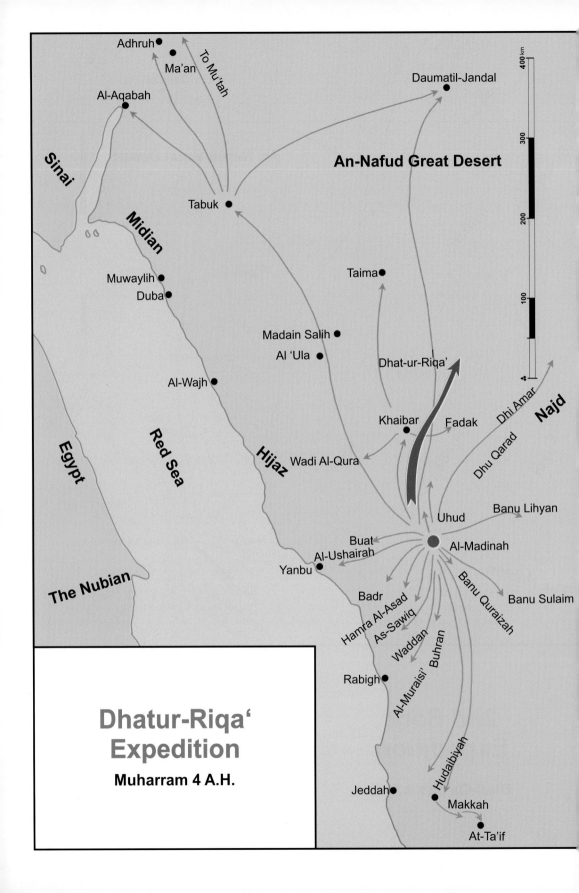

Adhruh
Ma'an
To Mu'tah
Al-Aqabah
Daumatil-Jandal
Sinai
An-Nafud Great Desert
Midian
Tabuk
Muwaylih
Duba
Taima
Madain Salih
Al 'Ula
Dhat-ur-Riqa'
Dhi Amar
Najd
Al-Wajh
Khaibar
Fadak
Dhu Qarad
Egypt
Red Sea
Hijaz
Wadi Al-Qura
Banu Lihyan
Uhud
The Nubian
Buat
Al-Ushairah
Al-Madinah
Yanbu
Banu Quraizah
Banu Sulaim
Badr
Hamra Al-Asad
As-Sawiq
Waddan
Buhran
Al-Muraisi'
Rabigh
Hudaibiyah
Jeddah
Makkah
At-Ta'if

400 km
300
200
100

Dhatur-Riqa' Expedition

Muharram 4 A.H.

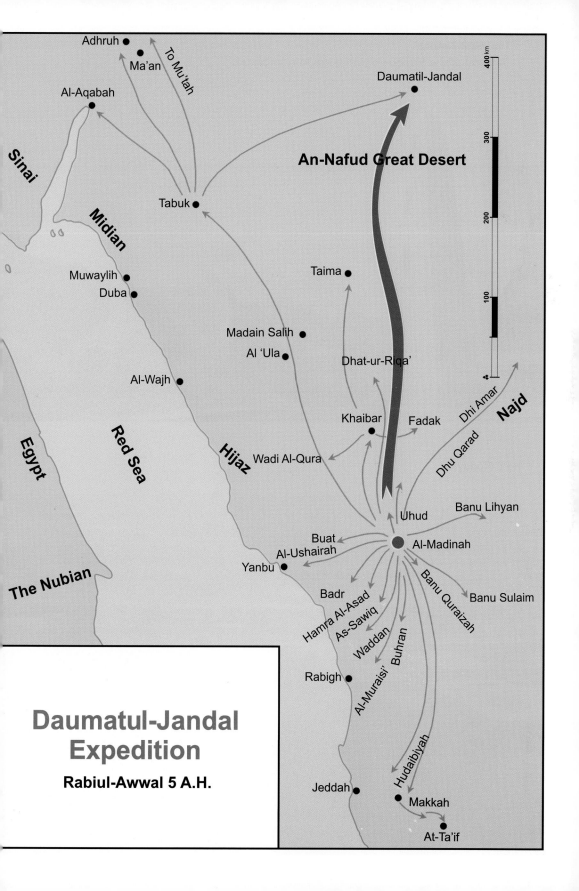

Adhruh

Ma'an

To Mu'tah

Al-Aqabah

Daumatil-Jandal

Sinai

Midian

An-Nafud Great Desert

Tabuk

Muwaylih

Duba

Taima

Madain Salih

Al 'Ula

Dhat-ur-Riqa'

Al-Wajh

Red Sea

Hijaz

Khaibar

Fadak

Dhi Amar

Najd

Egypt

Wadi Al-Qura

Dhu Qarad

Uhud

Banu Lihyan

The Nubian

Buat

Al-Ushairah

Yanbu

Al-Madinah

Banu Quraizah

Banu Sulaim

Badr

Hamra Al-Asad

As-Sawiq

Waddan

Al-Muraisi'

Buhran

Rabigh

Hudaibiyah

Jeddah

Makkah

At-Ta'if

Daumatul-Jandal Expedition

Rabiul-Awwal 5 A.H.

400 km

300

200

100

Daumatil-Jandal
(Minaret of the Mosque of Umar bin Al-Khattab ﷺ)

Ha'il (Today)

had gone to the Jews of Banu An-Nadir to ask them for help in paying the blood money for two men of Banu 'Aamir, because of the treaty that the Messenger of Allâh ﷺ had with them. But Banu An-Nadir said: "Let us kill him and take his companions as prisoners to Makkah, where we can sell them to Quraish."

After they were besieged, they asked the Messenger of Allâh ﷺ to send them into exile, and not kill them, and to let them take whatever of their wealth their camels could carry, except weapons. So they left Al-Madinah and settled in Khaibar, and some of them went on to Adhra'ât.

The final campaign of Badr, also known as Badr Al-Maw'id or the third battle of Badr, in Dhul-Qa'dah 4 AH.

Abu Sufyân, along with Quraish, wanted to march on Al-Madinah, so the Prophet ﷺ and his Companions came out to Badr and waited for him, as they had agreed to meet one year on from Uhud. The Prophet ﷺ stayed there for eight days, then he went back to Al-Madinah. Safwân ibn Umaiyyah said to Abu Sufyân: "By Allâh, I told you not to agree to meet with them the next year. They do not fear us any more, and they have seen that we did not appear, and all that stopped us was our weakness."

The campaign of Dhâtur-Riqâ' in Muharram 5 AH.

The Prophet ﷺ went to Najd with four hundred of his Companions, looking for Banu Muhârib and Banu Tha'labah of Ghatafân, who had assembled an army to fight him. This campaign was called Dhâtur-Riqâ', as was reported by Al-Bukhâri from Abu Mûsa Al-Ash'ari who said: "We went out with the Prophet ﷺ on a campaign, and there was one camel for every six persons, which we took turns to ride. So (due to excessive walking) our feet became injured, and my feet became injured and my toenails fell off, and we wrapped our feet with pieces of cloth (*Riqâ'*), and for this reason the campaign was named Dhâtur-Riqâ' as we wrapped our feet with rags (*Riqâ'*)."

But no fighting took place between the Muslims and the *Mushrikin*.

The campaign of Daumatil-Jandal in Rabi'ul-Awwal 5 AH.

The Prophet ﷺ heard that in Daumatil-Jandal there was a large group who wanted to approach Al-Madinah, so he mobilized the

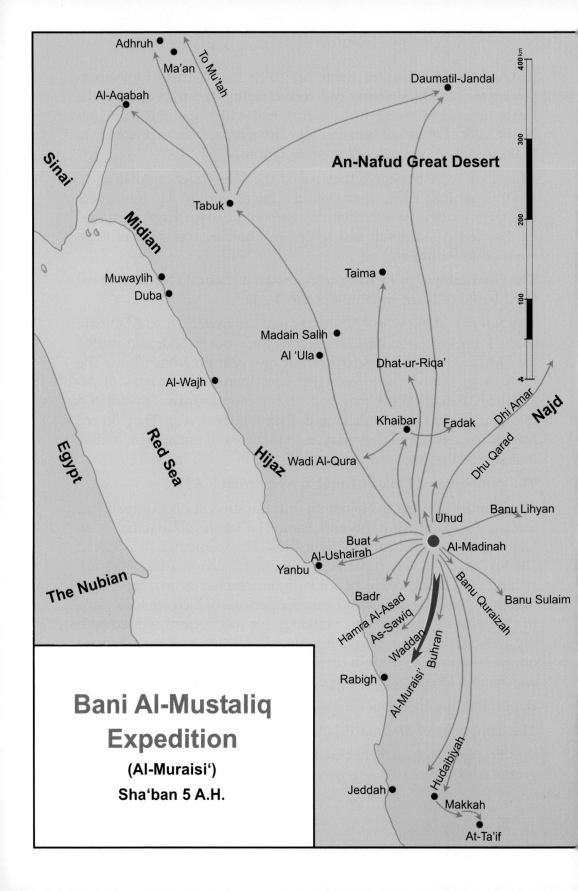

Bani Al-Mustaliq
Expedition
(Al-Muraisi')
Sha'ban 5 A.H.

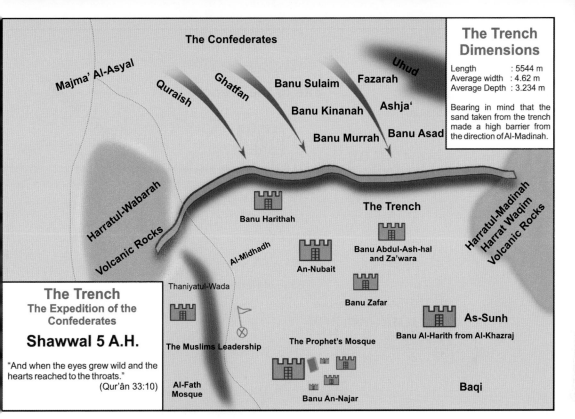

The Confederates

Majma' Al-Asyal

Quraish

Ghatfan

Banu Sulaim

Fazarah

Uhud

Banu Kinanah

Ashja'

Banu Murrah

Banu Asad

The Trench Dimensions

Length : 5544 m
Average width : 4.62 m
Average Depth : 3.234 m

Bearing in mind that the sand taken from the trench made a high barrier from the direction of Al-Madinah.

Harratul-Wabarah
Volcanic Rocks

Banu Harithah

The Trench

Al-Midhadh

An-Nubait

Banu Abdul-Ash-hal and Za'wara

Harratul-Madinah
Harrat Waqim
Volcanic Rocks

Thaniyatul-Wada

Banu Zafar

As-Sunh

Banu Al-Harith from Al-Khazraj

The Muslims Leadership

The Prophet's Mosque

The Trench
The Expedition of the Confederates

Shawwal 5 A.H.

"And when the eyes grew wild and the hearts reached to the throats."
(Qur'ân 33:10)

Al-Fath Mosque

Banu An-Najar

Baqi

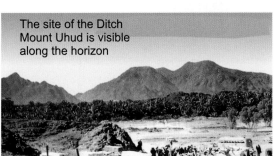

The site of the Ditch Mount Uhud is visible along the horizon

The slope of Mount Sal '.

The site where the leaders were based, and where Al-Fath Mosque was subsequently built.

The mosques of Abu Bakr, Ali bin Abi Talib, and Salman Al-Farisi are also visible in this picture.

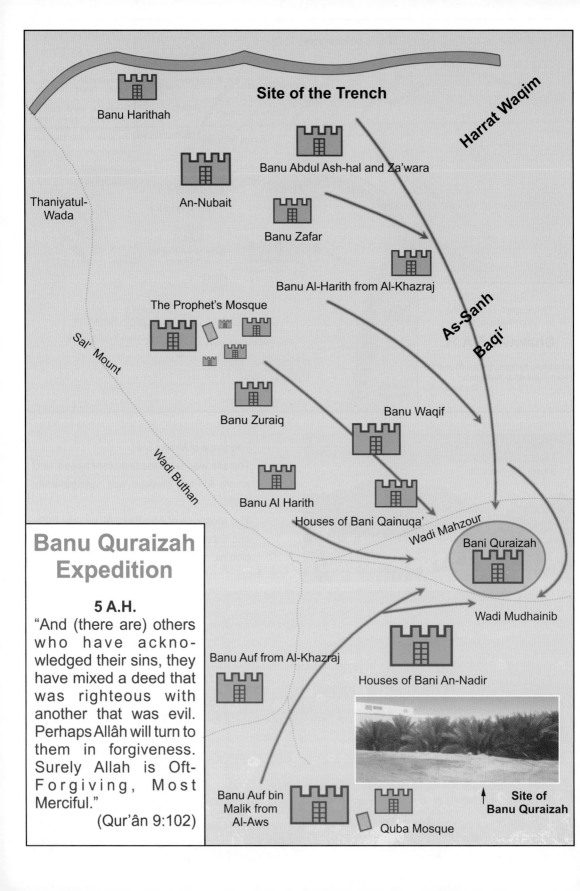

Site of the Trench

Banu Harithah

Harrat Waqim

Banu Abdul Ash-hal and Za'wara

An-Nubait

Thaniyatul-Wada

Banu Zafar

Banu Al-Harith from Al-Khazraj

As-Sanh

Baqi'

The Prophet's Mosque

Sal' Mount

Banu Zuraiq

Banu Waqif

Wadi Buthan

Banu Al Harith

Houses of Bani Qainuqa'

Wadi Mahzour

Bani Quraizah

Banu Quraizah Expedition

5 A.H.

"And (there are) others who have acknowledged their sins, they have mixed a deed that was righteous with another that was evil. Perhaps Allâh will turn to them in forgiveness. Surely Allah is Oft-Forgiving, Most Merciful."

(Qur'ân 9:102)

Wadi Mudhainib

Banu Auf from Al-Khazraj

Houses of Bani An-Nadir

Banu Auf bin Malik from Al-Aws

Quba Mosque

Site of Banu Quraizah

people and set out with one thousand Muslims. When he got near to Daumatil-Jandal, the group dispersed, so he ﷺ sent raiding parties in several directions, then they came back, and did not encounter anyone.

The campaign against Banu Mustaliq (Al-Muraisi') in Sha'bân 5 AH.

The reason for this battle was that Al-Hârith ibn Dirâr, the leader of Banu Mustaliq, who were Banu Judhaimah ibn Ka'b from Khuzâ'ah, had mobilized his people to wage war on the Messenger of Allâh ﷺ, so he went out with 700 of his Companions, and he met the *Mushrikin* at the oasis of Al-Muraisi'. The Muslims were victorious; they took men and women captive and took their camels and sheep as booty.

The battle of Al-Khandaq (*Al-Ahzâb* or the Confederates) in Shawwâl 5 AH.

The reason for this was that the Jews had incited Quraish and told them, "We will be with you against him until we eradicate him." So Quraish and the tribes who were with them, and Ghatafân, Banu Murrah, Ashja', Sulaim and Asad, marched forth. The ditch (Al-Khandaq) was dug on the north of Al-Madinah, on the suggestion of Salmân Al-Fârisi. Its length was 5544 meters, with an average width of 4.62 meters and an average depth of 3.234 meters.

After a siege that lasted for one month, the Confederates split without having achieved anything, because of a wind that did not go anywhere beyond the camp of the *Mushrikin*, even though the Jews of Banu Quraizah had broken their treaty with the Messenger of Allâh ﷺ.

The campaign against Banu Quraizah in Dhul-Qa'dah 5 AH.

The reason for this battle was fair retribution for an act of blatant treachery and violation of a signed treaty (i.e., treason), at the time when the Confederates had gathered. The Prophet ﷺ marched to their fortresses, and after a siege, Sa'd ibn Mu'âdh passed judgement on them, based on their own request. He ruled that the men should be killed, their wealth should be shared out, and the children and women should be taken captive. Banu Quraizah did not question

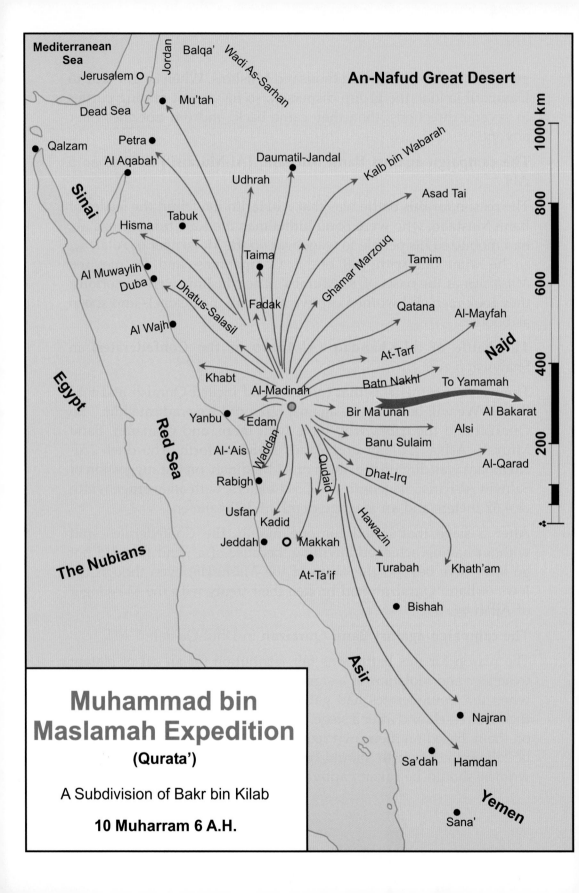

Muhammad bin Maslamah Expedition

(Qurata')

A Subdivision of Bakr bin Kilab

10 Muharram 6 A.H.

this siege or this retribution, because they knew what they had done.

The expedition of Muhammad ibn Maslamah Al-Ansâri to Al-Qurata' on 10 Muharram 6 AH.

He led thirty riders to Al-Qurata', which is a valley in (the land of) Banu Bakr of Kilâb.

The killing of
Salâm ibn Abi Huqaiq

A group of Jewish leaders, including Abu Râfi' Salâm ibn Abi-Huqaiq traveled from Khaibar and went to Quraish in Makkah, and called on them to wage war on the Messenger of Allâh ﷺ. They said: "We will be with you against him, until we eradicate him." Quraish said to them: "Welcome; the dearest of people to us are those who help us to fight Muhammad, but we will not trust you until you prostrate to our gods, then we will trust you." So they did that, and Quraish said to those Jews: "O Jews, you are the people of the first Book and of knowledge. Tell us about the differences between us and Muhammad. Is our religion better or that of Muhammad? Are we more guided or is Muhammad?" They said, "Nay, your religion is better than his, you are closer to the truth than him, and you are more guided, because you venerate this House and provide water to the pilgrims; you offer sacrifices and you worship as your forefathers worshipped. So, you are closer to the truth than him."[1]

Concerning them, Allâh revealed the words:

﴿أَلَمْ تَرَ إِلَى ٱلَّذِينَ أُوتُوا۟ نَصِيبًا مِّنَ ٱلْكِتَـٰبِ يُؤْمِنُونَ بِٱلْجِبْتِ وَٱلطَّـٰغُوتِ وَيَقُولُونَ لِلَّذِينَ كَفَرُوا۟ هَـٰٓؤُلَآءِ أَهْدَىٰ مِنَ ٱلَّذِينَ ءَامَنُوا۟ سَبِيلًا ۝ أُو۟لَـٰٓئِكَ ٱلَّذِينَ لَعَنَهُمُ ٱللَّهُ وَمَن يَلْعَنِ ٱللَّهُ فَلَن تَجِدَ لَهُۥ نَصِيرًا ۝﴾

"Have you not seen those who were given a portion of the Scripture? They believe in *Jibt* and *Tâghut*[2] and say to the

---

[1] Ibn Hishâm, 3/127; At-Tabari, 2/564' *'Uyun Al-Athar*, 2/55; Ibn Khaldun, 2/29; *Al-Bidâyah wan-Nihâyah*, 4/92; *Ar-Rawdul-Unuf*, 3/276; *Al-Iktifa'*, 1/113; *Al-Seerah An-Nabawiyyah* by Ibn Kathir, 1/181.

[2] The words '*Jibt* and *Tâghut''* cover wide meanings: They mean anything worshipped other than the Real God (Allâh), i.e., all the false deities, it may be an idol, Satan, graves, stone, sun, star, angel, saints or any human being.

disbelievers that they are better guided as regards the way than the believers (Muslims). They are those whom Allâh has cursed, and he whom Allâh curses, you will not find for him (any) helper."

[Qur'ân 4:51-52]

Quraish were pleased with what the Jewish delegation had said. At that point fifty men came forth from the clans of Quraish and made a pact whilst pressing their chests to the Ka'bah and clinging to its coverings, that they would not let one another down and that they would be united against Muhammad and would persist until the last man.

Then Ibn Abi-Huqaiq and those who were with him went to Ghatafân – from Qais 'Ailân – and incited them to join the war against the Messenger of Allâh ﷺ. They said to them: "We will be with you and Quraish has promised to be with us." And the Jews offered Ghatafân half the produce of Khaibar every year.

When the battle of Al-Khandaq – the direct cause of which was the Jews' incitement of others against the Muslims – was over, and the affair of Banu Quraizah who had broken the treaty at the most critical moment, had been dealt with, Khazraj asked the Messenger of Allâh ﷺ for permission to kill Salâm ibn Abi-Huqaiq, who was in Khaibar, and he gave them permission. So five people from Al-Khazraj, from Banu Salamah, went out: 'Abdullâh ibn 'Atik, Mas'ud ibn Sinân, 'Abdullâh ibn Unais, Abu Qatâdah (Al-Hârith ibn Rab'i Al-Ansâri) and Khuzâ'i ibn Aswad, an ally of theirs from Aslam. The Messenger of Allâh ﷺ appointed 'Abdullâh ibn 'Atik in charge of them, and forbade them to kill any child or woman. They set out for Khaibar, where they came to the house of Ibn Abi-Huqaiq at night, where they were able to kill him as a punishment for his incitement of others.

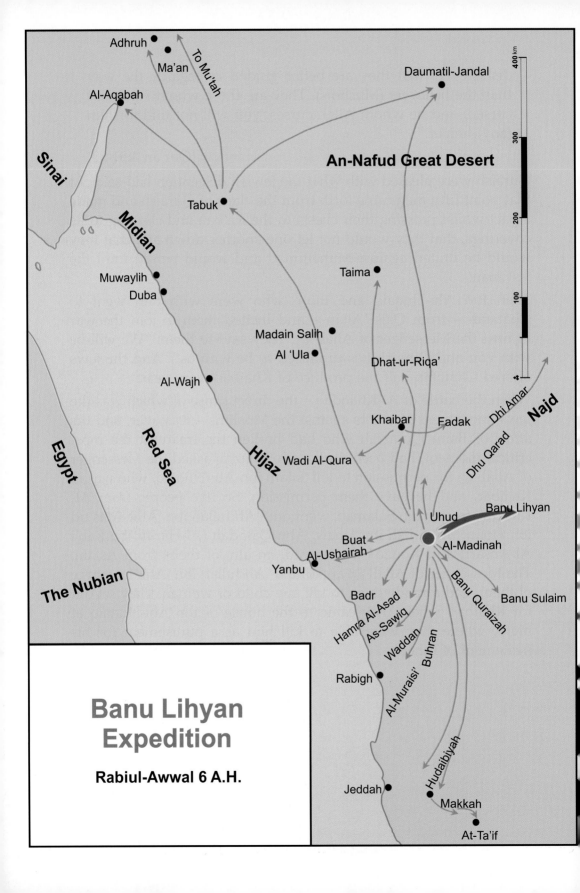

Adhruh

Ma'an

To Mu'tah

Al-Aqabah

Daumatil-Jandal

Sinai

An-Nafud Great Desert

Midian

Tabuk

400 km

300

200

Muwaylih

Duba

Taima

100

Madain Salih

Al 'Ula

Dhat-ur-Riqa'

Al-Wajh

Dhi Amar

Najd

Khaibar

Fadak

Egypt

Red Sea

Hijaz

Wadi Al-Qura

Dhu Qarad

The Nubian

Uhud

Banu Lihyan

Al-Madinah

Buat

Al-Ushairah

Banu Quraizah

Yanbu

Banu Sulaim

Badr

Hamra Al-Asad

As-Sawiq

Waddan

Buhran

Rabigh

Al-Muraisi'

Hudaibiyah

Jeddah

Makkah

**Banu Lihyan
Expedition**

Rabiul-Awwal 6 A.H.

At-Ta'if

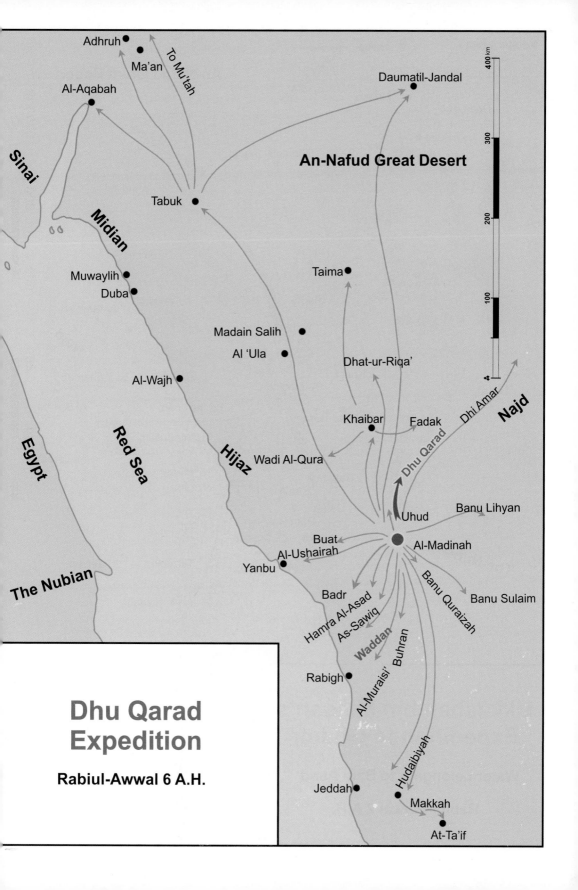

Adhruh
Ma'an
To Mu'tah
Al-Aqabah
Daumatil-Jandal

An-Nafud Great Desert

Sinai

Midian

Tabuk

Muwaylih
Duba

Taima

Madain Salih
Al 'Ula

Dhat-ur-Riqa'

Al-Wajh

Red Sea

Hijaz

Khaibar
Fadak
Dhi Amar
Najd
Dhu Qarad

Wadi Al-Qura

Egypt

Uhud
Banu Lihyan

The Nubian

Buat
Al-Ushairah
Al-Madinah

Yanbu

Badr
Hamra Al-Asad
As-Sawiq
Banu Quraizah
Banu Sulaim

Waddan
Buhran

Al-Muraisi'

Rabigh

Dhu Qarad
Expedition

Rabiul-Awwal 6 A.H.

Hudaibiyah

Jeddah
Makkah
At-Ta'if

400 km

300

200

100

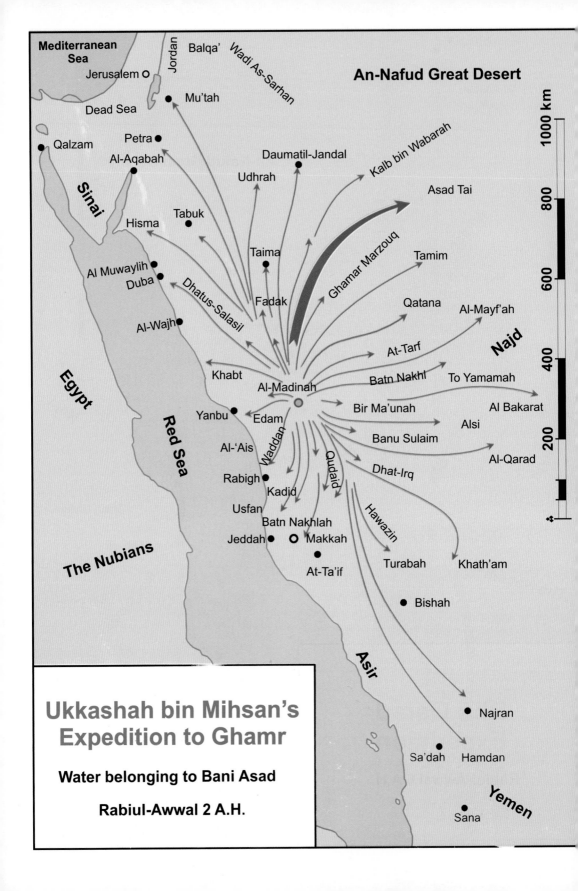

Mediterranean
Sea

An-Nafud Great Desert

Jerusalem ○

Jordan

Balqa'

Wadi As-Sarhan

Mu'tah

Dead Sea

Qalzam

Petra ●

Al-Aqabah

Daumatil-Jandal

Kalb bin Wabarah

Udhrah

Asad Tai

Sinai

Tabuk

Hisma

Taima

Ghamar Marzouq

Tamim

Al Muwaylih ●
Duba ●

Dhatus-Salasil

Fadak

Qatana

Al-Mayf'ah

Najd

Al-Wajh ●

At-Tarf

Egypt

Khabt

Batn Nakhl

To Yamamah

Red Sea

Al-Madinah

Bir Ma'unah

Al Bakarat

Yanbu ●
Edam

Banu Sulaim

Alsi

Al-'Ais

Waddan

Al-Qarad

Rabigh ●
Kadid

Qudaid

Dhat-Irq

Usfan

Batn Nakhlah

Hawazin

The Nubians

Jeddah ● ○ Makkah

At-Ta'if

Turabah

Khath'am

Asir

Bishah

1000 km

800

600

400

200

Ukkashah bin Mihsan's Expedition to Ghamr

Water belonging to Bani Asad

Rabiul-Awwal 2 A.H.

Najran

Sa'dah   Hamdan

Yemen

Sana

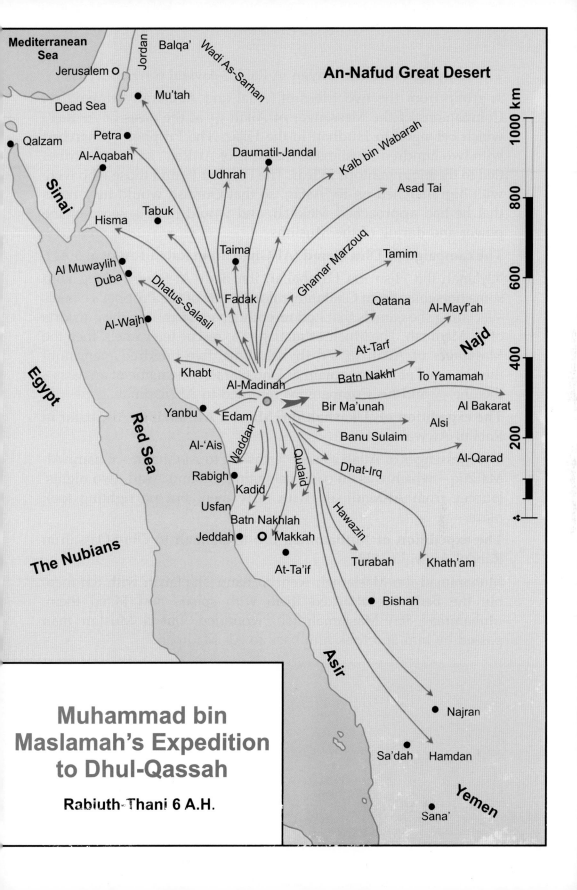

Muhammad bin Maslamah's Expedition to Dhul-Qassah

Rabiuth-Thani 6 A.H.

The campaign of Bani Lihyân in Rabiul-Awwal 6 AH.

A group from the two tribes of 'Adal and Al-Qârah betrayed six Companions of the Messenger of Allâh ﷺ at the oasis of Ar-Raji', which belonged to Hudhail in the Hijâz. The Prophet ﷺ marched with two hundred Muslims to the oasis of Ar-Raji', so the two tribes fled to the mountaintops in fear. The Prophet ﷺ and those who were with him marched on to 'Asfân, so that Quraish would hear news that he had approached Makkah, and would have a sense of the power and daring of the Muslims.

The campaign of Dhu Qarad (Al-Ghâbah) in Rabi'ul-Awwal 6 AH.

'Uyainah ibn Hisn ibn Hudhaifah ibn Badr Al-Fazâri, along with some horsemen from Ghatafân, raided some of the Prophet's camels – lactating she-camels that had recently given birth – on the outskirts of Al-Madinah. The Muslims managed to rescue ten camels, then the Messenger of Allâh ﷺ led the Muslims, five hundred men, until they stopped at the mountain of Dhu Qarad – the name of an oasis – then he ﷺ and his Companions returned to Al-Madinah.

The expedition of 'Ukâshah ibn Mihsan Al-Asadi to Al-Ghamr in Rabi'ul-Awwal 6 AH.

The Messenger of Allâh ﷺ sent 'Ukâshah to Al-Ghamr – Ghamr Al-Marzuq – which was an oasis belonging to Banu Asad, two nights' journey from Al-Madinah, with forty men. But no fighting took place.

The expedition of Muhammad ibn Maslamah to Dhul-Qassah in Rabi'ul-Awwal 6 AH.

Muhammad ibn Maslamah went to Banu Tha'labah with ten men, but the Bedouins attacked them with spears and killed them. Muhammad ibn Maslamah fell, wounded, but a Muslim man passed by him and took him back to Al- Madinah.

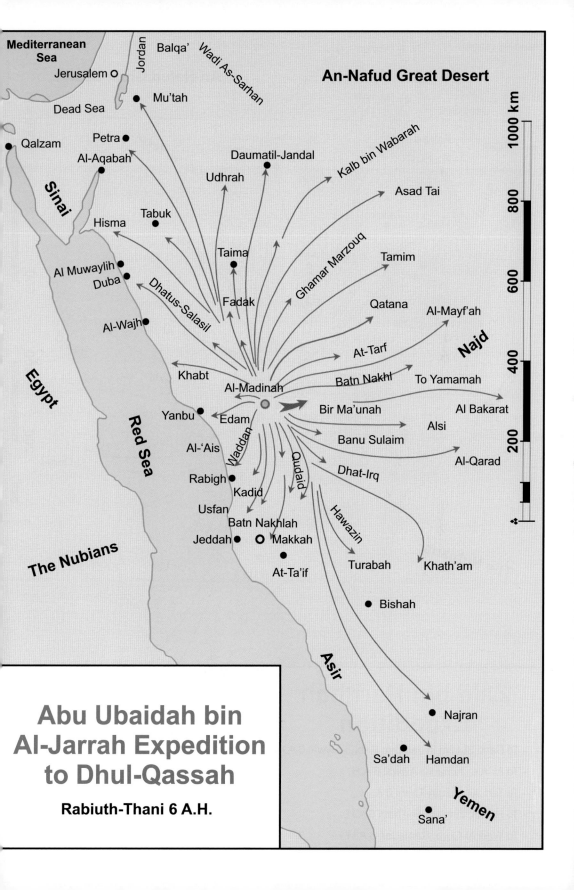

Abu Ubaidah bin Al-Jarrah Expedition to Dhul-Qassah

Rabiuth-Thani 6 A.H.

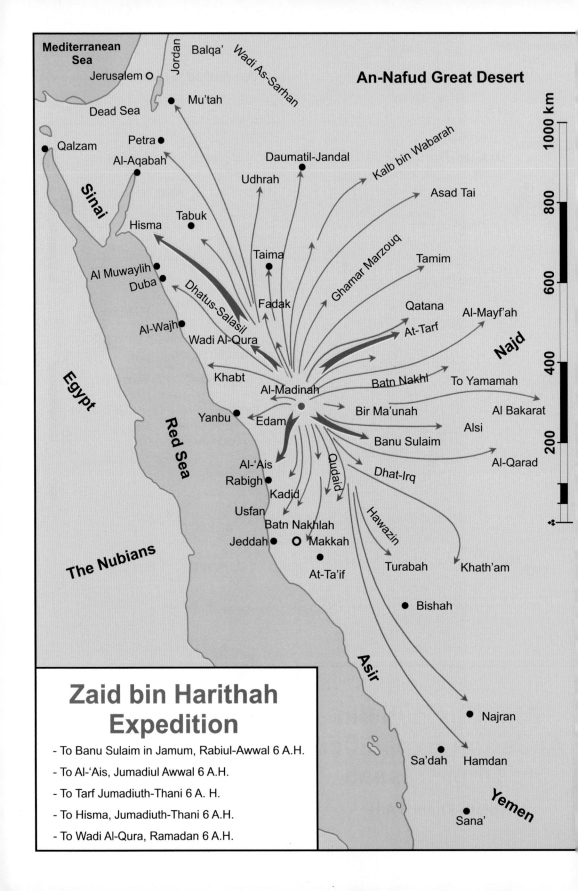

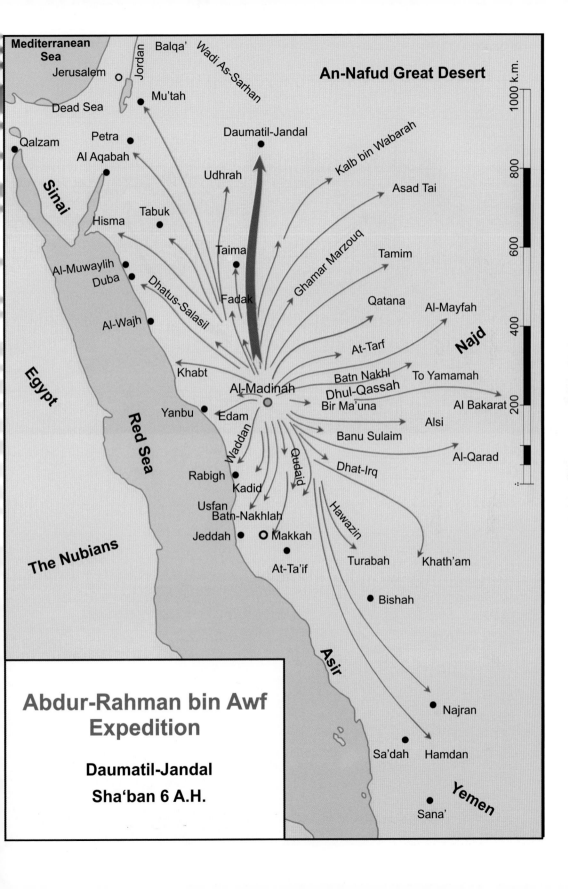

Mediterranean Sea

An-Nafud Great Desert

Jerusalem

Balqa'

Jordan

Wadi As-Sarhan

Mu'tah

Dead Sea

Daumatil-Jandal

Kalb bin Wabarah

Qalzam

Petra

Al Aqabah

Udhrah

Asad Tai

Sinai

Hisma

Tabuk

Taima

Ghamar Marzouq

Tamim

Al-Muwaylih

Duba

Dhatus-Salasil

Fadak

Qatana

Al-Mayfah

Al-Wajh

Najd

At-Tarf

Egypt

Khabt

Batn Nakhl

To Yamamah

Al-Madinah

Dhul-Qassah

Bir Ma'una

Al Bakarat

Red Sea

Yanbu

Edam

Alsi

Banu Sulaim

Al-Qarad

Waddan

Qudaid

Dhat-Irq

Rabigh

Kadid

Usfan

Batn-Nakhlah

Hawazin

The Nubians

Jeddah

Makkah

At-Ta'if

Turabah

Khath'am

Bishah

Asir

Najran

Abdur-Rahman bin Awf Expedition

Daumatil-Jandal

Sha'ban 6 A.H.

Sa'dah

Hamdan

Yemen

Sana'

1000 k.m.

800

600

400

200

Al-Jawf

Ha'il

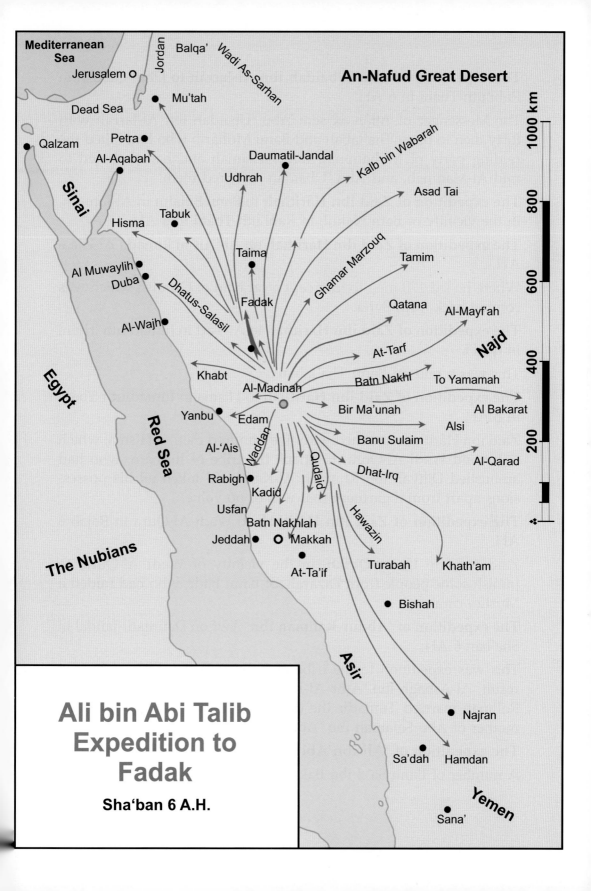

Mediterranean Sea

Jordan

Balqa'

Wadi As-Sarhan

An-Nafud Great Desert

Jerusalem O

Mu'tah

Dead Sea

Qalzam

Petra

Al-Aqabah

Daumatil-Jandal

Kalb bin Wabarah

Udhrah

Asad Tai

Sinai

Hisma

Tabuk

Taima

Ghamar Marzouq

Tamim

Al Muwaylih

Duba

Dhatus-Salasil

Fadak

Qatana

Al-Mayf'ah

Al-Wajh

At-Tarf

Najd

Khabt

Batn Nakhl

To Yamamah

Al-Madinah

Egypt

Red Sea

Yanbu

Edam

Bir Ma'unah

Al Bakarat

Al-'Ais

Waddan

Banu Sulaim

Alsi

Al-Qarad

Rabigh

Qudaid

Dhat-Irq

Kadid

Usfan

Hawazin

Batn Nakhlah

Jeddah

O Makkah

The Nubians

At-Ta'if

Turabah

Khath'am

Bishah

Asir

Najran

Sa'dah

Hamdan

Yemen

Sana'

1000 km

800

600

400

200

Ali bin Abi Talib Expedition to Fadak

Sha'ban 6 A.H.

The expedition of Abu 'Ubaidah ibn Al-Jarrâh to Dhul-Qassah in Rabi'uth-Thâni in 6 AH.

The Messenger of Allâh ﷺ sent Abu 'Ubaidah ibn Al-Jarrâh with forty men to Banu Tha'labah and Banu Muhârib who had killed the raiding party of Muhammad ibn Maslamah and had gathered to raid Al-Madinah, and Abu 'Ubaidah scattered them.

The expedition of Zaid ibn Hârithah to Banu Sulaim in Al-Jamum, in the vicinity of Batn Nakhl, in Rabi'uth-Thâni in 6 AH.

The expedition of Zaid ibn Hârithah on Al-'Ais in Jumâda Al-Ula 6 AH.

Where he led 170 men to intercept a caravan of Quraish which was coming back from Syria.

The expedition of Zaid ibn Hârithah to At-Tarf in Jumadiuth-Thâni in 6 AH.

This was a raid on Banu Tha'labah.

The expedition of Zaid ibn Hârithah to Hisma in Jumadiuth-Thâni in 6 AH.

Zaid ibn Hârithah marched with five hundred men to Hisma, which is beyond Wadi Al-Qura, to attack the tribe of Judhâm, who had ambushed Dihyah ibn Khalifah Al-Kalbi and taken all his possessions apart from a garment that was of no value.

The expedition of Zaid ibn Hârithah to Wadi Al-Qura in Rajab 6 AH.

Zaid went to Umm Qirfah, in the vicinity of Wadi Al-Qura, to punish some people from Fazârah, of Banu Badr, who had raided a Muslim caravan.

The expedition of 'Abdur-Rahmân ibn 'Awf on Daumatil-Jandal in Sha'bân 6 AH.

This was expedition to the tribe of Kalb in Daumatil-Jandal. As a result, Al-Asbagh ibn 'Amr Al-Kalbi became Muslim, and 'Abdur-Rahman married Tumâdir the daughter of Al-Asbagh, who is the mother of Abu Salamah ibn 'Abdur-Rahmân.

The expedition of 'Ali ibn Abi Tâlib to Fadak in Sha'bân 6 AH.

A number of Banu Sa'd ibn Bakr had assembled in Fadak with the

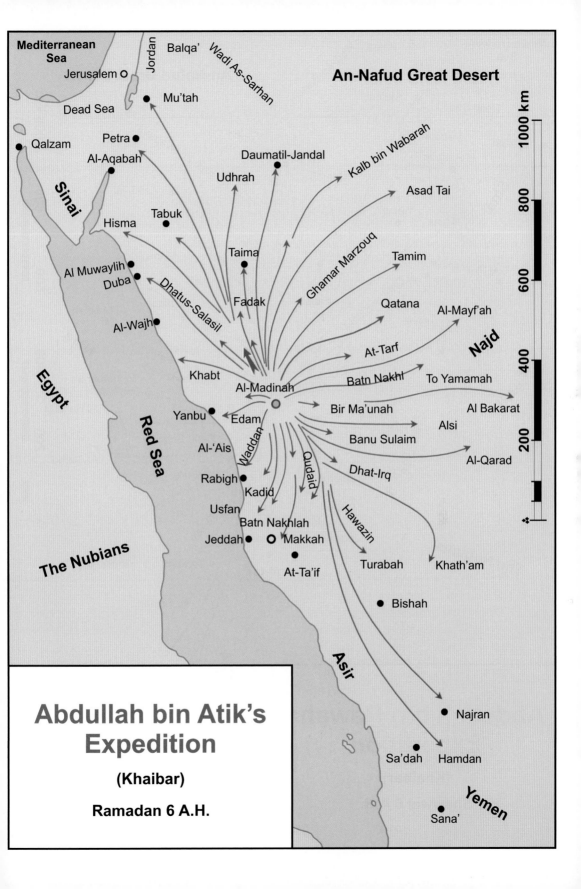

Abdullah bin Atik's Expedition

(Khaibar)

Ramadan 6 A.H.

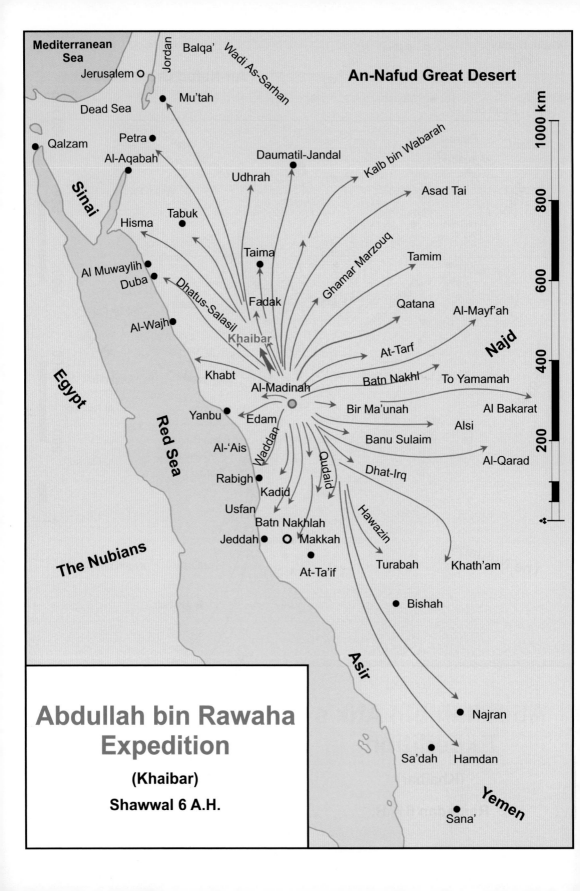

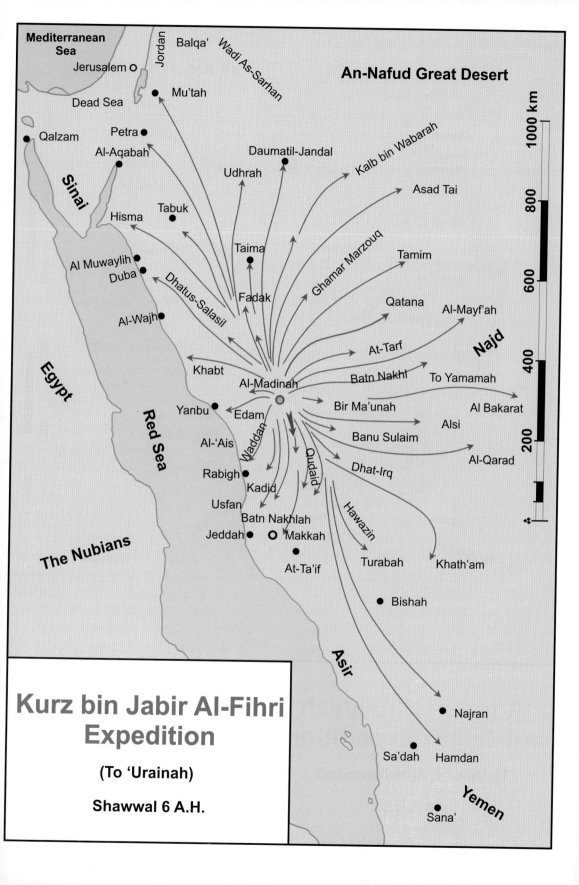

Kurz bin Jabir Al-Fihri
Expedition

(To 'Urainah)

Shawwal 6 A.H.

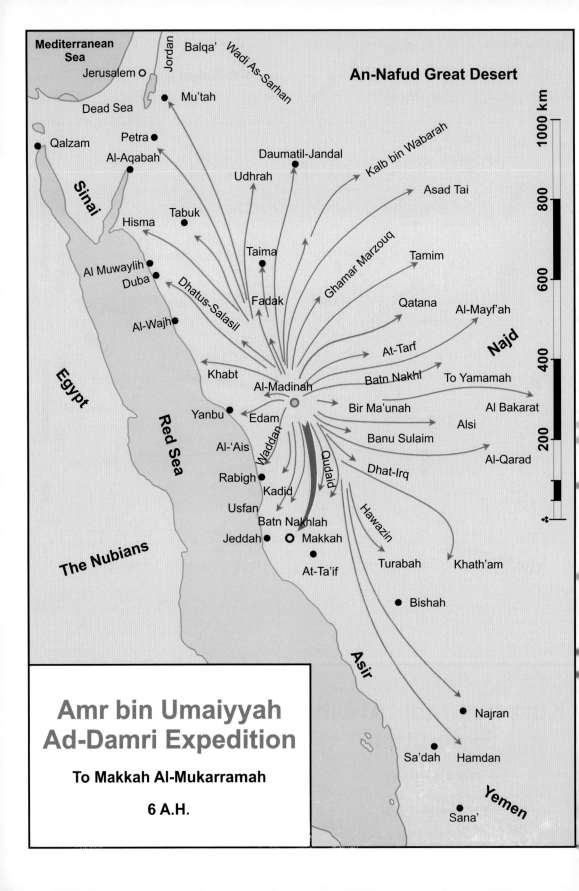

**Amr bin Umaiyyah
Ad-Damri Expedition**

To Makkah Al-Mukarramah

6 A.H.

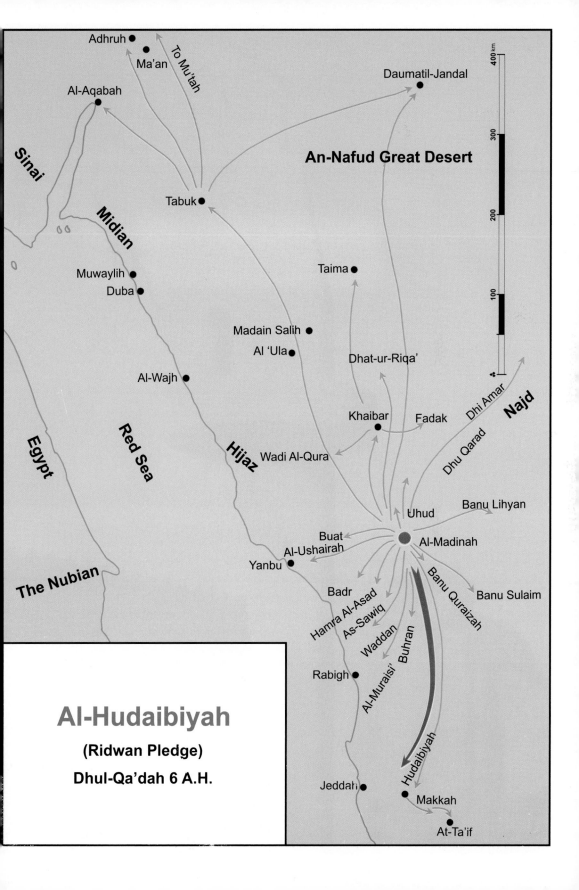

Adhruh

Ma'an

To Mu'tah

Al-Aqabah

Sinai

Midian

Tabuk

An-Nafud Great Desert

Daumatil-Jandal

Muwaylih

Duba

Taima

Madain Salih

Al 'Ula

Dhat-ur-Riqa'

Al-Wajh

Khaibar

Fadak

Dhi Amar

Najd

Red Sea

Egypt

Hijaz

Wadi Al-Qura

Dhu Qarad

The Nubian

Uhud

Banu Lihyan

Buat

Al-Madinah

Al-Ushairah

Yanbu

Badr

Hamra Al-Asad

As-Sawiq

Waddan

Al-Muraisi'

Buhran

Banu Quraizah

Banu Sulaim

Rabigh

Al-Hudaibiyah

(Ridwan Pledge)

Dhul-Qa'dah 6 A.H.

Jeddah

Hudaibiyah

Makkah

At-Ta'if

400 km

300

200

100

Masjid Al-Hudaibiyah (Ar-Ridwan)

intention of supporting the Jews of Khaibar. So 'Ali marched on them with one hundred men. Banu Sa'd fled and 'Ali came back to Al-Madinah, and no fighting took place.

The expedition of 'Abdullâh ibn 'Atik to Khaibar in Ramadân 6 AH.

'Abdullâh went, with two men, to Abu Râfi' Salâm ibn Abul-Huqaiq Al-Nadari, and killed him in Khaibar. He was the one who had incited Ghatafân and the surrounding *Mushrik* Arabs to wage war against the Muslims.

The expedition of 'Abdullâh ibn Rawâhah to the Jew Usair ibn Zârim in Khaibar in Shawwâl 6 AH.

He went to Usair ibn Zârim in Khaibar because he was the one who had gone to Ghatafân to gather them to fight the Messenger of Allâh ﷺ. Ibn Rawâhah was accompanied by thirty men. After being granted a promise of safety, Usair tried to commit an act of treachery so he and those who were with him were killed.

The expedition of Kurz ibn Jâbir Al-Fihri to 'Urainah in Shawwâl 6 AH.

Kurz went with twenty men to punish eight men of 'Urainah who had committed an act of treachery and killed Yasâr, the freed slave of the Messenger of Allâh ﷺ. They caught up with them and took them prisoner, then brought them back to Al-Madinah where they were crucified for their act of treachery.

The expedition of 'Amr ibn Umaiyyah Ad-Damari and Salamah ibn Aslam to Makkah in 6 AH.

'Amr ibn Umaiyyah and Salamah ibn Aslam went to Abu Sufyân in Makkah, when he had sent someone to kill the Prophet ﷺ. They hoped to find Abu Sufyân unprotected, but Mu'âwiyah recognized them and Quraish said: " 'Amr has not come for any good reason," so they gathered to attack him. Then 'Amr went back with Salamah to Al-Madinah.

The campaign of Al-Hudaibiyah (and the pledge of Al-Ridwân) in Dhul-Qa'dah 6 AH.

The Messenger of Allâh ﷺ set out with 1400 men, taking seventy sacrificial camels with him, and he entered *Ihrâm* for '*Umrah* so that the people would know that he had not come to fight and that he had only

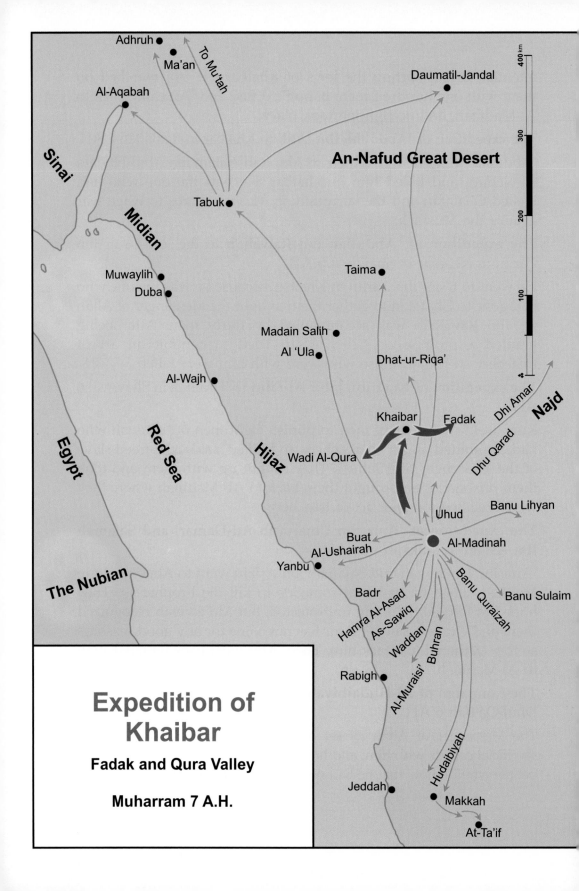

Expedition of Khaibar

Fadak and Qura Valley

Muharram 7 A.H.

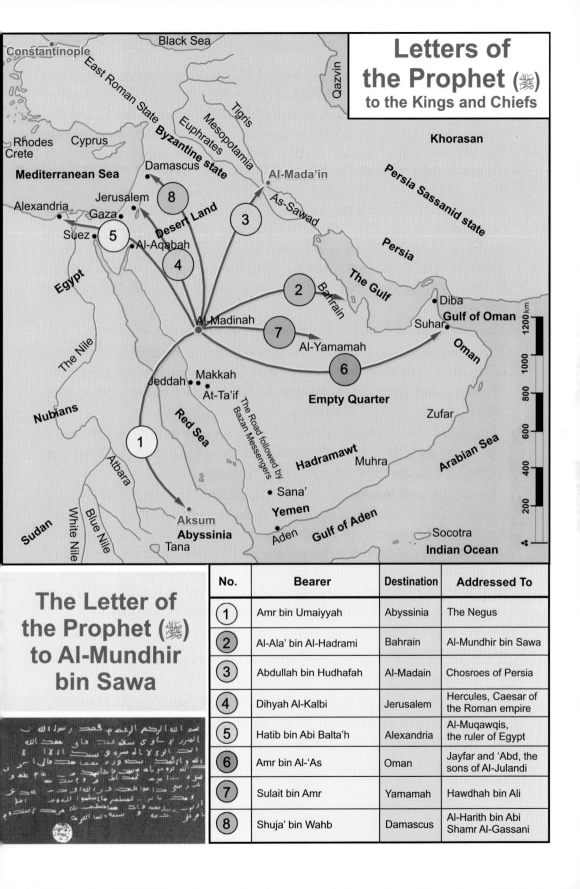

Letters of the Prophet (ﷺ)
to the Kings and Chiefs

Black Sea
Constantinople
East Roman State
Mediterranean Sea
Rhodes
Crete
Cyprus
Alexandria
Gaza
Suez
Al-Aqabah
Egypt
The Nile
Nubians
Sudan
Atbara
White Nile
Blue Nile
Red Sea
Jeddah
Makkah
At-Ta'if
The Road followed by Bazan Messengers
Aksum
Abyssinia
Tana
Damascus
Jerusalem
Desert Land
Byzantine state
Tigris
Euphrates
Mesopotamia
Al-Mada'in
As-Sawad
Qazvin
Khorasan
Persia Sassanid state
Persia
The Gulf
Bahrain
Al-Madinah
Al-Yamamah
Empty Quarter
Sana'
Yemen
Aden
Gulf of Aden
Hadramawt
Muhra
Zufar
Diba
Gulf of Oman
Suhar
Oman
Arabian Sea
Socotra
Indian Ocean

1200 km
1000
800
600
400
200

The Letter of the Prophet (ﷺ) to Al-Mundhir bin Sawa

No.	Bearer	Destination	Addressed To
1	Amr bin Umaiyyah	Abyssinia	The Negus
2	Al-Ala' bin Al-Hadrami	Bahrain	Al-Mundhir bin Sawa
3	Abdullah bin Hudhafah	Al-Madain	Chosroes of Persia
4	Dihyah Al-Kalbi	Jerusalem	Hercules, Caesar of the Roman empire
5	Hatib bin Abi Balta'h	Alexandria	Al-Muqawqis, the ruler of Egypt
6	Amr bin Al-'As	Oman	Jayfar and 'Abd, the sons of Al-Julandi
7	Sulait bin Amr	Yamamah	Hawdhah bin Ali
8	Shuja' bin Wahb	Damascus	Al-Harith bin Abi Shamr Al-Gassani

come to visit and venerate the Sacred House. The Prophet ﷺ and the people with him reached Al-Hudaibiyah where Quraish resolved never to let the Messenger of Allâh ﷺ enter Makkah. Quraish sent Budail ibn Warqa' Al-Khuzâ'i, then Mikraz ibn Hafs ibn Al-Akhyaf, then Al-Hils ibn 'Alqamah (the leader of the *Ahâbesh* or the tribes dwelling at suburbs), then 'Urwah ibn Mas'ud At-Thaqafi. After all these delegations had come to the Prophet ﷺ, the Companions swore the pledge of Ar-Radwân, promising the Messenger of Allâh ﷺ that they would die before they would flee. Then Quraish sent Suhail ibn 'Amr, and the treaty of Al-Hudaybiyah was drawn up, establishing a ten-year truce. This was official recognition of the Islamic state on the part of Quraish. It was also agreed that the Muslims would perform *'Umrah* the following year.

The campaigns of Khaibar, Fadak and Wadi Al-Qura in Muharram 7 AH.

The cause of these campaigns was the ongoing hostility of the Jews in Khaibar, and their contacting Ghatafân to incite them against the Muslims, and their alliance with the leaders of Khaibar, the aim of which was to raid Al-Madinah.

The aim of these campaigns was to put an end to the conspiracy of the Jews and their allies against the Muslims, and to stop the incitement of the tribes against the Muslims.

The Muslims conquered the fortresses of Khaibar: An-Natât (Nâ'im, As-Sa'b and Qillah); Ash-Shiqq (Ubayy and Al-Bari') and Al-Katibah (Al-Qamus, Al-Watih and Al-Sulâlim). The Messenger of Allâh ﷺ left the land for the people of Khaibar in return for half of its produce and "we will let you have what we want". He made a deal with the Jews of Fadak parallel to the deal of Khaibar. Then he conquered Wadi Al-Qura by force, and Taima' peacefully.

In order to explain the sequence of events, I have prepared some explanatory maps:

– The Prophet's letters to the kings and rulers
– The two envoys of Badhân who came from San'a' to Al-Madinah
– The journey of Mâriyah Al-Qibtiyah from Hafn to Al-Madinah
– The journey of the envoy of the Messenger of Allâh ﷺ to Heraclius.

The Dome making the location of the Well of Aris
(where the Prophet's Ring fell)

The Well into which the Ring of
the Prophet ﷺ fell from the Hand
of Uthman bin Affan ﷺ.

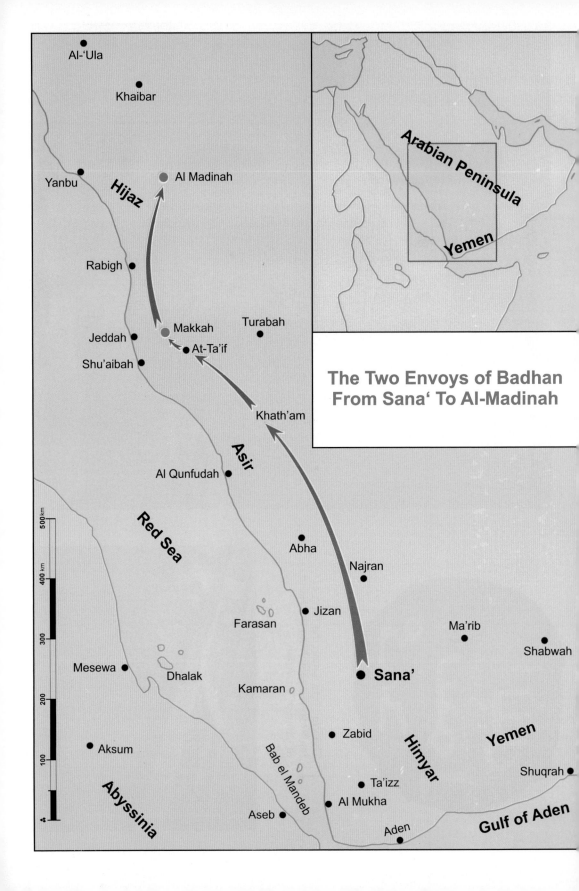

Al-'Ula

Khaibar

Yanbu

Hijaz

Al Madinah

Rabigh

Makkah

Turabah

Jeddah

At-Ta'if

Shu'aibah

Khath'am

Asir

Al Qunfudah

Red Sea

Abha

Najran

Jizan

Farasan

Ma'rib

Shabwah

Mesewa

Dhalak

Kamaran

Sana'

Aksum

Zabid

Himyar

Yemen

Bab el Mandeb

Shuqrah

Ta'izz

Abyssinia

Al Mukha

Aseb

Aden

Gulf of Aden

Arabian Peninsula

Yemen

The Two Envoys of Badhan From Sana' To Al-Madinah

500 km

400 km

300

200

100

The Arch of Chosroes

The two Envoys of Badhân (Badhâm)
From San'a' to Al-Madinah

When the Prophet ﷺ wanted to write to the kings and call them to Islam, it was said to him: "O Messenger of Allâh, they will not read any letter unless it has a seal." That was to indicate that the contents were not to be read by anyone else. It was also a precaution against forgery, because forgery could not take place if the document was sealed. So the Prophet ﷺ had made a ring of silver on which the words Muhammad Rasul Allâh (Muhammad the Messenger of Allâh) were written in three lines from bottom to top.[1]

The writing on this ring was inverted so that when it was pressed into the seal the words would appear the right way round. The ring was worn by the Prophet ﷺ, then by Abu Bakr, then 'Umar, then 'Uthmân. Then it fell into the well of Aris[2] in the year in which 'Uthmân died. They searched for it for three days but did not find it.

The Prophet ﷺ used to wear the ring on the smallest finger of his left hand. This was narrated from most of the Companions. And it was said that he wore it on the smallest finger of his right hand. This was narrated from several, including Ibn 'Abbâs and 'Āishah.

The letter of the Messenger of Allâh ﷺ to Chosroes (Epervaiz ibn Hormuz)

This letter was carried by 'Abdullâh ibn Hudhâfah As-Sahami to Ctesiphon (Al-Madâ'in), the capital of Persia. It read as follows:

"In the Name of Allâh, the Most Gracious, the Most Merciful.

---

[1] The Prophet ﷺ sent these letters to the kings and rulers in 6 AH, after Al-Hudaibiyah and before Khaibar.

[2] The well of Aris was a well known well near the Mosque of Quba' at Al-Madinah. [*Mu'jamul-Buldân* 1/298]

From Muhammad the Messenger of Allâh, to Chosroes the emperor of Persia. Peace be upon those who follow true guidance and believe in Allâh and His Messenger, and bear witness that there is no God except Allâh, with no partner or associate, and that Muhammad is His slave and Messenger. I invite you to the call of Allâh, for I am the Messenger of Allâh ﷺ to mankind, so that I may give warning to him who is living and that the word (or the charge) may be established against the disbelievers.[1] Become Muslim and you will be safe, but if you refuse then the sin of the Magians (Persians) will be upon you."[2]

'Abdullâh ibn Hudhâfah said: When I reached his door, I asked for permission to enter. When I reached him, I handed the letter of the Messenger of Allâh ﷺ to him. It was read to him and he said: "How dare he write these words to me when he is my slave?!"[3] Then he took the letter and tore it up. When news of that reached the Messenger of Allâh ﷺ, he said: "May Allâh tear apart his kingdom."[4]

Then Chosroes wrote to Badhân[5] - his deputy in Yemen – telling him, "Send two strong men to this man in the Hijâz, to bring him to me." So Badhân sent Kharkharah and Bâbawaih.[6] He sent a letter with them to the Messenger of Allâh ﷺ, telling him to go with them to Chosroes.

So they set out, and when they reached At-Tâ'if, they found a man from Quraish in At-Tâ'if, so they asked him about the Prophet ﷺ. He said: "He is in Al-Madinah." The people of At-Tâ'if and Quraish rejoiced when they saw these two men, and said to one another: "Be of good cheer, for Chosroes, the king of kings, will deal with him. The man will be dealt with."

---

[1] cf. *Ya-Sin* 30:70
[2] *'Uyun Al-Athr*, 2/262, 263; *At-Tabaqât Al-Kubra*, 1/259; *Al-Kâmil fit-Târikh*, 2/ 145; *Ibn Khaldun*, 2/37; *As-Seerah An-Nabawiyyah* by Ibn Kathir, 3/507, 508, 509; *At-Tabari*, 2/654; *I'lâm us-Sâ'ilin 'an Kutub Sayyidil-Mursalin*, 9.
[3] *Al-Seerah An-Nabawiyyah* by Ibn Kathir, 3/508
[4] *I'lâm Al-Sâ'ilin* 9
[5] Badhân or Badhâm, as it appears in *Al-Bidâyah wan-Nihâyah*, 4/269; *At-Tabaqât Al-Kubra*, 1/260; *Al-Seerah An-Nabawiyyah* by Ibn Kathir, 3/508
[6] According to Ibn Kathir their names were Kharkharah and Abâdhuwaih.

When they came to the Messenger of Allâh ﷺ, Bâbwaih spoke to him and said: "The King of kings Chosroes wrote to King Bâdhân and told him to send to you someone who will bring you to him. He has sent me to you so that you will go with me. If you do that, (Badhân) will write a letter in your favour so that Chosroes will not harm you, but if you refuse then you know who he is, and he will destroy you and your people, and devastate your land."

The Prophet ﷺ said to them: "Go and come back to me tomorrow." Then news from heaven came to the Messenger of Allâh ﷺ that Allâh had caused Chosroes' son Sherwaih turn against him and kill him. So he called them back and told them that. He ﷺ told them: "My Lord has killed your lord this night." And, "Tell him that my Lord has killed his lord this night."[1] They said: "Do you know what you are saying? We became angry with you for less than this. Should we write to King Badhân and tell him about this?" The Prophet ﷺ said: "Yes, tell him what I said, and tell him that my religion and my power will reach wherever Chosroes reached, and will reach everywhere. And tell him: If you become Muslim I will give you whatever is under your control and will appoint you as the ruler of your people the *Abna'*."[2]

The two men went back to Badhân and told him what had happened. He said: "By Allâh, these are not the words of a king. I think that the man is a Prophet as he says. I am going to find out, and I am certain that what he said is true. If what he said is true then he is indeed a Prophet who has been sent, and if it is not then we shall decide about him."

Soon Badhân received a letter from Sherwaih which said: "I have killed Chosroes, and the only reason I killed him was in order to avenge the Persian people because he killed many of their nobles

---

[1] Chosroes was killed by his son Shirwaih on the night of 10 Jumâdauth-Thâni 7 AH. *As-Seerah An-Nabawiyyah* by Ibn Kathir, 3/511

[2] *Abna'*: descendents of the Persians who were sent by Chosroes with Saif ibn Dhi Yazan, when he asked for his help against the Abyssinians. They defeated the Abyssinians and took control of Yemen, and intermarried with the Arabs, so their descendents were known as *Al-Abna'* (the sons). They were known by this name because their mothers were of a different race than their fathers.

and others who were defending their land. When this letter of mine reaches you, then take an oath of allegiance to me from those who are under your control, then go to this man concerning whom Chosroes wrote and do not provoke him until further notice."[1]

When the letter of Sherwaih reached Badhân, he said: "This man is indeed a Messenger". So he became Muslim and the descendents of the Persians in Yemen also became Muslim. Bâbwaih said to Badhân: "I have never spoken to any man who made me feel so much respect for him" – meaning the Messenger of Allâh ﷺ. Badhân said to him: "Were there any bodyguards with him?" He said: "No."

---

[1] For more information on Badhân: *At-Tabaqât Al-Kubra*, 1/260; *Al-Bidâyah wn-Nihâyah*, 4/269; *'Uyun Al-Athr*, 2/263; At-Tabari, 2/655; *Al-Kâmil fi't-Târikh*, 2/145; Ibn Khaldun, 2/38; *As-Seerah An-Nabawiyyah* by Ibn Kathir, 3/509; *As-Seerah Al-Halabiyyah*, 3/278; *As-Seerah An-Nabawiyyah wal-Athâr Al-Muhammadiyyah*, 2/65.

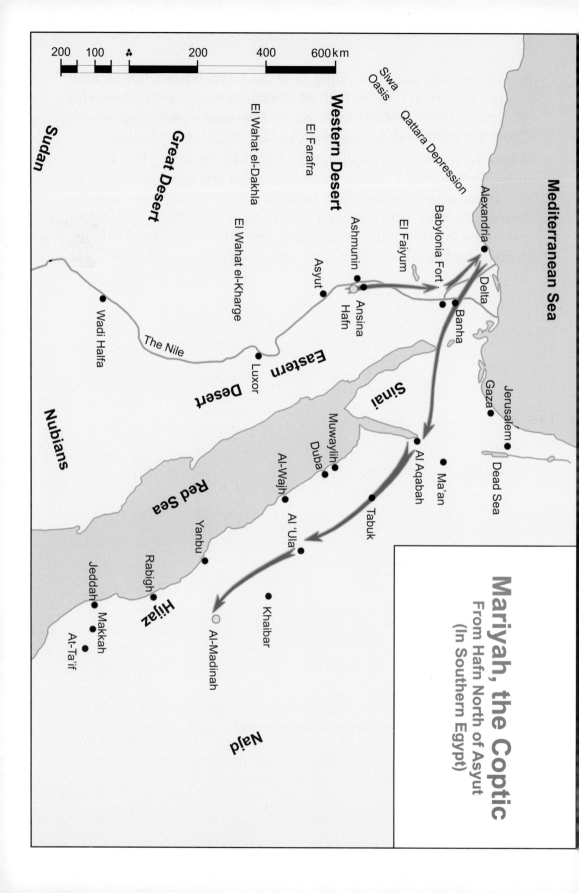

Mariyah, the Coptic
From Hafn North of Asyut
(In Southern Egypt)

Mâriyah Al-Qibtiyah
(Hafn on the outskirts of Ansina, a village in Upper Egypt)

After the Messenger of Allâh ﷺ returned from Al-Hudaibiyah in Dhul-Qa'dah 6 AH, he said: "O people, which of you will take this letter of mine to the ruler of Egypt, and his reward will be with Allâh? Hâtib ibn Abi Balta'ah leapt up and said, "I will, O Messenger of Allâh." The Prophet ﷺ said: "May Allâh bless you O Hâtib."[1]

Hâtib came to Alexandria, and asked about Al-Muqawqis.[2] He was told that he was at a gathering on the shore. So Hâtib rode in a boat and drew close to him, and pointed to the letter he held in his hand. When Al-Muqawqis saw it, he issued orders that Hâtib be brought before him.

The text of the letter:

"In the Name of Allâh, the Most Gracious, the Most Merciful.

From Muhammad the Messenger of Allâh,[3] to Al-Muqawqis the ruler of Egypt. Peace be upon those who follow true guidance. I invite you to the call of Islam. Become Muslim, you will be safe; become Muslim and Allâh will give you a double reward. But if you turn away, the sins of the Egyptians will be upon you.

﴿يَٰٓأَهۡلَ ٱلۡكِتَٰبِ تَعَالَوۡاْ إِلَىٰ كَلِمَةٖ سَوَآءِۭ بَيۡنَنَا وَبَيۡنَكُمۡ أَلَّا نَعۡبُدَ إِلَّا ٱللَّهَ وَلَا نُشۡرِكَ بِهِۦ شَيۡـٔٗا وَلَا يَتَّخِذَ بَعۡضُنَا بَعۡضًا أَرۡبَابٗا مِّن دُونِ ٱللَّهِۚ فَإِن تَوَلَّوۡاْ فَقُولُواْ ٱشۡهَدُواْ بِأَنَّا مُسۡلِمُونَ﴾

---

[1] *Al-Seerah Al-Halabiyyah*, 3/280; *As-Seerah An-Nabawiyyah wal-Athâr Al-Muhammadiyyah*, 2/69, where it says Hâtib was accompanied by Jabra or Jubaira – the freed slave of Abu Ruhm Al-Ghifâri.

[2] His name was Juraij ibn Mina Al-Qibti; the word Muqawqis means "the one who constructs tall buildings".

[3] In *I'lâmus-Sâ'ilin* (19) it says: "From Muhammad the son of 'Abdullâh to Al-Muqawqis..."

"O people of the Scripture (Jews and Christians): Come to a word that is just between us and you, that we worship none but Allâh (Alone), and that we associate no partners with Him, and that none of us shall take others as lords besides Allâh. Then, if they turn away, say: "Bear witness that we are Muslims." [Qur'ân 3:64]

Hâtib said to Al-Muqawqis: "We have a religion which we will never give up except for something better than it, namely Islam. This Prophet Muhammad ﷺ called the people, and those who were most vehemently opposed to him were Quraish; the most hostile were the Jews and the closest to him were the Christians. The glad tidings of Musa concerning 'Îsa are like the glad tidings of 'Îsa concerning Muhammad ﷺ, and our calling you to the Qur'ân is like your calling the people of the Torah to the Gospel. Every Prophet who came to a people is part of his (Muhammad's) *Ummah*, so they should obey him. You are among those to whom he has come. We do not tell you not to follow the religion of the Messiah, rather we enjoin you to follow it."[1]

Al-Muqawqis said: "Is not your companion (meaning the Messenger of Allâh ﷺ) a Prophet?"

Hâtib said: "Yes, he is the Messenger of Allâh."

Al-Muqawqis said: "Why did he not pray against his people when they drove him out of his land?"

Hâtib said: "What about 'Îsa ibn Maryam, do you not bear witness that he was a Messenger of Allâh? So why did he not pray against his people when they wanted to crucify him, until Allâh raised him up?"

Al-Muqawqis said: "You have spoken well. You are a wise man who has come from a wise man."[2]

Then he called for a scribe of his who could write Arabic, and wrote the following to the Prophet:

"In the Name of Allâh, the Most Gracious, the Most Merciful.

To Muhammad ibn 'Abdullâh from Al-Muqawqis the ruler of

[1] 'Uyun Al-Athr, 2/265; I'lâmus-Sâ'ilin, 20.
[2] Usdul-Ghâbah, 1/432; As-Seerah An-Nabawiyyah by Ibn Kathir, 3/514; As-Seerah Al-Halabiyyah, 3/281..

Egypt. Peace be upon you. I have read your letter and understood what you said in it and to what you call (people). I know that there is a Prophet still to come, and I thought that he would appear in Syria. I have honoured your envoy[1] and I am sending to you two girls[2] who are of high status in Egypt, and some clothes, and a mule for you to ride. Peace be upon you."

Hâtib said: So I left him, and I only stayed with him for five days. When I came to the Messenger of Allâh ﷺ I told him what he had said to me. He said: "He was worried about his kingdom but it will not abide."

The Messenger of Allâh ﷺ married Mariyah Al-Qibtiyyah, who became the mother of his son Ibrâhim, and Hassân ibn Thâbit married Shireen.

The rest of the gifts of Al-Muqawqis included the grey mule Duldul who lived until the time of Mu'âwiyah ibn Abi Sufyân. He also sent some honey from Binha', some perfume, twenty garments of fine Egyptian linen and a glass cup which the Prophet ﷺ used to drink from. He also sent to him a doctor, but the Prophet ﷺ said to him: "Go back to your people, for we are a people who do not eat until we get hungry and when we eat we do not eat our fill."[3]

The important places through which she passed include:

Egypt and Alexandria, both of which are well known.

Mariyah Al-Qibtiyyah came from Hafn,[4] which was on the outskirts of Ansina[5]. In *Al-Intisâr* by Ibn Daqmâq[6] is mentioned: "Ansina is an ancient town in which there are great ruins, and a

---

[1] Al-Muqawqis gave Hâtib one hundred dinars and five garments, and he sent a guard with him so that he could travel safely, and he said to him: "Your companion will prevail over the land."

[2] Mariyah Al-Qibtiyyah and Shireen

[3] *Al-Tabaqât Al-Kubra*, 1/260

[4] See *Mu'jamul-Buldân*, 2/276

[5] See *Mu'jamul-Buldân*, 1/265

[6] Ibrâhim ibn Muhammad ibn 'Aidmir ibn Daqmâq Al-Qâhiri [750-809 AH; 1349-1407 CE]. An Egyptian historian who wrote nearly two hundred books on history, both his own work and copies of others. He was known for his fair-minded approach to history. His books include *Nazmul-Jamân; Nuzhatul-Amân fi Târikhul-Islam; Al-Intisâr li Wâsitah 'Aqdul-Amsâr...* (*Al-A'lâm*, 1/64)

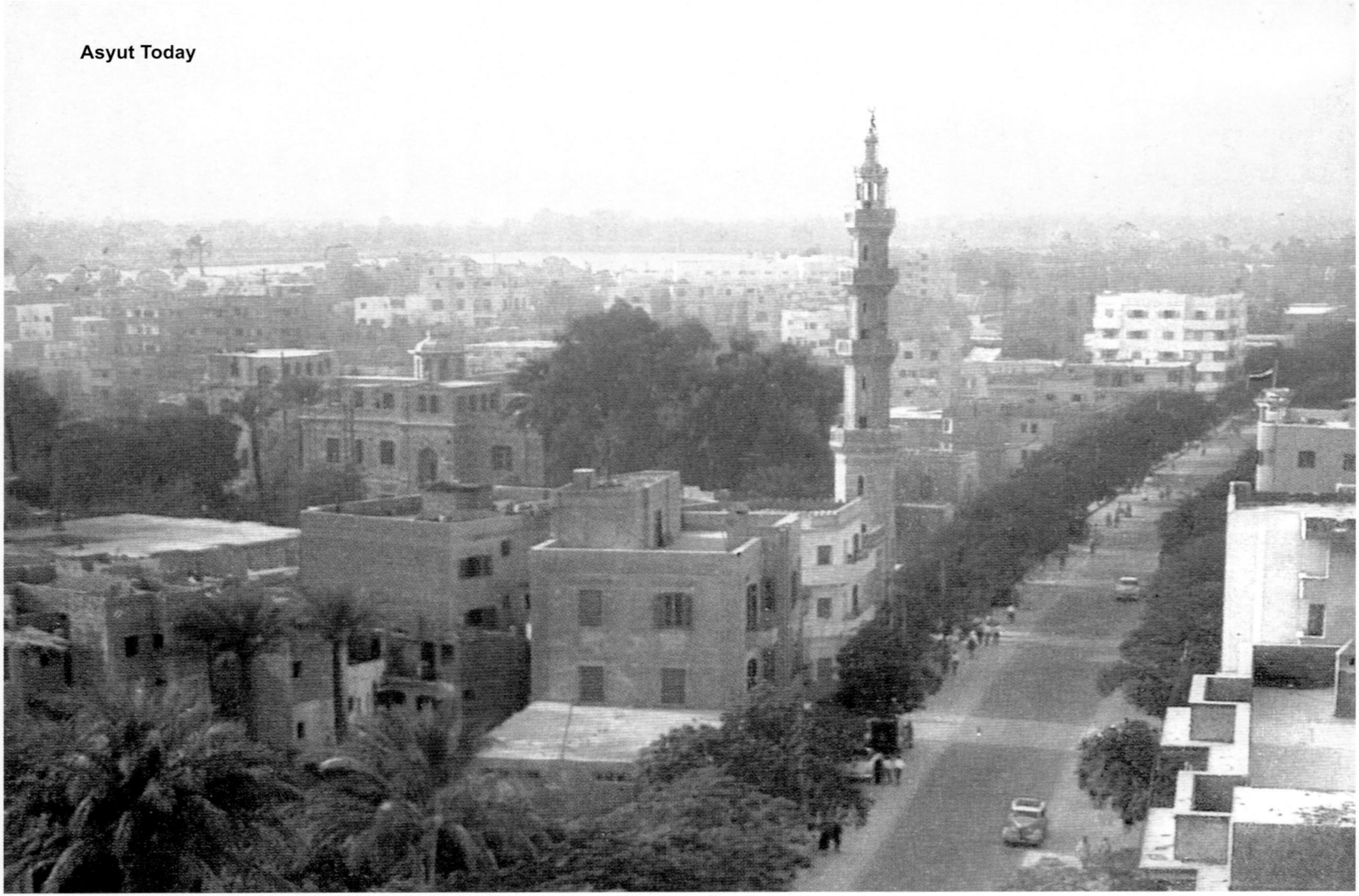

Asyut Today

small Nilometer to measure the level of the Nile. Part of it still remains to this day. It is on the eastern bank of the Nile opposite Al-Ashmunin." The village of Al-Ashmunin is in the province of Asyut, in Upper Egypt.

Binha'[1] is one of the villages of Egypt, which is known nowadays as Banha'. It is situated on a branch of the Nile. The best quality of honey in Egypt comes from Banha' and its environs.

It says in *Al-Bidâyah wan-Nihâyah* (5/303) concerning Mâriyah Al-Qibtiyyah: She was from a village in the land of Egypt called Hafn, on the outskirts of Ansina. Mu'âwiyah ibn Abi Sufyân spared the people of this village from having to pay the *Khirâj* tax during the days of his governorship, as an honour to them, because she had borne the Messenger of Allâh ﷺ a male child, namely Ibrâhim.

* * *

---

[1] *Mu'jamul-Buldân*, 1/501; *Subhul-A'sha*, 3/378

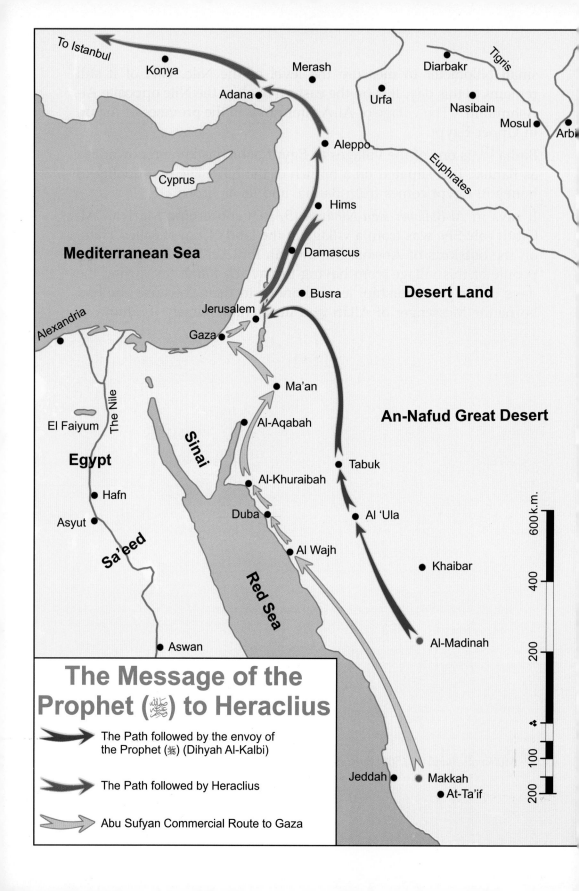

To Istanbul

Konya

Merash

Diarbakr

Tigris

Adana

Urfa

Nasibain

Mosul

Arbi

Aleppo

Cyprus

Euphrates

Hims

Mediterranean Sea

Damascus

Desert Land

Busra

Jerusalem

Gaza

Ma'an

An-Nafud Great Desert

Alexandria

Al-Aqabah

The Nile

El Faiyum

Sinai

Tabuk

Egypt

Al-Khuraibah

Hafn

Duba

Al 'Ula

Asyut

Al Wajh

Khaibar

Sa'eed

Red Sea

Al-Madinah

Aswan

600 k.m.

400

200

The Message of the
Prophet (ﷺ) to Heraclius

→ The Path followed by the envoy of
the Prophet (ﷺ) (Dihyah Al-Kalbi)

→ The Path followed by Heraclius

⇒ Abu Sufyan Commercial Route to Gaza

Jeddah

Makkah

At-Ta'if

100

200

The letter of the Messenger of Allâh ﷺ

To Caesar: Heraclius
(Early 7 AH; Autumn 628 CE)

Abu Sufyân set out to Gaza to engage in trade on behalf of Quraish after the treaty of Al-Hudaibiyah (Dhul-Qa'dah 6 AH), at a time when Heraclius was traveling from Hims to Jerusalem on foot, to go and pray there, in thanksgiving for his victory over the Persians. He woke up one morning feeling anxious, looking up at the sky. His bishops said to him: "O king, you seem anxious this morning." He said: "Yes." They said: "Why is that?" He said: "Last night I was shown the one who will prevail over me."

Then Heraclius called the leader of his guard and said to him: "Search Syria from top to bottom and bring me someone from his people (meaning the people of the Messenger of Allâh ﷺ) so that I can ask him about him."

Abu Sufyân narrated: By Allâh, my companions and I were in Gaza when he came to us and asked us: "Where are you from?" We told him, and he took all of us to him (to Heraclius). When we reached him, he said: "Who among you is most closely related to him?" Abu Sufyân said: I am. He said: "Bring him closer to me." So he sat me in front of him then told my companions to sit behind me, and said: "If he lies, correct him." Abu Sufyân said: I knew that if I lied, they would not correct me, but I was a man of high standing and I would have been ashamed to lie. I knew that the least that would happen as a result would be that news of that would be spread and they would talk about me in Makkah, so I did not lie.

After some questions and a discussion between Heraclius and Abu Sufyân, Heraclius said: "You said that he is one of the best of you in lineage, and this is the kind of person whom Allâh chooses as a Prophet;

195

He only chooses a Prophet from among the best of his people.

I asked you whether anyone else in his family says the same as he says so he is imitating him, and you said no. I asked you whether he had a position of leadership which had been taken away from him and he was saying these things in order to regain his position, and you said no. I asked you about his followers, whether they love him and honour him, or forsake him and abandon him, and you said that it is rare for someone to join him and then forsake him. This is the sweetness of faith; it rarely enters a person's heart and then leaves it. I asked you how the war is going between you and him, and you said that it alternates; sometimes you win and sometimes he wins. This is how the wars of the Prophets are, but in the end they prevail. I asked you whether he is treacherous, and you said he is not treacherous. I asked you what he enjoins upon you and you said that he enjoins you to worship Allâh (alone) and not associate anything with Him, and he forbids you to worship idols; he tells you to pray, give in charity and be chaste. If you are telling the truth then he will prevail over (the land) beneath these two feet of mine. I knew that he would appear but I did not think that he would be from among you. If I knew that I would be safe, I would take the trouble to go to him, and if I were in his presence I would wash his feet."[1]

Then he said: "Go and take care of your business."

Abu Sufyân said: So I stood up, striking one of my hands against the other, and said: "O slaves of Allâh, the affair of Ibn Abi Kabshah[2] has become serious! The kings of Banu-Asfar[3] have started to fear

---

[1] *Al-Kâmil fit-Târikh*, 2/143; *Al-Bidâyah wan-Nihâyah*, 4/262; Ibn Khaldun, 2/36; *I'lâmus-Sâ'ilin*, 10; *As-Seerah An-Nabawiyyah* by Ibn Kathir, 3/495; *As-Seerah Al-Halabiyyah*, 3/272; *As-Seerah An-Nabawiyyah wal-Athâr Al-Muhammadiyyah*, 2/58

[2] Ibn Abi Kabshah: i.e., the Messenger of Allâh ﷺ. The *Kuffâr* of Quraish used to name him after his father through breastfeeding (*Ridâ'ah*). Abu Kabshah was the husband of Halimah As-Sa'diyyah who breastfed him.

[3] The Byzantines (Ar-Rum, the "Romans") were called Banu-Asfar because they were the descendents of Rum ibn Al-'Ais ibn Ishâq ﷺ the Prophet of Allâh. He was called *Al-Asfar* because his skin had a yellowish tone (*Asfar* yellow). Or it was said that it was his father, Al-'Ais, who was yellowish in colour. (*As-Seerah Al-Halabiyyah*, 3/150.

that he will take over their kingdom."

The letter was carried by Dihyah[1] Al-Kalbi, and its text was as follows:

"In the Name of Allâh, the most Gracious, the most Merciful.

From Muhammad, the Messenger of Allâh[2] to Heraclius the ruler of Rome (Byzantium). Peace be upon those who follow true guidance. I invite you to the call of Islam. Become Muslim and you will be safe, and Allâh will give you a two-fold reward, but if you turn away then the sins of the *Arisiyyin*[3] will be upon you.

﴿يَـٰٓأَهْلَ ٱلْكِتَـٰبِ تَعَالَوْا۟ إِلَىٰ كَلِمَةٍ سَوَآءٍۭ بَيْنَنَا وَبَيْنَكُمْ أَلَّا نَعْبُدَ إِلَّا ٱللَّهَ وَلَا نُشْرِكَ بِهِۦ شَيْـًٔا وَلَا يَتَّخِذَ بَعْضُنَا بَعْضًا أَرْبَابًا مِّن دُونِ ٱللَّهِ فَإِن تَوَلَّوْا۟ فَقُولُوا۟ ٱشْهَدُوا۟ بِأَنَّا مُسْلِمُونَ ۝٦٤﴾

"O people of the Scripture (Jews and Christians): Come to a word that is just between us and you, that we worship none but Allâh (Alone), and that we associate no partners with Him, and that none of us shall take others as lords besides Allâh. Then, if they turn away, say: Bear witness that we are Muslims."

[Qur'ân 3:64]

Heraclius said to Dihyah: "By Allâh, I know that your companion is a Prophet who has been sent, and that he is the one for whom we are

---

[1] His name is given as Dihyah in *Usd Al-Ghâbah* and as Dahyah in *Al-Tabaqât Al-Kubra*. In the dialect of Yemen it means "leader."

[2] In *I'lâm As-Sâ'ilin* it says: "From Muhammad the slave and Messenger of Allâh".

[3] *Al-Arisiyyin*: i.e., the peasants. What is meant is: the sins of your subjects who follow you and obey your orders will be upon you. These people are mentioned in particular because they are quicker to obey than others, or because they were the majority of inhabitants, so their sins would be upon him, because if he became Muslim they would also become Muslims, but if he refused they would also refuse.

waiting, and we find him in our Scripture, but I fear what the Byzantines will do to me. Were it not for that, I would have followed him."

Al-Hâfiz ibn Hajar said: If only Heraclius had understood what the Prophet ﷺ said in his letter: 'Become Muslim, you will be safe,' and realized that this applied in a general sense, both in this world and in the Hereafter, and had become Muslim, he would have been safe from all that he feared. But guidance is in the Hand of Allâh.[1]

Heraclius traveled to Hims, and when he wanted to leave Syria and go back to Constantinople, he set off on his mule. When he reached the mountain pass, he looked back towards Syria and said: "Peace be upon you, O land of Syria, I bid you farewell." Then he went on to Constantinople.

---

[1] *Al-Seerah Al-Halabiyyah*, 3/274; *As-Seerah An-Nabawiyyah wal-Athâr Al-Muhammadiyyah*, 2/61

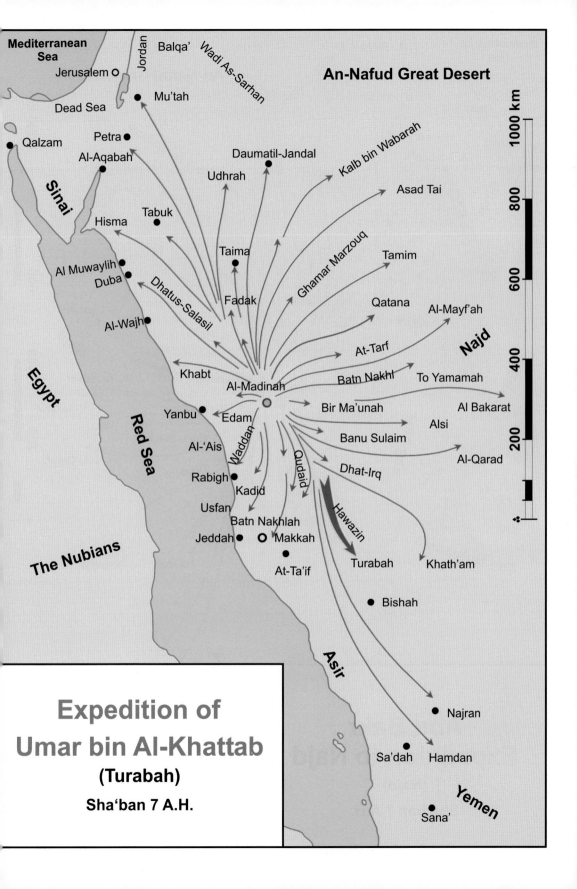

Expedition of
Umar bin Al-Khattab
(Turabah)
Sha'ban 7 A.H.

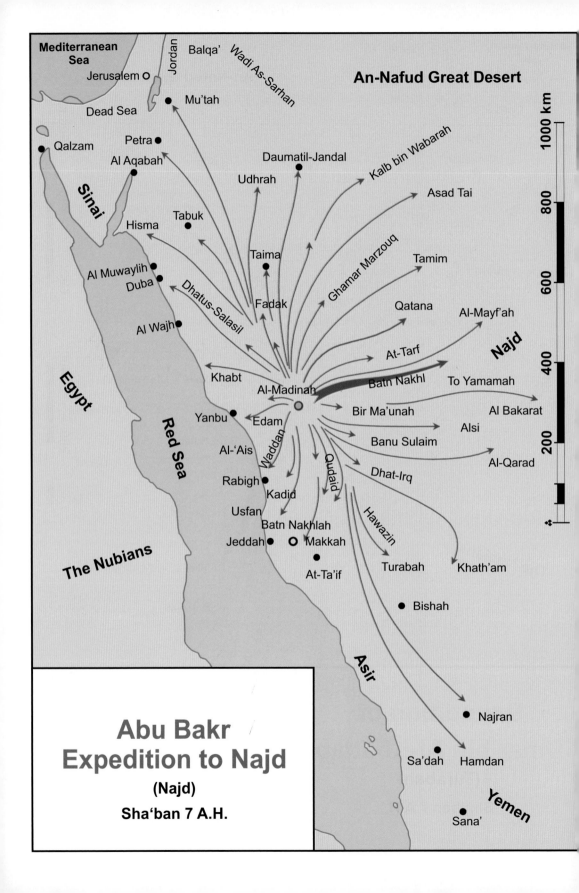

Abu Bakr
Expedition to Najd
(Najd)
Sha'ban 7 A.H.

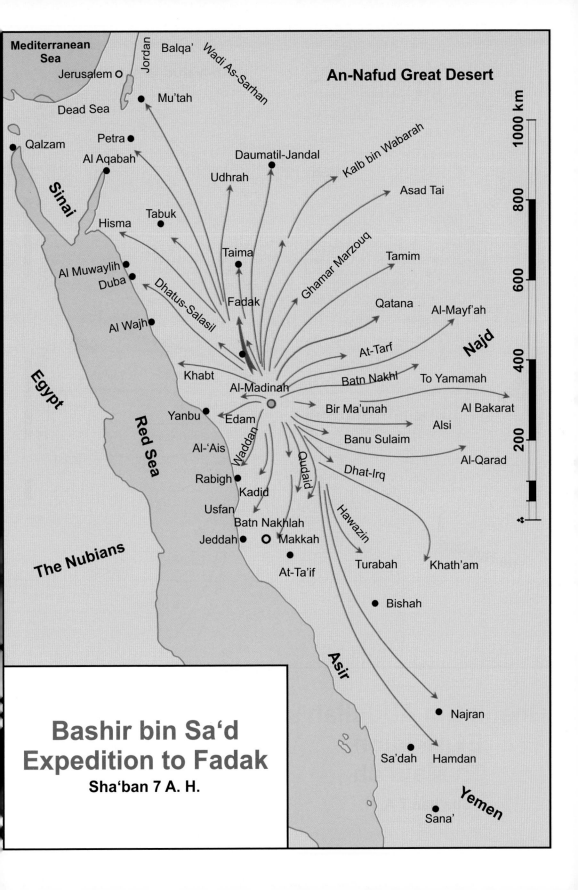

Bashir bin Sa'd
Expedition to Fadak
Sha'ban 7 A. H.

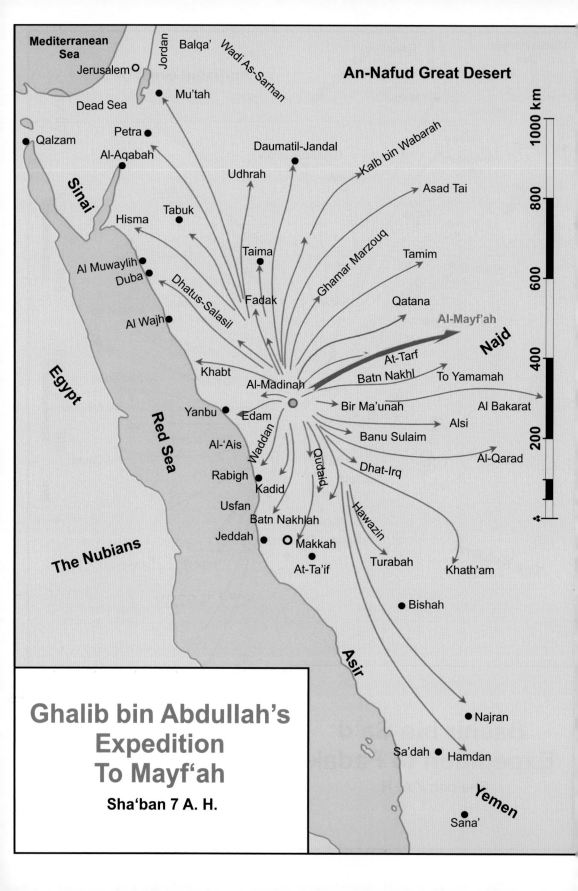

Ghalib bin Abdullah's Expedition To Mayf'ah

Sha'ban 7 A. H.

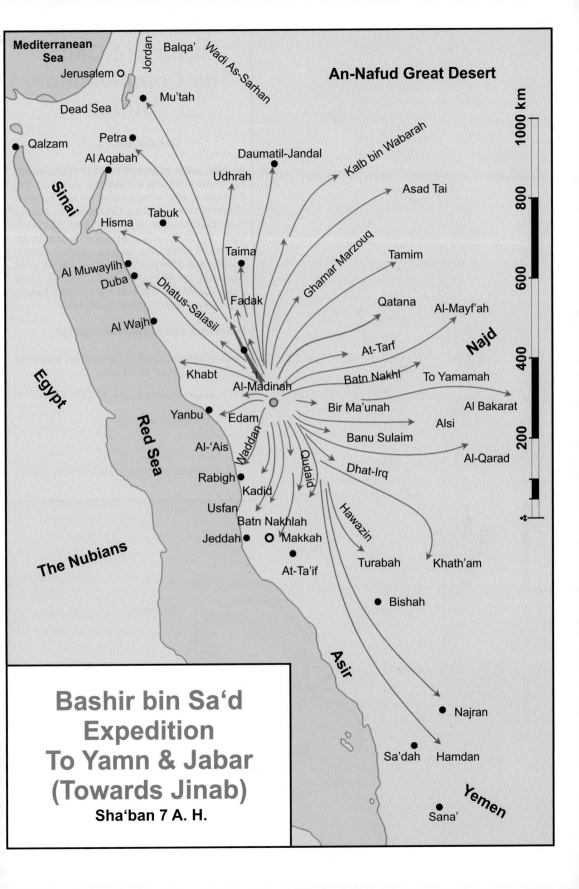

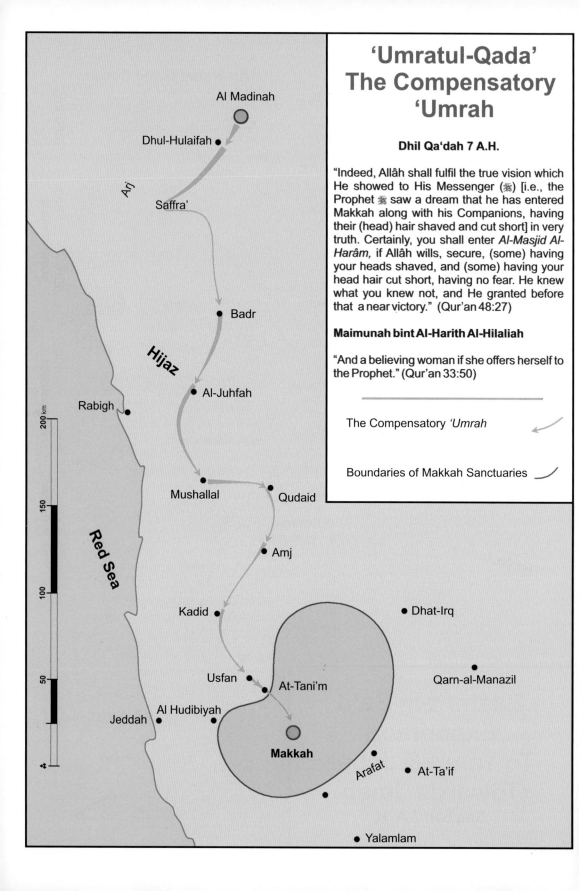

'Umratul-Qada' The Compensatory 'Umrah

Dhil Qa'dah 7 A.H.

"Indeed, Allâh shall fulfil the true vision which He showed to His Messenger (ﷺ) [i.e., the Prophet ﷺ saw a dream that he has entered Makkah along with his Companions, having their (head) hair shaved and cut short] in very truth. Certainly, you shall enter *Al-Masjid Al-Harâm*, if Allâh wills, secure, (some) having your heads shaved, and (some) having your head hair cut short, having no fear. He knew what you knew not, and He granted before that a near victory." (Qur'an 48:27)

Maimunah bint Al-Harith Al-Hilaliah

"And a believing woman if she offers herself to the Prophet." (Qur'an 33:50)

The Compensatory *'Umrah*

Boundaries of Makkah Sanctuaries

Al Madinah

Dhul-Hulaifah

Arj

Saffra'

Badr

Hijaz

Al-Juhfah

Rabigh

Mushallal

Qudaid

Amj

Kadid

Dhat-Irq

Usfan

At-Tani'm

Qarn-al-Manazil

Al Hudibiyah

Jeddah

Makkah

Arafat

At-Ta'if

Red Sea

Yalamlam

200 km

150

100

50

The expedition of 'Umar ibn Al-Khattâb to Turabah in Sha'bân 7 AH.

He led thirty men to the tribe of Hawâzin, who fled when they learned of his approach, so he returned to Al-Madinah.

The expedition of Abu Bakr As-Siddiq to Najd in Sha'bân 7 AH.

He went to Najd where there were groups of Banu Kilâb.

The expedition of Bashir ibn Sa'd Al-Ansâri to Fadak in Sha'bân 7 AH.

He went with thirty men to some groups of Banu Murrah.

The expedition of Ghâlib ibn 'Abdullâh Al-Laithi to Batn Nakhl in Ramadân 7 AH.

Ghâlib set out with 130 men to go to Banu 'Uwâl and Banu 'Abd of Tha'labah, who were in Al-Mayfa'ah, which is beyond Batn Nakhl heading towards Najd, and fighting took place. During this battle Usâmah ibn Zaid killed the man who said *Lâ ilâha illallâh*, and the Prophet ﷺ said to him: "Why did you not cut open his heart and see whether he was telling the truth or not?"

The expedition of Bashir ibn Sa'd Al-Ansâri to Yamn and Jabâr in Shawwâl 7 AH.

The Messenger of Allâh ﷺ sent him with three hundred men to disperse a group of Ghatafân, whom 'Uyaianah ibn Husn had promised to join and march on Al-Madinah. So he scattered the people.

'Umratul-Qada, (also known as 'Umratul-Qisâs or 'Umratul-Qadiyyah)[1] in Dhu'l-Qa'dah 7 AH.

The Prophet ﷺ and those who were accompanying him reached Makkah, where he made up the *'Umrah* he had missed. He entered the House, and Bilâl gave the call to prayer from atop the Ka'bah whilst Quraish were listening and watching. On the fourth day he announced that it was time to leave.

---

[1] This was neither a campaign nor an expedition. It is mentioned here so as to follow the sequence of events; it has been mentioned above in conjunction with the campaign of Al-Hudaibiyah

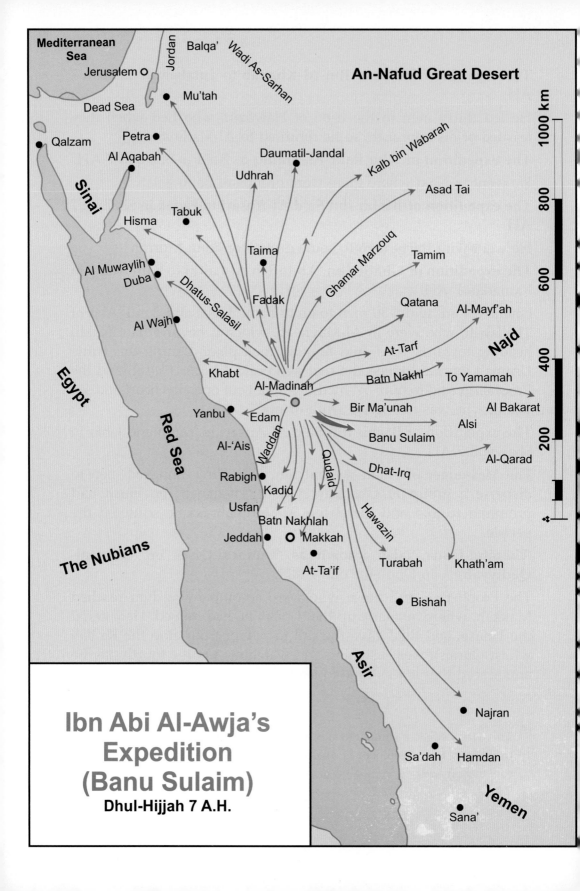

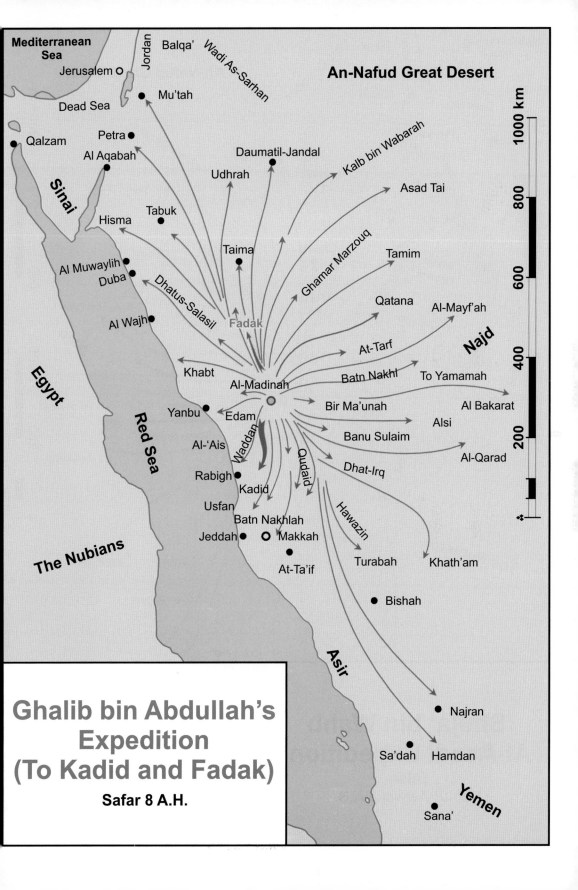

Mediterranean
Sea
Jerusalem ○
Jordan
Balqa'
Wadi As-Sarhan
An-Nafud Great Desert
Dead Sea
Mu'tah
Qalzam
Petra
Al Aqabah
Daumatil-Jandal
Udhrah
Kalb bin Wabarah
Asad Tai
Sinai
Hisma
Tabuk
Taima
Ghamar Marzouq
Tamim
Al Muwaylih
Duba
Dhatus-Salasil
Fadak
Qatana
Al-Mayf'ah
Al Wajh
At-Tarf
Najd
Khabt
Al-Madinah
Batn Nakhl
To Yamamah
Egypt
Red Sea
Yanbu
Edam
Bir Ma'unah
Al Bakarat
Al-'Ais
Waddan
Banu Sulaim
Alsi
Rabigh
Kadid
Dhat-Irq
Al-Qarad
Usfan
Qudaid
Batn Nakhlah
Hawazin
Jeddah
Makkah
The Nubians
At-Ta'if
Turabah
Khath'am
Bishah
1000 km
800
600
400
200
Najran
Asir
Sa'dah
Hamdan
Yemen
Sana'

Ghalib bin Abdullah's Expedition (To Kadid and Fadak)

Safar 8 A.H.

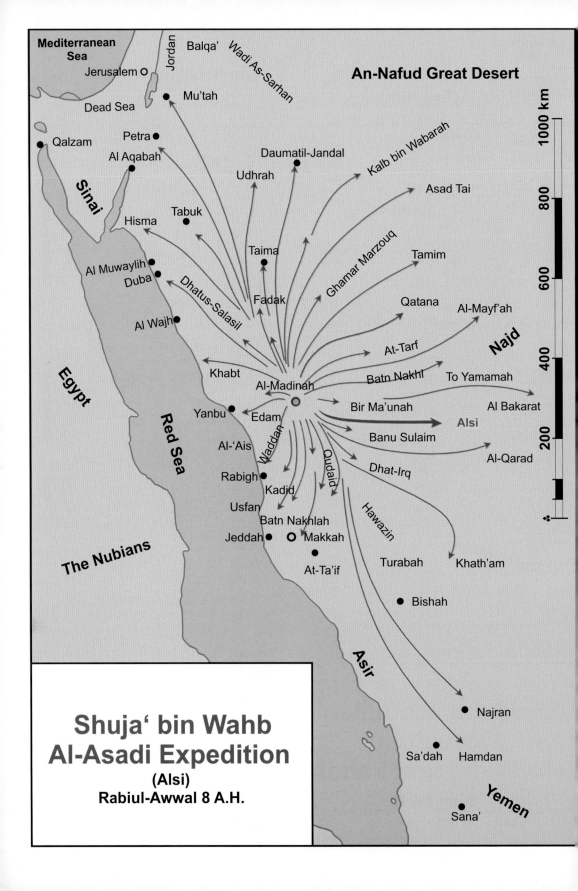

Shuja' bin Wahb
Al-Asadi Expedition
(Alsi)
Rabiul-Awwal 8 A.H.

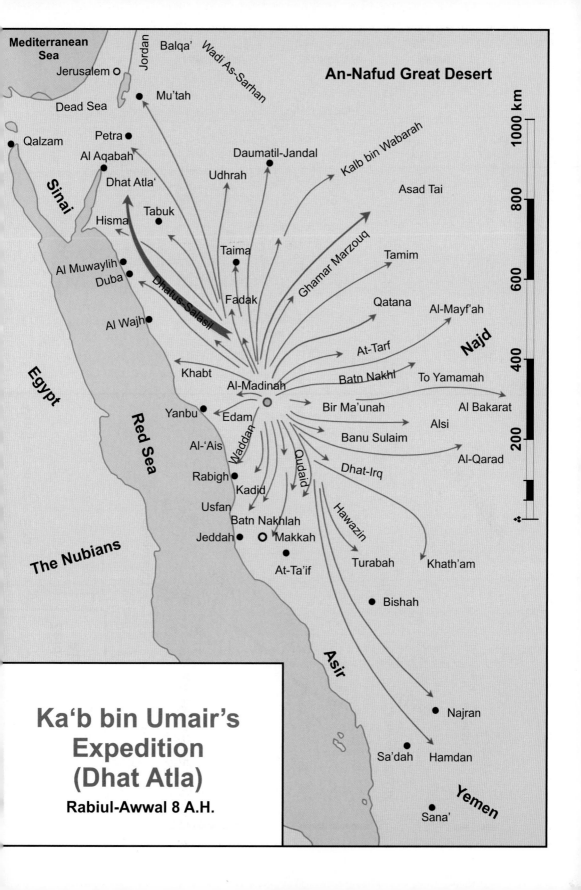

Ka'b bin Umair's Expedition (Dhat Atla)

Rabiul-Awwal 8 A.H.

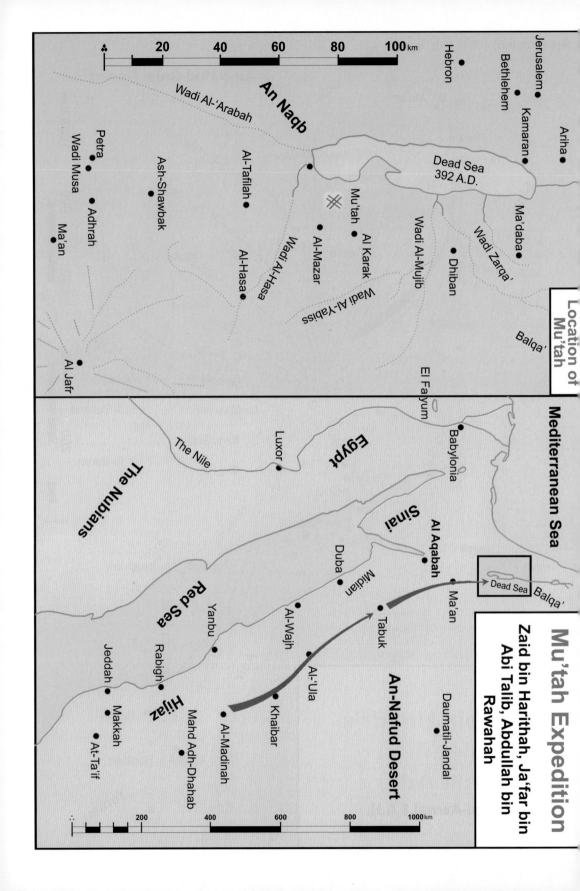

← The plain where the Battle of Mu'tah took place. At distance some of the hills to which Khalid bin Al-Walid withdrew could be seen.

Maqam Abdullah bin Rawahah ↓

Al-Mashhad ↑

Maqam Zaid bin Harithah ↓

Maqam Ja'far bin Abi Talib ↓

The expedition of Ibn Abil-'Awja' As-Sulami to Bani Sulaim in Dhul-Hijjah 7 AH.

Ibn Abi'l-'Awja' went with fifty men to Banu Sulaim, where intense fighting took place in which most of the enemy were killed and Ibn Abil-'Awja' was injured. He was carried back to the Messenger of Allâh ﷺ, and returned to Al-Madinah on the first day of Safar 8 AH.

The expedition of Ghâlib ibn 'Abdullâh Al-Laithi to Al-Kadid in Safar 8 AH.

Ghâlib and the people who were with him set out towards Banu Al-Mulawwih, who were from Banu Laith.

The expedition of Ghâlib ibn 'Abdullâh Al-Laithi to Fadak in Safar 8 AH.

The Prophet ﷺ said to Ghâlib Al-Laithi: "Go to the place where the companions of Bashir ibn Sa'd were killed." So he went with 200 men and managed to wreak vengeance for what had happened to the raiding party of Bashir ibn Sa'd.

The expedition of Shujâ' ibn Wahb Al-Asadi to Alsi in Rabi'ul-Awwal 8 AH.

He took twenty-four men with him, to a group of Hawâzin who were in Alsi.

The expedition of Ka'b ibn 'Umair Al-Ghifâri to Dhât Atlâ' in Rabi'ul-Awwal 8 AH.

There were fifteen men with Ka'b. He set out with them for Dhât Atlâ' – beyond Wadi Al-Qura – where they were killed except for one wounded man who managed to reach Al-Madinah and tell the Messenger of Allâh ﷺ what had happened, which upset him greatly.

The battle of Mu'tah, the battle of Jaish Al-Umara' in Jumâda Al-Ula 8 AH.

The Muslim army marched to Al-Balqa' – in southern Jordan – to punish Shurahbil ibn 'Amr Al-Ghassâni who had killed the envoy of the Messenger of Allâh ﷺ, Al-Hârith ibn 'Umair Al-Azdi.

This army numbered three thousand, led by Zaid ibn Hârithah; if he was killed, Ja'far ibn Abi Tâlib was to take over; and if he was killed,

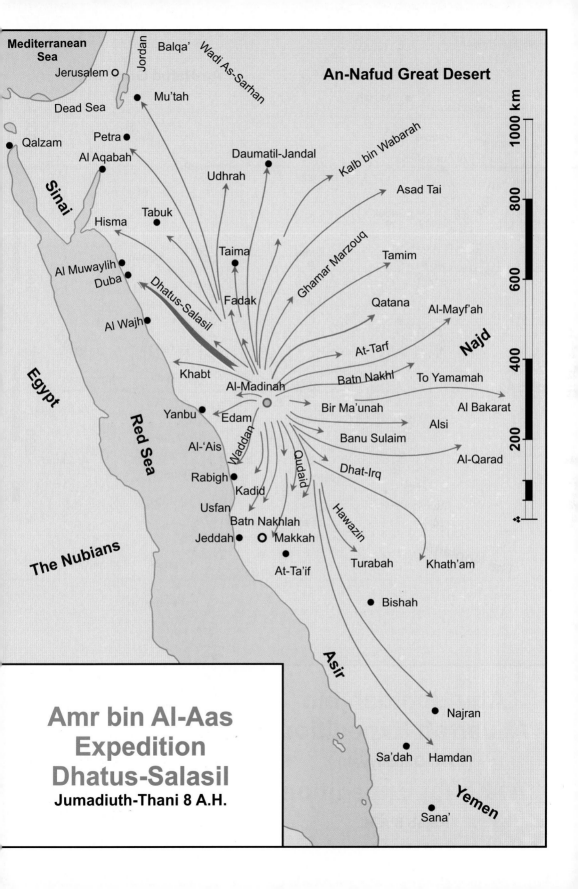

Mediterranean
Sea

Jerusalem O

Dead Sea

Qalzam

Jordan

Balqa'

Wadi As-Sarhan

An-Nafud Great Desert

Mu'tah

Petra

Al Aqabah

Sinai

Udrah

Daumatil-Jandal

Kalb bin Wabarah

Asad Tai

1000 km

Hisma

Tabuk

Taima

800

Al Muwaylih

Duba

Dhatus-Salasil

Fadak

Ghamar Marzouq

Tamim

600

Al Wajh

Qatana

Al-Mayf'ah

Khabt

At-Tarf

Najd

400

Al-Madinah

Batn Nakhl

To Yamamah

Yanbu

Edam

Bir Ma'unah

Al Bakarat

Al-'Ais

Waddan

Banu Sulaim

Alsi

200

Egypt

Red Sea

Rabigh

Kadid

Qudaid

Dhat-Irq

Al-Qarad

Usfan

Batn Nakhlah

Hawazin

Jeddah

Makkah

The Nubians

At-Ta'if

Turabah

Khath'am

Bishah

Asir

Najran

Sa'dah

Hamdan

Yemen

Sana'

Amr bin Al-Aas
Expedition
Dhatus-Salasil
Jumadiuth-Thani 8 A.H.

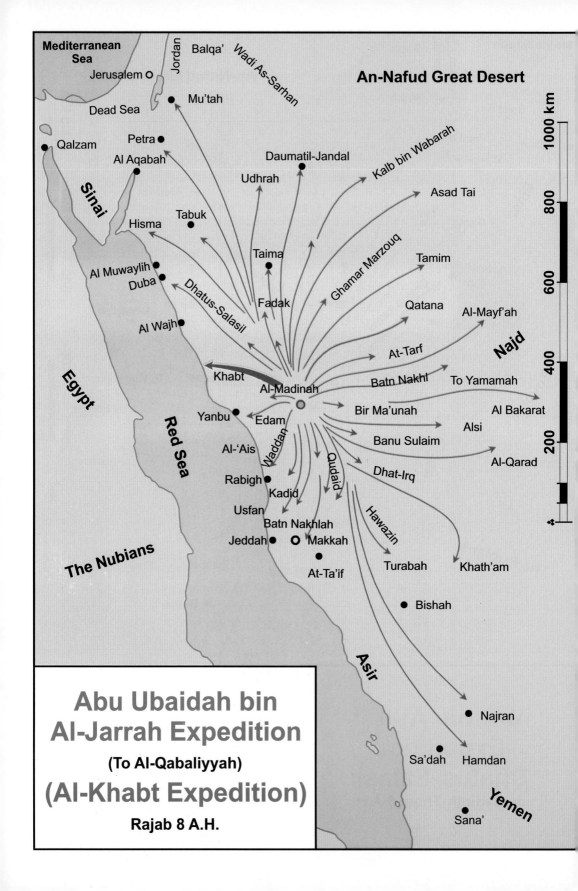

Abu Ubaidah bin
Al-Jarrah Expedition

(To Al-Qabaliyyah)

(Al-Khabt Expedition)

Rajab 8 A.H.

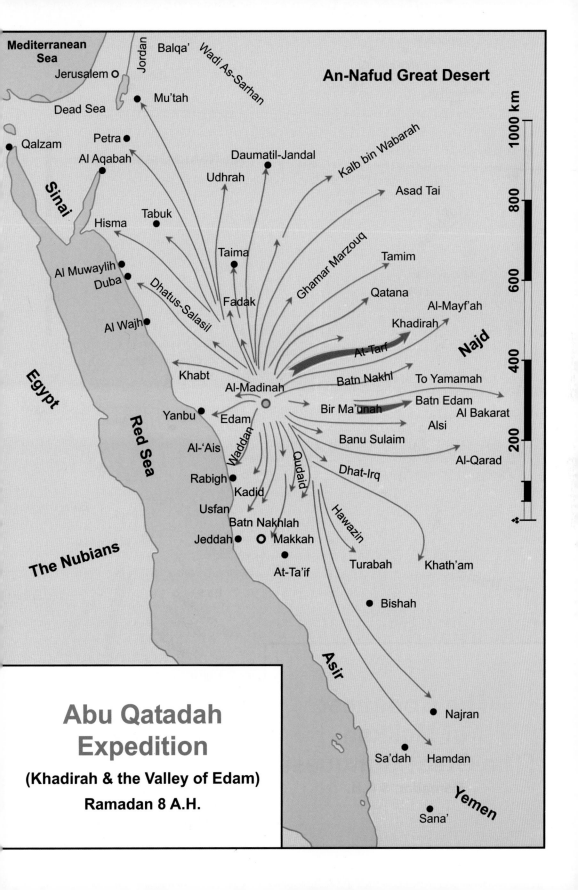

Abu Qatadah
Expedition

(Khadirah & the Valley of Edam)

Ramadan 8 A.H.

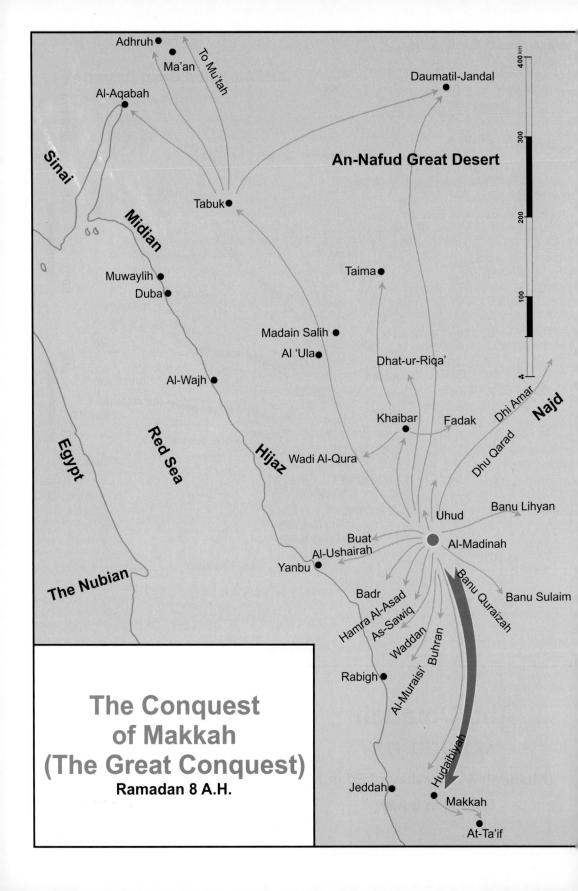

The Conquest
of Makkah
(The Great Conquest)
Ramadan 8 A.H.

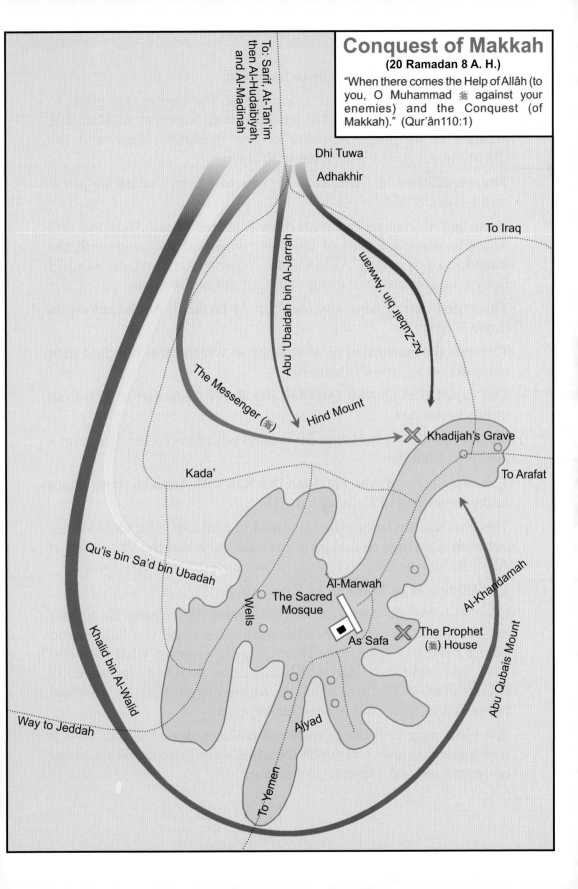

Conquest of Makkah
(20 Ramadan 8 A. H.)

"When there comes the Help of Allâh (to you, O Muhammad ﷺ against your enemies) and the Conquest (of Makkah)." (Qur'ân110:1)

To: Sarif, At-Tan'im then Al-Hudaibiyah, and Al-Madinah

Dhi Tuwa

Adhakhir

To Iraq

Abu 'Ubaidah bin Al-Jarrah

Az-Zubair bin 'Awwam

The Messenger (ﷺ)

Hind Mount

Khadijah's Grave

To Arafat

Kada'

Qu'is bin Sa'd bin Ubadah

Al-Marwah

The Sacred Mosque

Al-Khandamah

Wells

As Safa

The Prophet (ﷺ) House

Abu Qubais Mount

Khalid bin Al-Walid

Way to Jeddah

Ajyad

To Yemen

'Abdullâh ibn Rawâhah was to take over.

These three leaders were all martyred, so the banner was given to Khâlid ibn Al-Walid, who led a tactical withdrawal to Al-Madinah, because of the huge numbers of the Byzantine army and the Christianized Arabs who were with them.

The expedition of 'Amr ibn Al-'Aas to Dhatus-Salâsil in Juma-diuth-Thâni 8 AH.

'Amr ibn Al-'Aas set out with three hundred of the *Muhâjirin* and *Ansâr* to meet a group of Qudâ'ah who had gathered with the intention of attacking Al-Madinah. When he entered the land of Baliyy, he scattered the groups of 'Udhrah and Balqain.

The expedition of Abu 'Ubaidah ibn Al-Jarrâh to Al-Qabaliyyah in Rajab 8 AH.

This was the expedition of Al-Khabat, in which three hundred men marched on a clan of Juhainah.

The expedition of Abu Qatâdah ibn Rab'i Al-Ansâri to Khadirah in Sha'bân 8 AH.

He went to the land of Muhârib in Najd with fifteen men, to scatter a group of Ghatafân.

The expedition of Abu Qatâdah ibn Rab'i Al-Ansâri to Batn Edam at the beginning of Ramadân 8 AH.

This was shortly before the Conquest of Makkah. Abu Qatâdah set out with eight men so that people would think that the Messenger of Allâh ﷺ was headed in that direction, as a diversionary tactic.

The Conquest of Makkah in Ramadân 8 AH

Quraish broke the treaty of Al-Hudaibiyah by helping Banu Bakr against Khuzâ'ah, who were allies of the Messenger of Allâh ﷺ, and killing twenty of their men. Then Quraish regretted what they had done, and 'Amr ibn Sâlim Al-Khuzâ'i came with forty horsemen of Khuzâ'ah to Al-Madinah to tell the Messenger of Allâh ﷺ what had happened to them and to seek his support.

The Messenger of Allâh ﷺ marched with ten thousand men, and it was a great conquest in which the idols were broken and the word of *Tawhid* reigned supreme in Makkah.

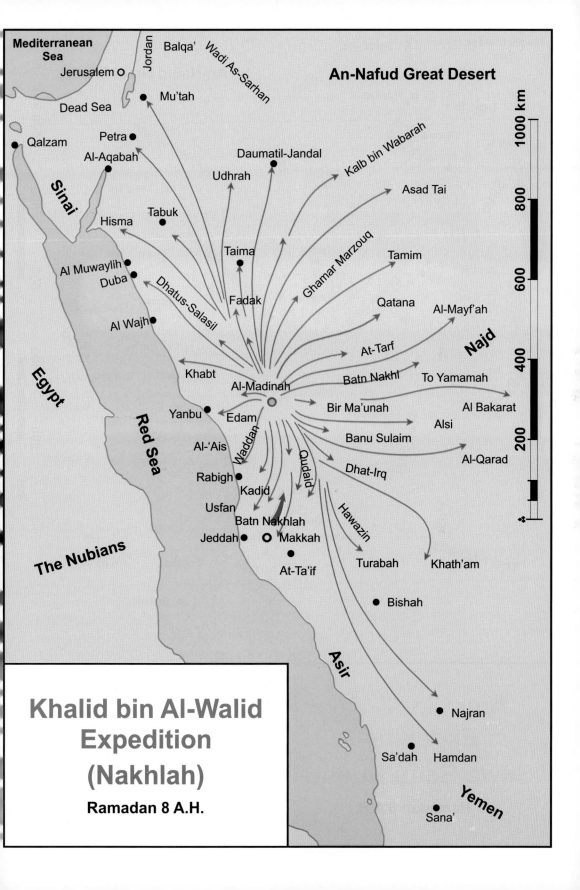

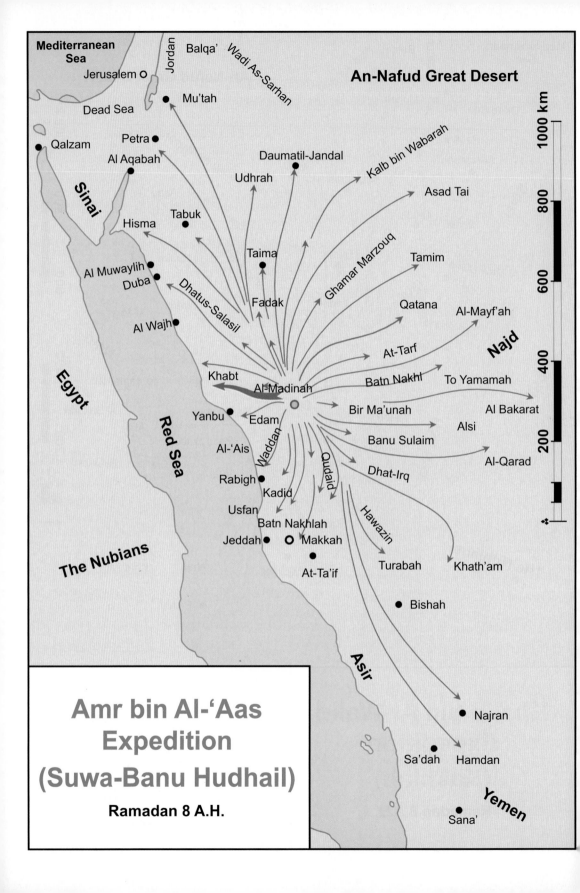

Mediterranean Sea
Jerusalem
Jordan
Balqa'
Wadi As-Sarhan
An-Nafud Great Desert
Mu'tah
Dead Sea
Petra
Qalzam
Al Aqabah
Daumatil-Jandal
Udhrah
Kalb bin Wabarah
Sinai
Tabuk
Asad Tai
Hisma
Taima
Al Muwaylih
Duba
Ghamar Marzouq
Tamim
Dhatus-Salasil
Fadak
Al Wajh
Qatana
Al-Mayf'ah
At-Tarf
Najd
Egypt
Khabt
Batn Nakhl
To Yamamah
Al-Madinah
Bir Ma'unah
Al Bakarat
Red Sea
Yanbu
Edam
Banu Sulaim
Alsi
Al-'Ais
Waddan
Al-Qarad
Rabigh
Qudaid
Dhat-Irq
Kadid
Usfan
Hawazin
Batn Nakhlah
Jeddah
Makkah
Turabah
Khath'am
The Nubians
At-Ta'if
Bishah
Asir
Najran
Sa'dah
Hamdan
Yemen
Sana'

Amr bin Al-'Aas Expedition (Suwa-Banu Hudhail)

Ramadan 8 A.H.

1000 km
800
600
400
200

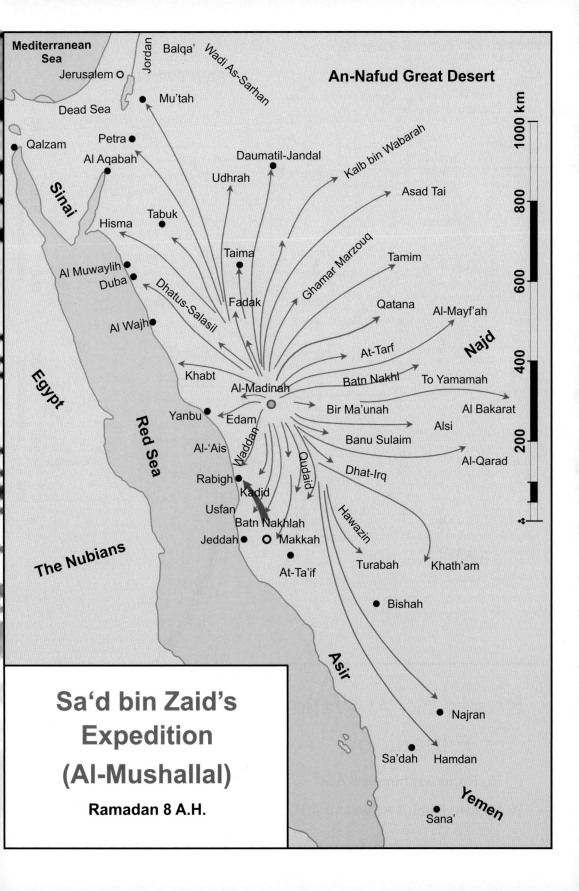

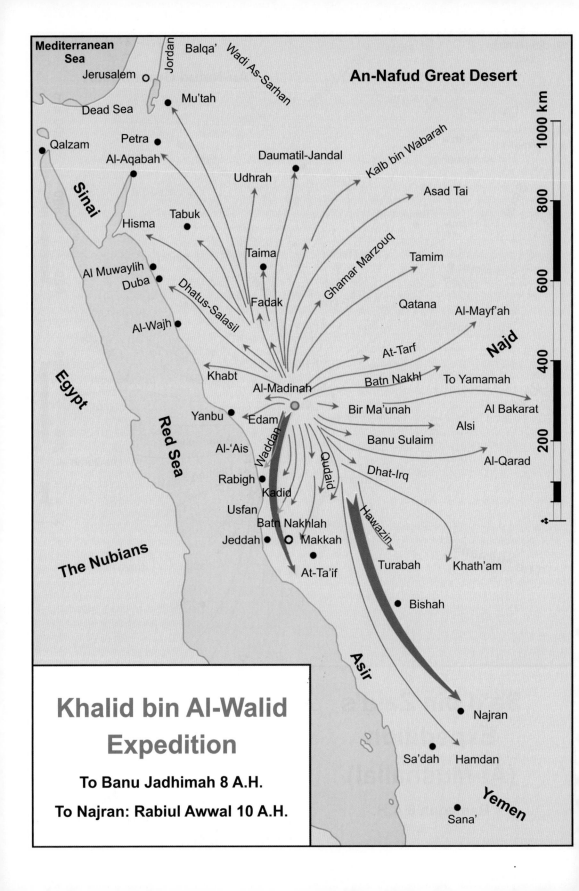

Khalid bin Al-Walid Expedition

To Banu Jadhimah 8 A.H.

To Najran: Rabiul Awwal 10 A.H.

Ruins of Ma'rib Dam (Yemen)

Ruins of Al-Ukhdud

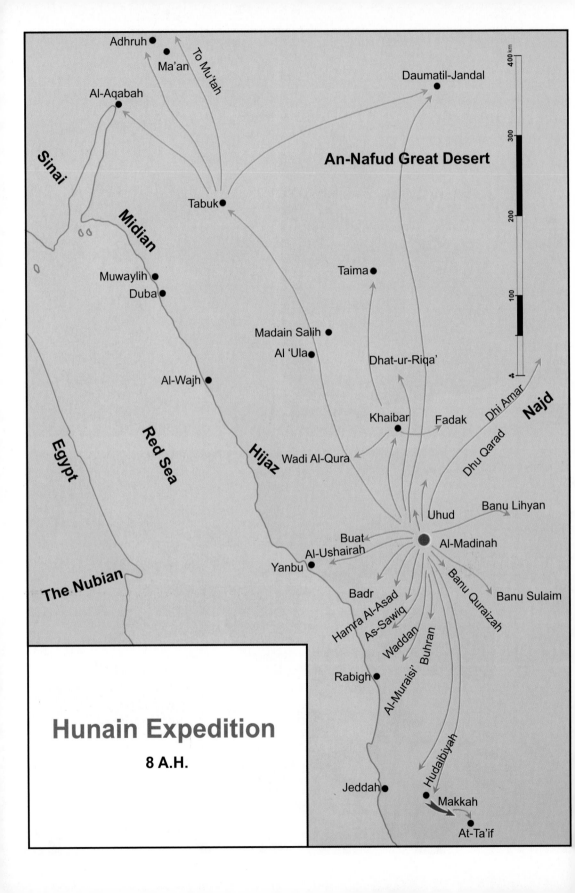

Hunain Expedition
8 A.H.

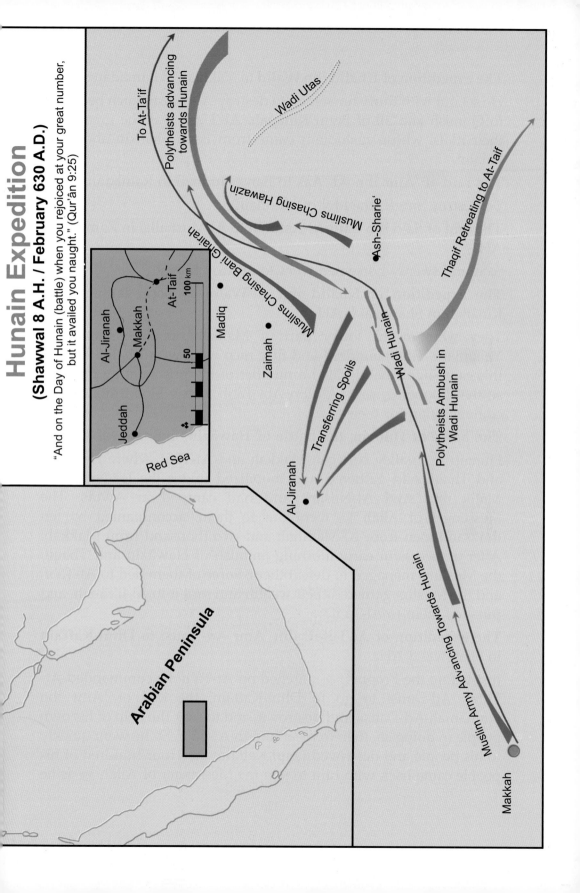

Hunain Expedition

(Shawwal 8 A.H. / February 630 A.D.)

"And on the Day of Hunain (battle) when you rejoiced at your great number, but it availed you naught." (Qur'ân 9:25)

Arabian Peninsula

Red Sea

Al-Jiranah
Makkah
At-Taif
Jeddah
Madiq
Zaimah

100 km
50

To At-Ta'if

Polytheists advancing towards Hunain

Wadi Utas

Muslims Chasing Hawazin

Ash-Sharie'

Muslims Chasing Bani Ghairah

Thaqif Retreating to At-Taif

Transferring Spoils

Wadi Hunain

Al-Jiranah

Polytheists Ambush in Wadi Hunain

Muslim Army Advancing Towards Hunain

Makkah

The expedition of Khâlid ibn Walid to Nakhlah in Ramadân 8 AH.

He set out with thirty horsemen to destroy Al-'Uzza which belonged to Quraish and all of Banu Kinanah. Al-'Uzza was the greatest of their idols, whose custodians came from Banu Shaibân and Banu Sulaim.

The raid of 'Amr ibn Al-'Aas to Banu Hudhail in Ramadân 8 AH.

To destroy Suwâ', the idol of Hudhail.

The raid of Sa'd ibn Zaid Al-Ashhali to Al-Mushallal in Ramadân 8 AH.

Sa'd and twenty horsemen went to destroy Manât.

The expedition of Khâlid ibn Al-Walid to Banu Jadhimah of Kinânah in Shawwâl 8 AH.

They were in the lower part of Makkah, in the direction of Yalamlam. Three hundred and fifty men went with Khâlid. During this campaign Khâlid killed a number of the prisoners by mistake, so the Prophet ﷺ sent 'Ali ibn Abi Tâlib to pay blood money and compensation for their loss.

The battle of Hunain, the battle of Hawâzin, in Shawwâl 8 AH.

Hunain is a valley between Makkah and At-Tâ'if, where Hawâzin and Thaqif had gathered and mobilized under the leadership of Mâlik ibn 'Awf Al-Nasari, and had camped in Awtâs. The Messenger of Allâh ﷺ went out to them, accompanied by ten thousand men from Al-Madinah and two thousand from Makkah. After a successful early-morning ambush of Hawâzin and Thaqif, the Muslims managed to defeat them. Some of them fled to At-Tâ'if, and the Muslim gathered their wealth and sent it to Al-Ji'rânah, and pursued them to Al-Tâ'if.

The expedition of At-Tufail ibn 'Amr Ad-Dausi to Dhul-Kaffain in Shawwâl 8 AH.

Just before the Prophet ﷺ marched on At-Tâ'if, he commanded At-Tufail Ad-Dausi to go to Dhul-Kaffâin, the idol of 'Amr ibn Humamah Ad-Dausi, and destroy it, and to seek the help of his own people in doing so, then to meet him in At-Tâ'if. So he went quickly to his people and destroyed Dhul-Kaffâin, then four hundred of his people came back with him to join the Messenger of Allâh ﷺ as he

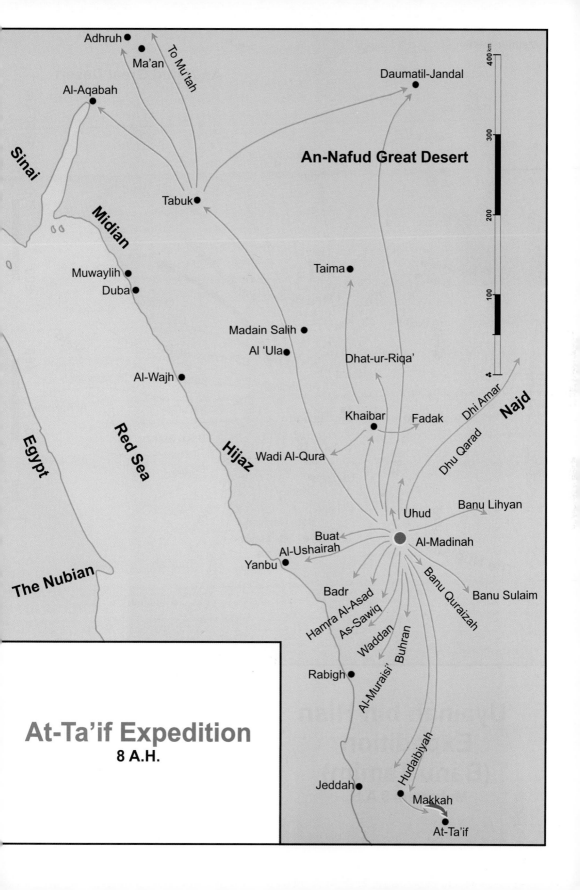

Adhruh •

Ma'an •

To Mu'tah

Al-Aqabah •

Sinai

Midian

Daumatil-Jandal •

An-Nafud Great Desert

Tabuk •

Muwaylih •

Duba •

Taima •

Madain Salih •

Al 'Ula •

Dhat-ur-Riqa'

Al-Wajh •

Dhi Amar

Khaibar •   Fadak

Najd

Egypt

Red Sea

Hijaz

Wadi Al-Qura

Dhu Qarad

Uhud   Banu Lihyan

Buat

Al-Ushairah

Al-Madinah

The Nubian

Yanbu •

Badr

Hamra Al-Asad

As-Sawiq

Waddan

Buhran

Banu Quraizah

Banu Sulaim

Rabigh •

Al-Muraisi'

At-Ta'if Expedition
8 A.H.

Hudaibiyah

Jeddah •

Makkah •

At-Ta'if

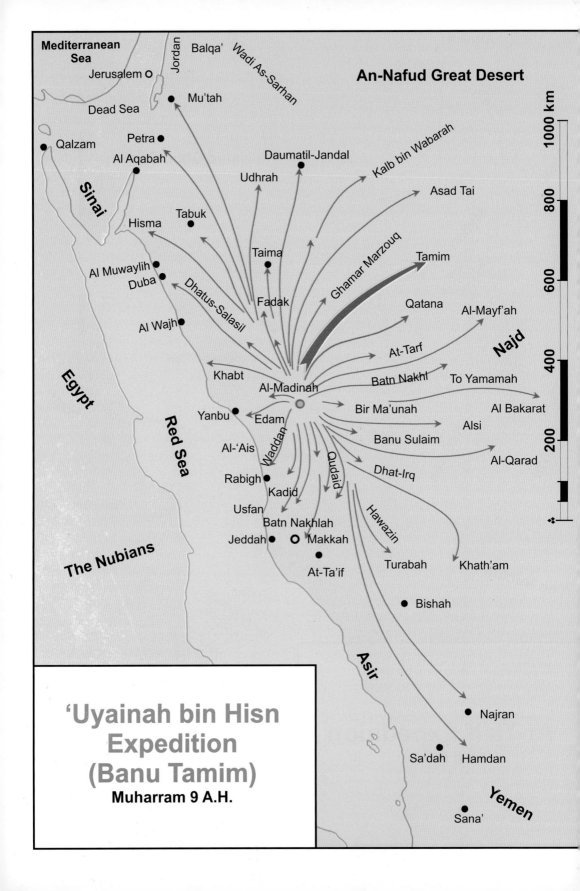

Mediterranean Sea

An-Nafud Great Desert

Jerusalem O

Jordan
Balqa'
Wadi As-Sarhan

Mu'tah

Dead Sea

Qalzam

Petra

Daumatil-Jandal

Kalb bin Wabarah

Al Aqabah

Udhrah

Asad Tai

Sinai

Tabuk

Hisma

Taima

Ghamar Marzouq

Tamim

Al Muwaylih

Duba

Dhatus-Salasil

Fadak

Qatana

Al-Mayf'ah

Al Wajh

At-Tarf

Najd

Khabt

Batn Nakhl

To Yamamah

Al-Madinah

Bir Ma'unah

Al Bakarat

Egypt

Yanbu

Edam

Alsi

Red Sea

Al-'Ais

Banu Sulaim

Al-Qarad

Waddan

Rabigh

Qudaid

Dhat-Irq

Kadid

Usfan

Hawazin

Batn Nakhlah

The Nubians

Jeddah

O Makkah

Turabah

Khath'am

At-Ta'if

Bishah

Asir

'Uyainah bin Hisn
Expedition
(Banu Tamim)
Muharram 9 A.H.

Najran

Sa'dah

Hamdan

Yemen

Sana'

1000 km

800

600

400

200

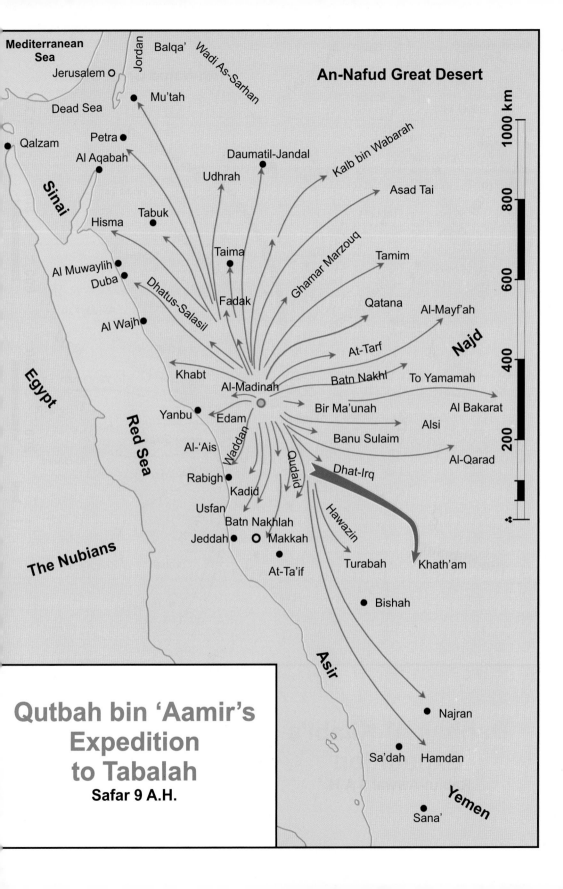

Qutbah bin 'Aamir's Expedition to Tabalah
Safar 9 A.H.

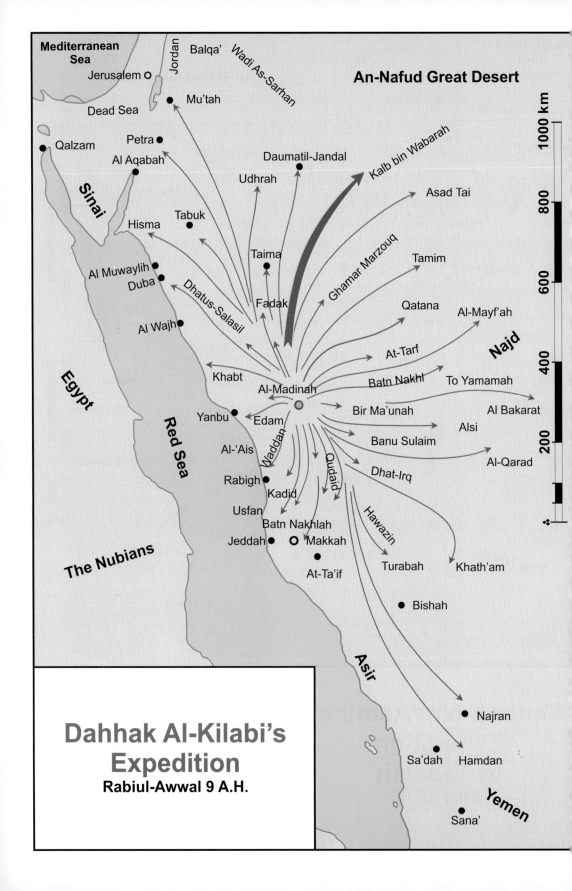

Dahhak Al-Kilabi's
Expedition
Rabiul-Awwal 9 A.H.

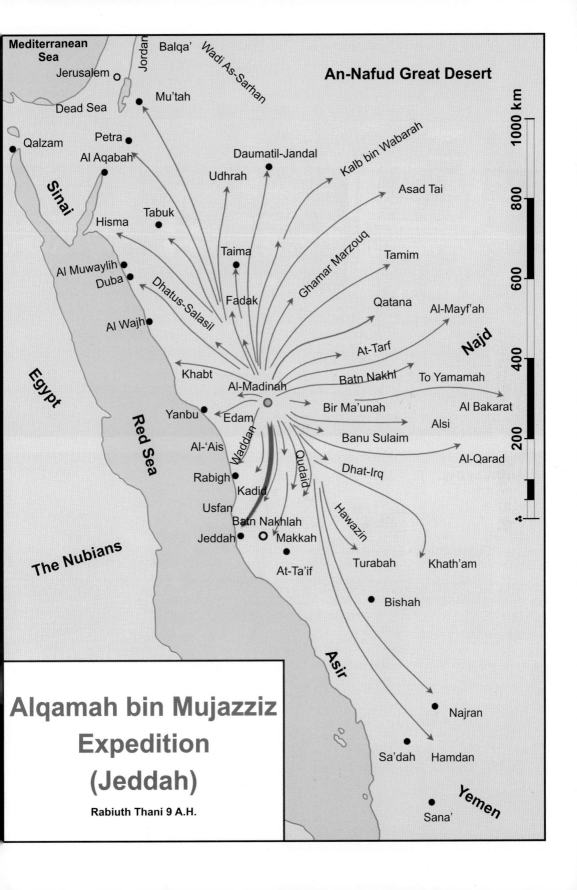

Jeddah by Night

Jeddah by Day

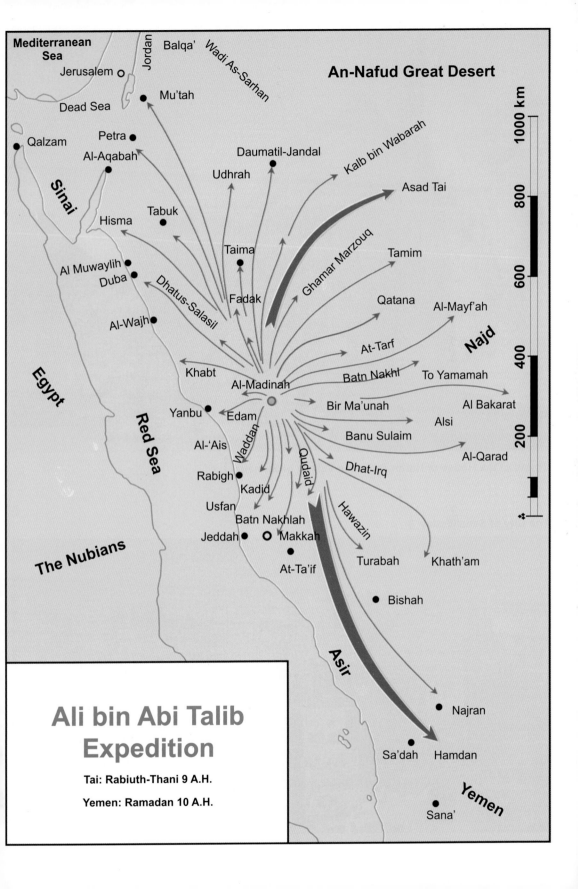

Ali bin Abi Talib Expedition

Tai: Rabiuth-Thani 9 A.H.

Yemen: Ramadan 10 A.H.

Ruins of the House of Hatim Tai in the Village of Sumaira ↑

The City of Sana' Today ↓

was besieging At-Tâ'if.

The campaign of At-Tâ'if in Shawwâl 8 AH.

The Muslims besieged At-Tâ'if for eighteen days, and used a catapult against it. The Prophet ﷺ said on the day of At-Tâ'if "Any slave who comes out to us will be free." So a number of their slaves came out and he set them free, and handed over each one of them to a Muslim man to spend on him.

The Messenger of Allâh ﷺ lifted the siege after Thaqif realized that they did not have the strength to fight the Arabs around them who had become Muslim and pledged their allegiance to the Prophet ﷺ. They sent a delegation in 9 AH to declare their Islam.

The expedition of 'Uyainah ibn Hisn Al-Fazâri to Banu Tamim in Muharram 9 AH.

'Uyainah set out with fifty horsemen to go to Banu Tamim, who were between As-Saqiya and the land of Banu Tamim. They took some of them captive, but the Messenger of Allâh ﷺ showed mercy and let them go.

The expedition of Qutbah ibn 'Aamir to Tabâlah in Safar 9 AH.

This is where the tribe of Khath'am were, towards Baishah, near Turabah. Fighting took place between the Muslims and Khath'am.

The expedition of Ad-Dahhâk ibn Sufyân Al-Kilâbi to Banu Kilâb in Rabul-Awwal 9 AH.

Al-Dahhâk and the men with him marched on Banu Kilâb and met them in Az-Zujj (Zujji Lawâh), where fighting took place.

The expedition of 'Alqamah ibn Mujazziz Al-Mudliji to Jeddah in Rabi'uth-Thâni in 9 AH.

Three hundred men went with him, to repel a group who had come by sea from Abyssinia.

The expedition of 'Ali ibn Abi Tâlib to Tai in Rabi'uth-Thâni 9 AH

'Ali marched with one hundred men to the tribe of Tai to destroy their idol Al-Fuls, which he demolished. Among the prisoners captured at Tai was Saffânah the sister of 'Adi ibn Hâtim, who had fled to Syria. The Messenger of Allâh ﷺ freed her and her brother came as a Muslim to the Messenger of Allâh ﷺ, after he heard from

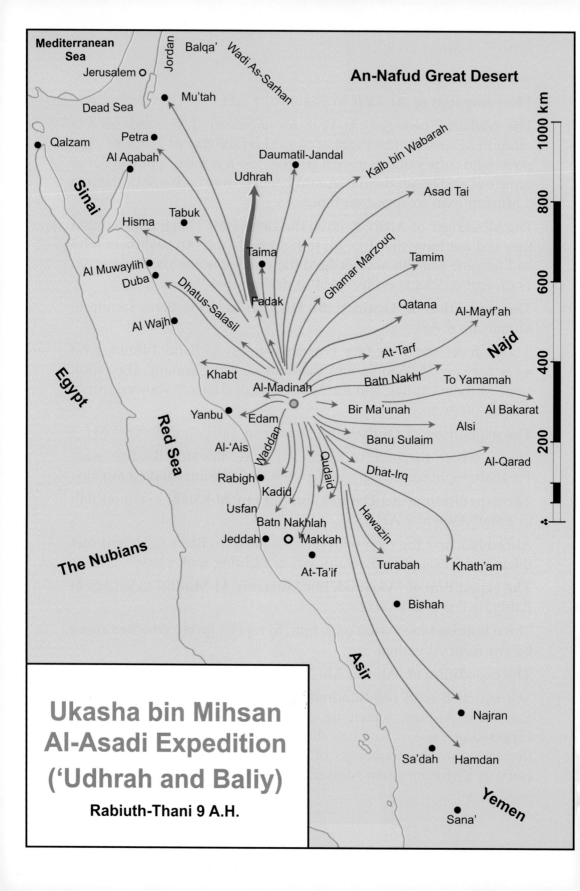

Mediterranean Sea
Jordan
Balqa'
Wadi As-Sarhan
An-Nafud Great Desert
Jerusalem
Mu'tah
Dead Sea
Petra
Al Aqabah
Daumatil-Jandal
Udhrah
Kalb bin Wabarah
Asad Tai
Qalzam
Sinai
Hisma
Tabuk
Taima
Ghamar Marzouq
Tamim
Al Muwaylih
Duba
Dhatus-Salasil
Fadak
Qatana
Al-Mayf'ah
Al Wajh
At-Tarf
Najd
Khabt
Al-Madinah
Batn Nakhl
To Yamamah
Egypt
Yanbu
Edam
Bir Ma'unah
Al Bakarat
Red Sea
Al-'Ais
Waddan
Banu Sulaim
Alsi
Rabigh
Kadid
Qudaid
Dhat-Irq
Al-Qarad
Usfan
Batn Nakhlah
Hawazin
The Nubians
Jeddah
Makkah
Turabah
Khath'am
At-Ta'if
Bishah
Asir
Najran
Sa'dah
Hamdan
Yemen
Sana'

1000 km
800
600
400
200

Ukasha bin Mihsan Al-Asadi Expedition ('Udhrah and Baliy)

Rabiuth-Thani 9 A.H.

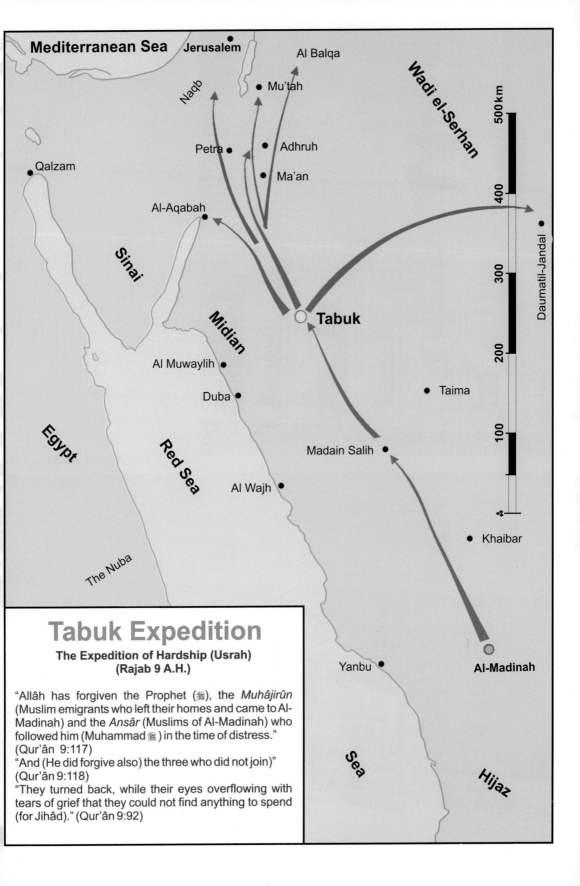

Mediterranean Sea   Jerusalem

Al Balqa

Naqb   ● Mu'tah

Petra ●   ● Adhruh

Qalzam ●   ● Ma'an

Al-Aqabah ●

Sinai

Midian   ○ **Tabuk**

Al Muwaylih ●

Duba ●   ● Taima

Egypt   Red Sea

Al Wajh ●

Madain Salih ●

The Nuba   ● Khaibar

Wadi el-Serhan

Daumatil-Jandal ●

500 km
400
300
200
100

Tabuk Expedition

The Expedition of Hardship (Usrah)
(Rajab 9 A.H.)

"Allâh has forgiven the Prophet (ﷺ), the *Muhâjirûn* (Muslim emigrants who left their homes and came to Al-Madinah) and the *Ansâr* (Muslims of Al-Madinah) who followed him (Muhammad ﷺ) in the time of distress." (Qur'ân 9:117)

"And (He did forgive also) the three who did not join)" (Qur'ân 9:118)

"They turned back, while their eyes overflowing with tears of grief that they could not find anything to spend (for Jihâd)." (Qur'ân 9:92)

Yanbu ●   **Al-Madinah**

Sea   Hijaz

← Tabuk

↓ Mada'in Salih

his sister about how the Muslims were and how she thought things would develop in the future.

The expedition of 'Ukâshah ibn Mihsanul-Asadi to Al-Jinâb in Rabi'uth-Thâni 9 AH.

He marched on the area where the tribes of 'Udhrah and Baliy were, and reached some land of theirs that was called Al-Jinâb.

The campaign of Tabuk, the campaign of hardship (*Ghazwatul-'Usrah*), in Rajab 9 AH.

The reason for this campaign was the massing of the Byzantines in southern Syria, along with the tribes of Lakhm, Judhâm, 'Aamilah and Ghassân. Their vanguard had reached Al-Balqa', so the Messenger of Allâh ﷺ set out at the time of distress [cf. *At-Tawbah* 9:117], during a period of drought and intense heat.

From Tabuk he sent Khâlid ibn Al-Walid to Daumatil-Jandal, then he ﷺ and those who were with him returned to Al-Madinah, after scattering the Byzantine army.

Tabuk was the last of the Prophet's campaigns.

In 9 AH, Abu Bakr As-Siddiq led the people in *Hajj*. He set out with three hundred men from Al-Madinah, and the Messenger of Allâh ﷺ sent with him twenty sacrificial camels. When he was in Al-'Arj, 'Ali caught up with him to recite *Surat Barâ'ah* [*Surat At-Tawbah*] to the people.

The expedition of Khâlid ibn Al-Walid to Najrân in Rab'ul-Awwal 10 AH.

The Messenger of Allâh ﷺ sent him to Banu 'Abdul-Madân in Najrân.

The expedition of 'Ali ibn Abi Tâlib to Yemen in Ramadân 10 AH.

It was said that 'Ali went to Yemen twice, one of which was in Ramadân.

He ﷺ went with three hundred horsemen, and these were the first horses to enter that land, namely Madhhij in Yemen.

'Ali came back and met the Messenger of Allâh ﷺ in Makkah, where he had come for *Hajj* in 10 AH.

The Year of Delegations

Ibn Ishaaq said: When the Messenger of Allâh ﷺ conquered Makkah and finished with Tabuk, and Thaqif had become Muslim and sworn their allegiance to him, delegations from the Arabs came to him from all directions. Most of the delegations came in 9 AH, hence it was dubbed The Year of Delegations.

The fact that Quraish had become Muslim was the direct cause of the delegations coming, because Quraish were the leaders of the Arabs, the servants of the House and the Sanctuary, and the Arabs did not deny that. Quraish were the ones who had instigated the war against the Messenger of Allâh ﷺ, and now here they were in Makkah, all of them entering the religion of Allâh in crowds, and destroying their idols.

After Badr, Uhud and Al-Khandaq, the Arabs said: Let him and his people fight it out; if he prevails over them then he is a true Prophet.

Ibn Sa'd listed more than seventy delegations in *At-Tabaqât Al-Kubra* (vol. 1, pp. 291-359), of which we will list the most well known and most important here:[1]

- The delegation of Mazeenah (in Rajab 5 AH). The Prophet ﷺ said to them: "You are muhaajireen wherever you are, so go back to your wealth and return to your country."[2]

- The delegation of Banu 'Abdul-Qais

- The delegation of Banu Hanifah

- The delegation of the people of Najrân

- The delegation of Banu 'Aamir

- Dimâm ibn Tha'labah on behalf of his people Banu Sa'd ibn Bakr

- The delegation of Tai with Zaid Al-Khail (Zaid Al-Khair) and

---

[1] *Al-Iktifa*, 1/163; *As-Seerah An-Nabawiyyah* by Ibn Kathir, 4/76; *Al-Kâmil fi't-Târikh*, 2/195; At-Tabari, 3/239; Ibn Khaldun, 2/51; *Al-Tabaqât Al-Kubra*, 1/291 ff.

[2] *Al-Bidâyah wa'n-Nihâyah*, 5/41

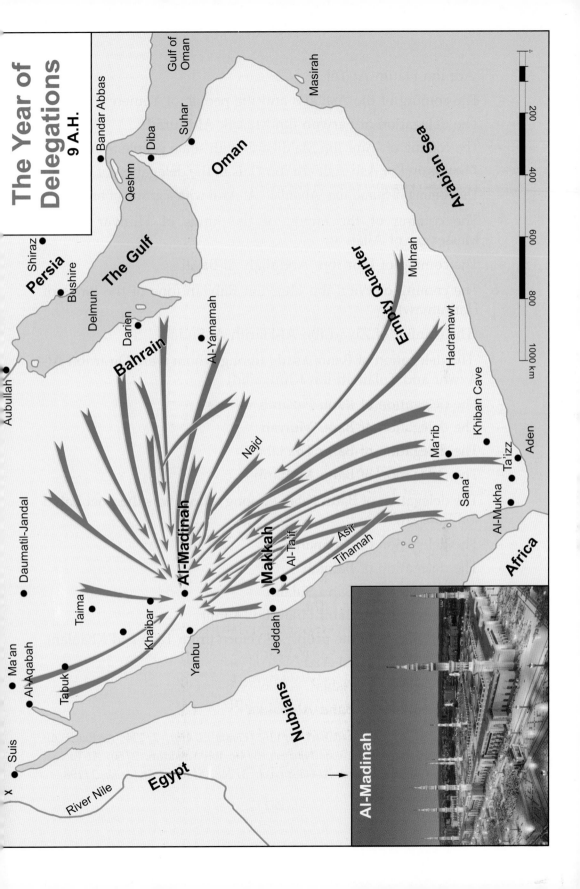

The Year of Delegations
9 A.H.

'Adi ibn Hâtim At-Tai

- The coming of the Ash'aris and the people of Yemen
- The delegation of Farwah ibn Musaik Al-Murâdi
- The coming of 'Amr ibn Ma'dikarib with some people from Zabid
- The coming of Ash-Ash'ath ibn Qais in the delegation of Kindah
- The coming of Surad ibn 'Abdullâh Al-Azdi with a group of his people
- The coming of the envoy of the kings of Himyar to the Messenger of Allâh ﷺ
- The coming of Jarir ibn 'Abdullâh Al-Bajali
- The coming of Wâ'il ibn Hujr ibn Rabi'ah (one of the kings of Hadramawt)
- The coming of Ziyâd ibn Al-Hârith Al-Sudâ'i
- The delegation of Banu Asad (among whom were Dirâr ibn Al-Azwar and Tulaihah ibn Khuwailid)
- The delegation of Banu Fazârah
- The delegation of Banu Murrah
- The delegation of Banu Tha'labah
- The delegation of Banu Muhârib
- The delegation of Banu Kilâb (among whom was the poet Labid ibn Rabi'ah)
- The delegation of Kinânah
- The delegation of Bâhilah
- The delegation of Banu Sulaim
- The delegation of Banu Hilâl ibn 'Aamir
- A delegation from the people of Yemen (from Tajib and Khaulân)
- The delegation of Al-Azd
- The delegation of Ashja'
- The delegation of Banu Al–Bakka'[1]

---

[1] Ibn Hishâm, 4/164; At-Tabari, 3/136; 'Uyun Al-Athr, 2/234; Ar-Rawd Al-Unuf, 4/220; Al-Bidâyah wan-Nihâyah, 5/46; Ibn Khaldun, 2/56; At-Tabaqât Al-Kubra, 1/357; As-Seerah Al-Halabiyyah, 3/248; Al-Kâmil fit-Târikh, 2/198.

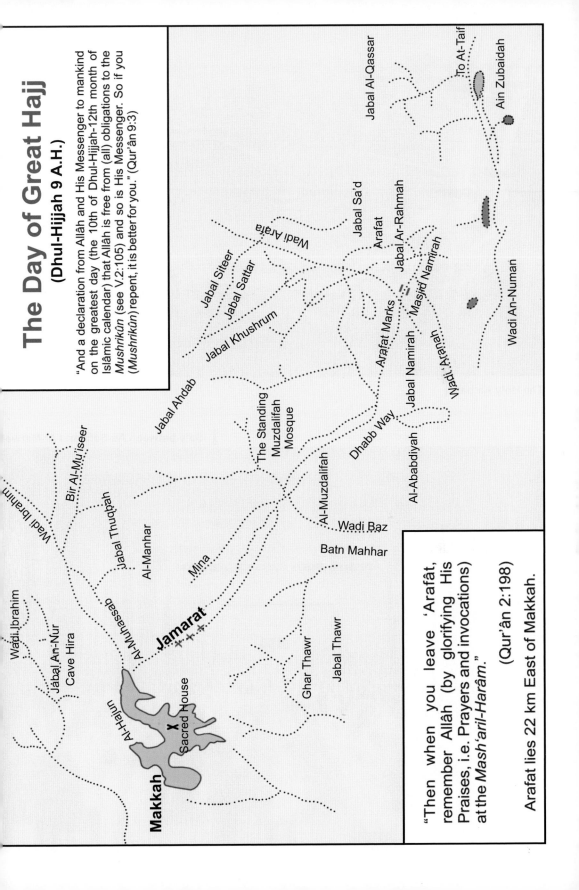

The Day of Great Hajj
(Dhul-Hijah 9 A.H.)

"And a declaration from Allâh and His Messenger to mankind on the greatest day (the 10th of Dhul-Hijjah-12th month of Islâmic calendar) that Allâh is free from (all) obligations to the Mushrikûn (see V.2:105) and so is His Messenger. So if you (Mushrikûn) repent, it is better for you." (Qur'ân 9:3)

"Then when you leave 'Arafât, remember Allâh (by glorifying His Praises, i.e. Prayers and invocations) at the Mash'aril-Harâm."

(Qur'ân 2:198)

Arafat lies 22 km East of Makkah.

Makkah

Jamarat

Sacred House

Al-Hajun

Al-Muhassab

Wadi Ibrahim

Jabal An-Nur

Cave Hira

Wadi Ibrahim

Bir Al-Mu'iseer

Jabal Thuqbah

Al-Manhar

Mina

Ghar Thawr

Jabal Thawr

Batn Mahhar

Wadi Baz

Al-Muzdalifah

The Standing
Muzdalifah
Mosque

Jabal Ahdab

Jabal Khushrum

Jabal Sattar

Jabal Siteer

Wadi Arafa

Dhabb Way

Al-Ababdiyah

Jabal Namirah

Wadi 'Aranah

Masjid Namirah

Arafat Marks

Jabal Ar-Rahmah

Arafat

Jabal Sa'd

Wadi An-Numan

Jabal Al-Qassar

To At-Taif

Ain Zubaidah

The Holy Ka'bah ↑

↓ Sa'y between As-Safa and Al-Marwah

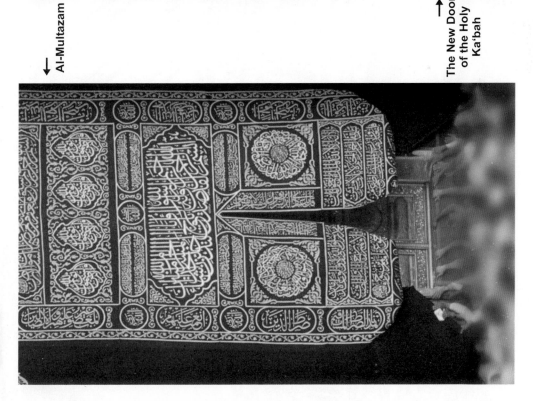

Al-Multazam

The New Door
of the Holy
Ka'bah

Jabalur-Rahmah (the Mount of Mercy) in Arafat

Mina (and stoning of the Jamarat)

Muzdalifah

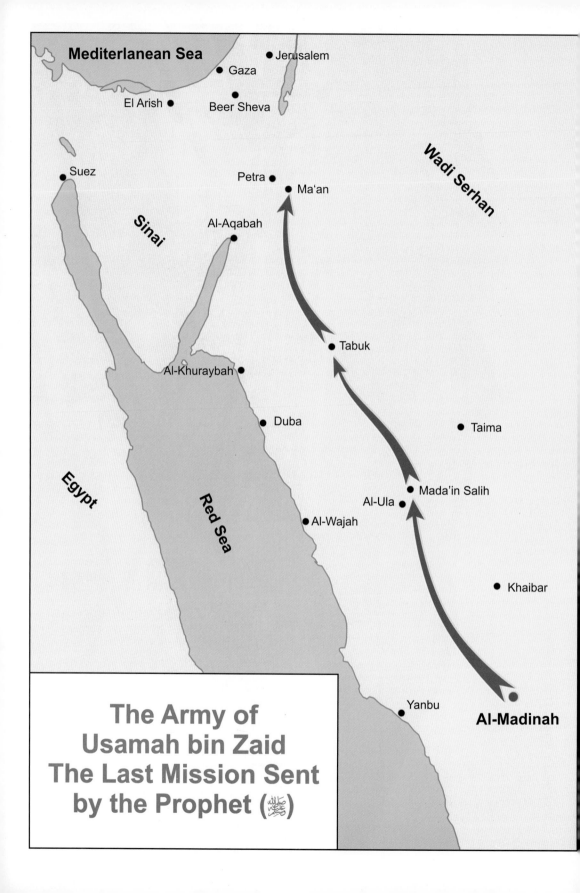

Mediterlanean Sea

Jerusalem

Gaza

El Arish

Beer Sheva

Suez

Petra

Ma'an

Sinai

Al-Aqabah

Wadi Serhan

Tabuk

Al-Khuraybah

Duba

Taima

Egypt

Red Sea

Mada'in Salih

Al-Ula

Al-Wajah

Khaibar

Yanbu

Al-Madinah

The Army of Usamah bin Zaid The Last Mission Sent by the Prophet (ﷺ)

The Farewell Pilgrimage

During this pilgrimage the Prophet ﷺ showed the people how to do the rituals and taught them the *Sunnahs* of *Hajj*. He addressed the people in the Farewell Sermon, during which he said:

"O people, listen to what I say, for I do not know if I will meet you again in this place after this year. O people, your blood and your wealth are sacred to you until you meet your Lord, as sacred as this day of yours, this month of yours. You will meet your Lord and He will ask you about your deeds. I have conveyed the message..."

"All *Riba* (usury) is abolished, but you will have the capital of your wealth. Do not wrong others and you will not be wronged. Allâh has decreed that there is no *Riba*, and the *Riba* of 'Abbaas ibn 'Abdul-Muttalib is all abolished..."

"O people, you have rights over your women, and your women have rights over you... I urge you to treat your women well..."

"Think about what I have said, O people, for I have conveyed the message..."

"O Allâh, bear witness."

***

The army of Usâmah ibn Zaid to Al-Balqa' in Safar 11 AH, the last mission dispatched by the Prophet ﷺ.

The Prophet ﷺ said: "Go to the place where your father was killed – the south of Al-Balqa' in Mu'tah – and let your cavalry march there." The army of Usâmah camped in Al-Jurf – three miles from Al-Madinah in the direction of Syria (*Mu'jamul-Buldân*, 2/128). The Prophet ﷺ said: "Send the army of Usâmah." Then the Messenger of Allâh ﷺ passed away, but Abu Bakr ؓ dispatched the army.

Ar-Rawdah Al-Mutahharah

The Burying Places of the Prophet ﷺ and his Companions Abu Bakr and Umar ﷺ

The Governors and Agents of the Messenger of Allâh ﷺ appointed in charge of the *Zakâh*

The Prophet ﷺ sent:

- Al-Muhâjir ibn Abi Umaiyyah ibn Al-Mughirah to San'a'
- Ziyâd ibn Labid Al-Ansâri to Hadramawt
- 'Adi ibn Hâtim to Tai' and Banu Asad
- Mâlik ibn Nuwairah Al-Yarbu'i to Banu Hanzalah
- Az-Zabarqân ibn Badr to one part of Banu Sa'd
- Qais ibn 'Aasim to another part of Banu Sa'd
- Al-'Ala' ibn Al-Hadrami to Bahrain, then Abân ibn Sa'eed ibn Al-'Aas.
- 'Ali ibn Abi Tâlib to Najrân, after sending 'Amr ibn Hazm with the delegation from Najrân, as their governor and to teach them Islam, and to take their *Zakâh* from them. The Prophet ﷺ wrote a letter to him giving guidelines on how to do his job. (Ibn Hishâm, 4/179, 182).

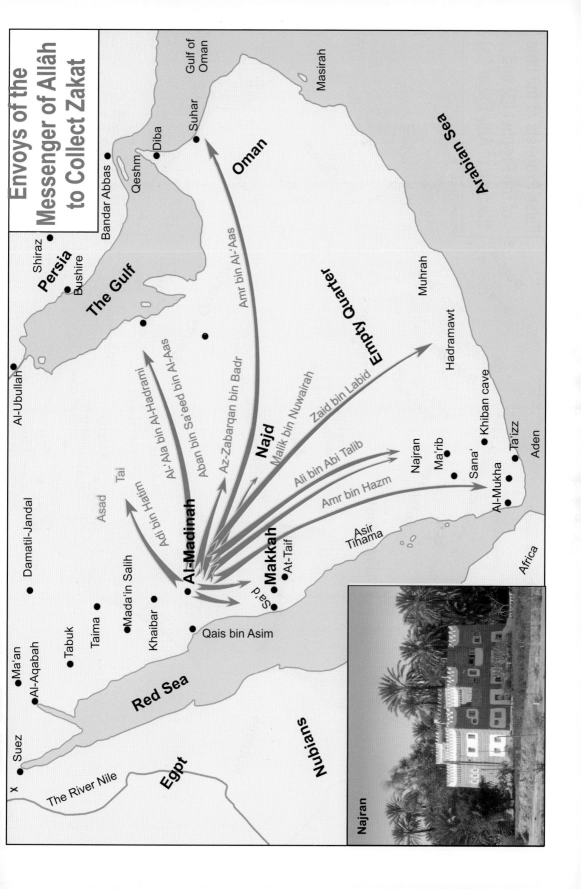

Envoys of the Messenger of Allâh to Collect Zakat

Gulf of Oman

Masirah

Suhar

Diba

Oman

Qeshm

Bandar Abbas

Amr bin Al-'Aas

Shiraz

Persia

Bushire

The Gulf

Muhrah

Al-Ubullah

Empty Quarter

Hadramawt

Al-'Ala bin Al-Hadrami

Aban bin Sa'eed bin Al-Aas

Az-Zabarqan bin Badr

Khiban cave

Tai

Zaid bin Labid

Asad

Malik bin Nuwairah

Najd

Ta'izz

Adi bin Hatim

Najran

Ma'rib

Ali bin Abi Talib

Sana'

Aden

Damatil-Jandal

Al-Mukha

Amr bin Hazm

Arabian sea

Mada'in Salih

Al-Madinah

Asir

Ma'an

Tabuk

Taima

Khaibar

Makkah

Tihama

Al-Aqabah

At-Taif

Sa'd

Africa

Qais bin Asim

Red Sea

Suez

Nubians

Egpt

The River Nile

x

Najran

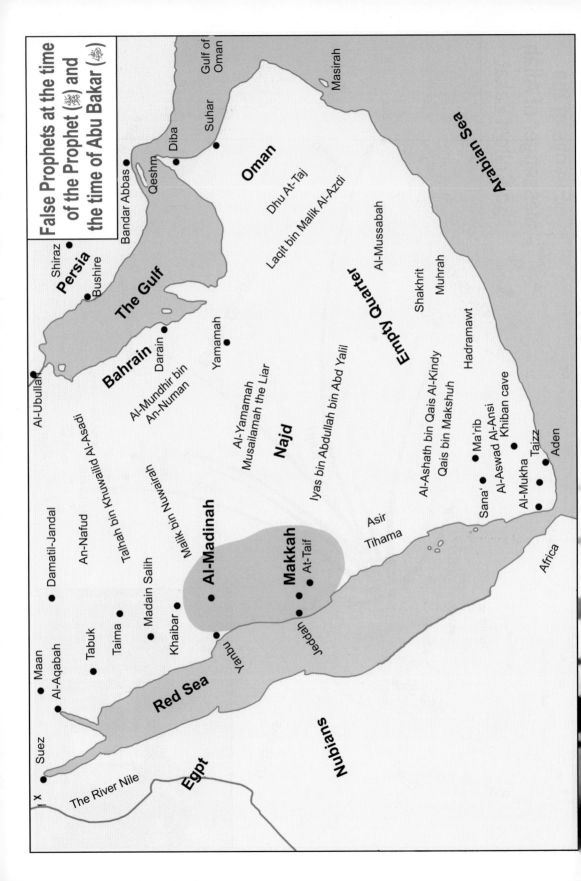

False Prophets at the time of the Prophet (ﷺ) and the time of Abu Bakar (ﷺ)

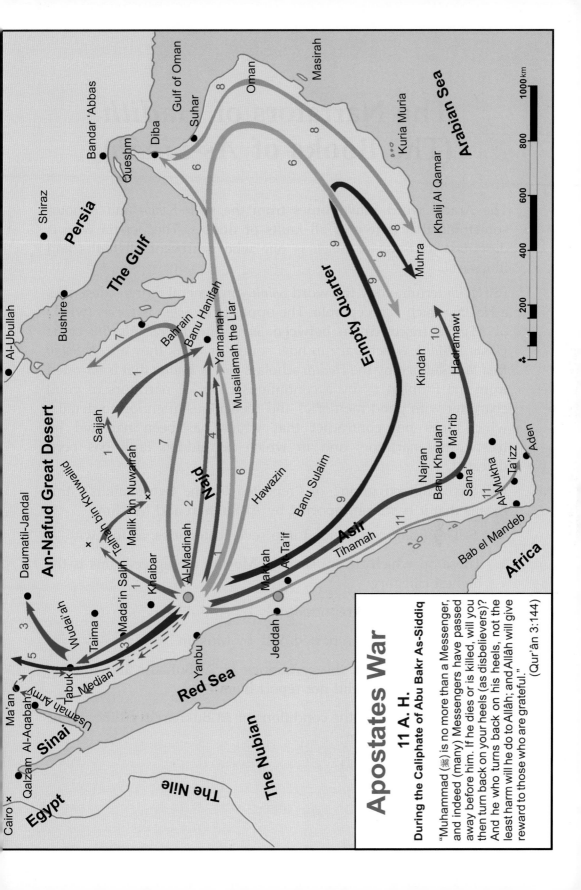

Apostates War
11 A. H.
During the Caliphate of Abu Bakr As-Siddiq

"Muhammad (ﷺ) is no more than a Messenger, and indeed (many) Messengers have passed away before him. If he dies or is killed, will you then turn back on your heels (as disbelievers)? And he who turns back on his heels, not the least harm will he do to Allâh; and Allâh will give reward to those who are grateful."

(Qur'ân 3:144)

The Narrators of *Hadith* (The Books of *As-Sihâh*)

The Arabic word *Sahih* comes from the verb *Sahha* and denotes something that is free of all faults or doubts. The person who is described as *Sahih* or *Sihâh* is one who is free of all faults and illnesses.

In *Hadith* terminology the word *Sahih* – in general terms – describes a *Hadith* which is acceptable. The opposite of *Sahih* is *Da'eef* (weak) or *Mardud* (rejected). In between *Sahih* and *Da'eef Ahadith* come *Hasan Ahadith* which vary in how sound or weak they are. A *Sahih Hadith* is defined by the *Hadith* scholars as: "A *Hadith* that is narrated from the Prophet ﷺ by a continuous chain of narrators of good character with good memories and meticulous attention to detail," which does not contradict that which has been narrated by trustworthy narrators and in which no hidden fault has been detected.[1]

If it says "agreed upon" or "reported by the two shaikhs", this means that it has been reported by Al-Bukhâri and Muslim.

The *Sahih Ahadith* are divided into seven categories, as follows:

1. Those on which *Al-Bukhâri* and Muslim are agreed; this is the highest category

2. Those which were reported only by Al-Bukhâri

3. Those which were reported only by Muslim

4. Those which meet the conditions of Al-Bukhâri and Muslim even though they did not report them

5. Those which meet the conditions of Al-Bukhâri even though he did not report them

---

[1] *Al-Qamus Al-Islami*, 4/253

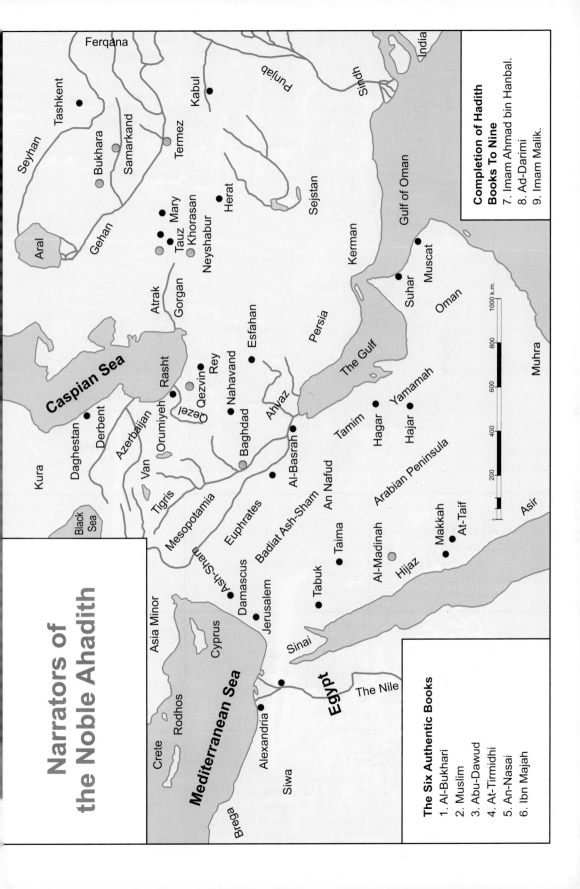

Narrators of
the Noble Ahadith

Completion of Hadith Books To Nine
7. Imam Ahmad bin Hanbal.
8. Ad-Darimi
9. Imam Malik.

The Six Authentic Books
1. Al-Bukhari
2. Muslim
3. Abu-Dawud
4. At-Tirmidhi
5. An-Nasai
6. Ibn Majah

Ferqana
India
Tashkent
Seyhan
Kabul
Punjab
Bukhara
Samarkand
Termez
Sindh
Aral
Gehan
Mary
Khorasan
Herat
Tauz
Neyshabur
Sejstan
Gulf of Oman
Atrak
Gorgan
Kerman
Muscat
Caspian Sea
Rasht
Esfahan
Persia
Suhar
Oman
Orumiyeh
Rey
Qezvin
Nahavand
The Gulf
Qezel
Van
Baghdad
Ahvaz
Yamamah
Muhra
Derbent
Azerbaijan
Al-Basrah
Tamim
Hagar
Hajar
Daghestan
Kura
Tigris
An Nafud
Arabian Peninsula
Black
Sea
Mesopotamia
Euphrates
Badiat Ash-Sham
Makkah
At-Taif
Asir
Ash-Sham
Damascus
Taima
Al-Madinah
Hijaz
Asia Minor
Jerusalem
Tabuk
Cyprus
Sinai
Rodhos
Crete
Mediterranean Sea
Egypt
The Nile
Alexandria
Siwa
Brega

1000 k.m.
800
600
400
200
0

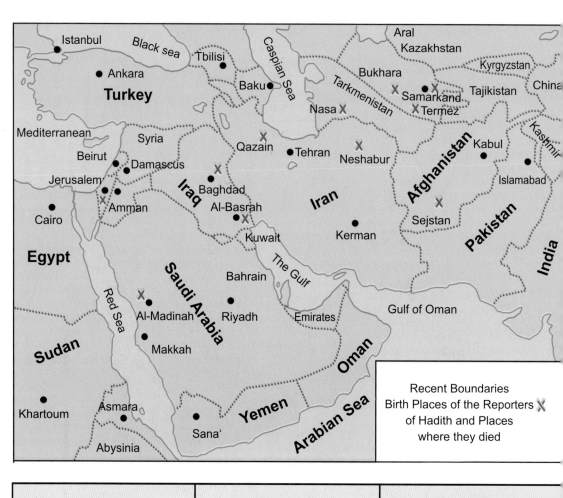

Recent Boundaries
Birth Places of the Reporters ✗
of Hadith and Places
where they died

Al-Bukhari	Muslim	Abu Dawud
Bukhara	Neshabur	Sejstan: Afghanistan
Khartenk: One of the villages of Samarkand	Suburb of Neshabur In Iran	Al-Basrah: South Iraq
At-Tirmidhi	**An-Nasai**	**Ibn Majah**
Termez	Nasa: Turkmenistan	Qazvin
Uzbekistan	Jerusalem: Palestine	Iran
Ibn Hanbal	**Ad-Darimi**	**Malik**
Baghdad	Samarkand	Al-Madinah
Iraq	Uzbekistan	Kingdom of Saudi Arabia

6. Those which meet the conditions of Muslim even though he did not report them

7. Those which are judged to be *Sahih* by scholars other than Al-Bukhâri and Muslim but which do not meet their conditions

The Messenger of Allâh ﷺ allowed some of his companions who were skilled in writing – as well as some who did not have good memories – to write down his words; then he gave permission for the *Ahadith* to be written down. Hence many of the *Tâbi'in* used to write down *Ahadith* in the presence of the *Sahâbah*, and Sa'd ibn 'Ubâdah Al-Ansâri had a book or books containing a number of *Ahadith* of the Messenger of Allâh ﷺ. Abu Râfi', the freed slave of the Messenger of Allâh ﷺ also had something similar. 'Abdullâh ibn 'Amr compiled *As-Sahifah As-Sâdiqah* at the time of the Messenger of Allâh ﷺ, and the *Sahifah* of Jâbir ibn 'Abdullâh Al-Ansâri was compiled during the time of the *Sahâbah*, and part of it during the time of the Messenger of Allâh ﷺ.

During the time of 'Umar ibn 'Abdul-'Aziz (99-101 AH), he wrote to the people of Al-Madinah, saying: "Look for the *Ahadith* of the Messenger of Allâh ﷺ and write them down. For I am afraid that knowledge and its people may disappear." Ibn Shihâb Az-Zuhri said: " 'Umar ibn 'Abdul-'Aziz commanded us to gather the *Sunnahs*, so we wrote them down in a book and made copies of it and he sent a copy to each of the lands over which he ruled."

* * *

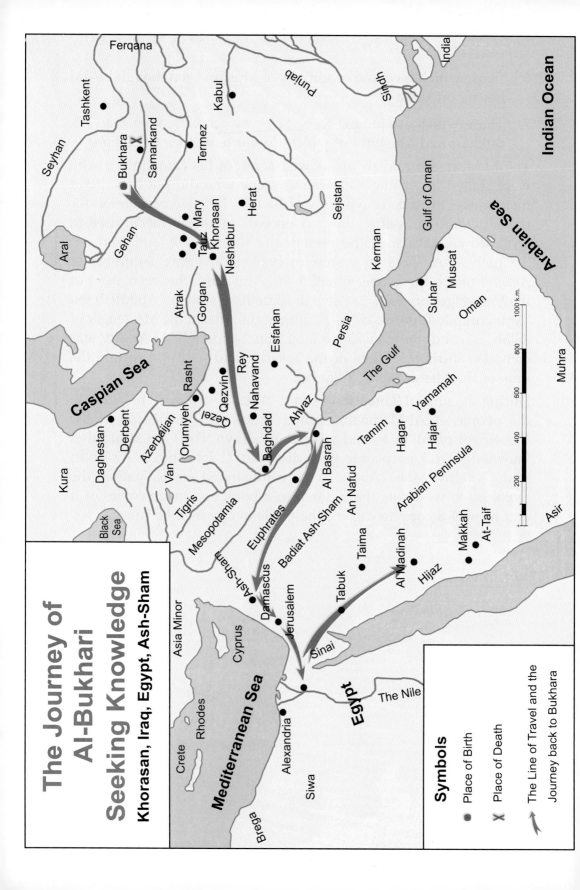

The Journey of Al-Bukhari

Seeking Knowledge
Khorasan, Iraq, Egypt, Ash-Sham

Symbols

● Place of Birth

✕ Place of Death

↗ The Line of Travel and the Journey back to Bukhara

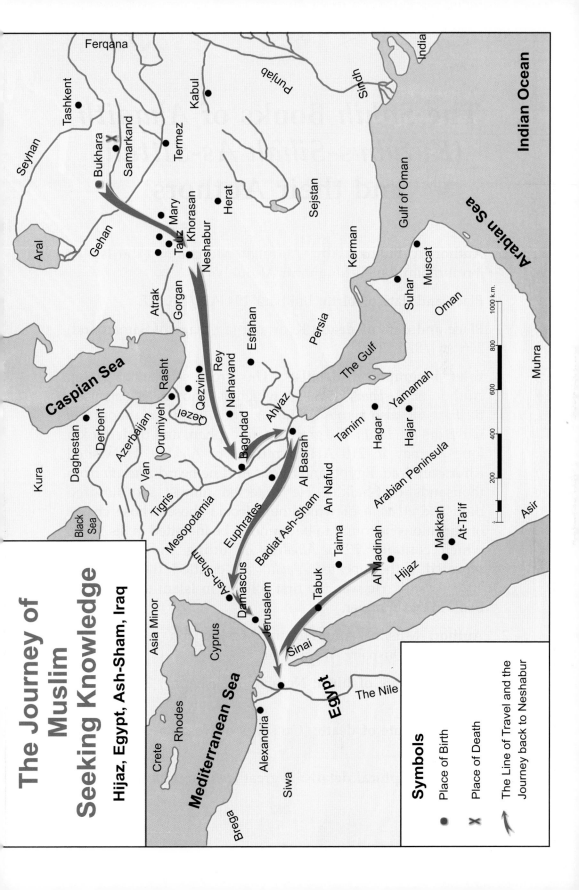

The Journey of Muslim Seeking Knowledge

Hijaz, Egypt, Ash-Sham, Iraq

India

Indian Ocean

Ferqana

Tashkent

Seyhan

Bukhara

Samarkand

Termez

Kabul

Punjab

Sindh

Gulf of Oman

Arabian Sea

Aral

Gehan

Tauz Mary

Khorasan

Herat

Sejstan

Muscat

Neshabur

Suhar

Oman

Caspian Sea

Atrak

Gorgan

Esfahan

Kerman

Rasht

Rey

Persia

Orumiyeh

Qezvin

Nahavand

The Gulf

Qezel

Baghdad

Ahvaz

Yamamah

Van

Al Basrah

Tamim

Hagar

Hajar

Azerbaijan

Tigris

Euphrates

An Nafud

Arabian Peninsula

Derbent

Daghestan

Mesopotamia

Badiat Ash-Sham

Muhra

Kura

Black Sea

Ash-Sham

Damascus

Taima

Tabuk

Al Madinah

Makkah

At-Ta'if

Asir

Asia Minor

Jerusalem

Hijaz

Cyprus

Sinai

Egypt

The Nile

Rhodes

Crete

Mediterranean Sea

Alexandria

Siwa

Brega

1000 k.m.

800 600 400 200

Symbols

● Place of Birth

✕ Place of Death

➤ The Line of Travel and the Journey back to Neshabur

The *Sahih* Books of *Ahadith* (*Kutubus-Sihâh As-Sittah*) and their Authors

1. **Author:** Al-Bukhâri Abu 'Abdullâh Muhammad ibn Ismâ'il ibn Ibrâhim ibn Al-Mughirah Al-Bukhâri

   Place and date of birth: Bukhara 194 AH/810 CE

   Place and date of death: Khartank (a village of Samarqand) 256 AH/870 CE

   Brief biographical details: The great scholar of Islam. Author of *Al-Jâmi' As-Sahih* which is known as *Sahih Al-Bukhâri*. He also wrote *At-Târikh*, and *Ad-Du'afa'*, about the narrators of *Hadith*. He grew up an orphan, and undertook a long journey in 210 AH in pursuit of *Ahadith*. He visited Khurasan, Iraq, Egypt, and Syria. And he heard *Ahadith* from thousands of Shaikhs. He collected almost six hundred thousand *Ahadith* of which he selected those whose chains of narrations he found to be sound to be included in his *Sahih*, which contains 7275 *Ahadith* including those that are repeated. If the repeated *Ahadith* are omitted, the number is 4000 *Ahadith*. He was the first scholar in Islam to compile a book in this manner.

2. **Author:** Muslim Abul-Husain Muslim ibn Al-Hajjâj ibn Muslim Al-Qushairi Al-Nesaburi

   Place and date of birth: Nesabur (Naishapur) 204 AH/820 CE

   Place and date of death: Outskirts of Nesabur 261 AH/875 CE

   Brief biographical details: A great *Hafiz* and *Imam* of *Hadith*

scholars. He traveled to the Hijâz, Egypt, Syria and Iraq. The most famous of his books is *Sahih Muslim*, which contains 4000 *Ahâdith*. He wrote it over a period of fifteen years. His other books include *Al-Musnad Al-Kabir*, which he organized in chapters according to the narrator of the *Hadith; Al-Jâmi'*, which is organized in chapters according to subject; and *Al-Kuna wal-Asma'*.

3. **Author**: Abu Dâwud As-Sijistâni. Sulaimân ibn Al-Ash'ath ibn Ishaq ibn Bashir Al-Azdi As-Sijistâni.

Place and date of birth: Sijistân 202 AH/817 CE

Place and date of death: Al-Basrah 275 AH/889 CE

Brief biographical details: The Imam of *Hadith* scholars of his time. He undertook a great journey (Baghdad, Al-Basrah, and the Islamic capitals). He wrote *As-Sunan* in which he compiled 4800 *Ahâdith; Al-Murâsil*, About *Hadith*; and *Kitâb Az-Zuhd* (the Book of Asceticism).

4. **Author:** At-Tirmidhi: Abu 'Isa Muhammad ibn 'Isa ibn Sawrah ibn Musa As-Sulami Al-Bughi

Place and date of birth: Tirmidh 209 AH/824 CE

Place and date of death: Tirmidh 279 AH/892 CE

Brief biographical details: He was a student of Al-Bukhâri and had some Shaykhs in common with him. He undertook a journey to Khurasan, Iraq and the Hijâz. He was famous for his memory. His works include *Al-Jâmi' 'Al-Kabir*, which is *Sahih At-Tirmidhi*, as well as *Ash-Shamâ'il An-Nabawiyyah, At-Târikh*, and *Al-'Ilal*, which is about *Hadith*.

5. **Author:** An-Nasâ'i. Abu 'Abdur-Rahmân Ahmad ibn 'Ali ibn Shu'aib ibn 'Ali ibn Sinân ibn Bahr ibn Dinâr

Place and date of birth: Nasa 215 AH/830 CE

Place and date of death: Al-Quds (Jerusalem) 303 AH/915 CE

Brief biographical details: He was a *Qâdi* (judge) and *Hâfiz*

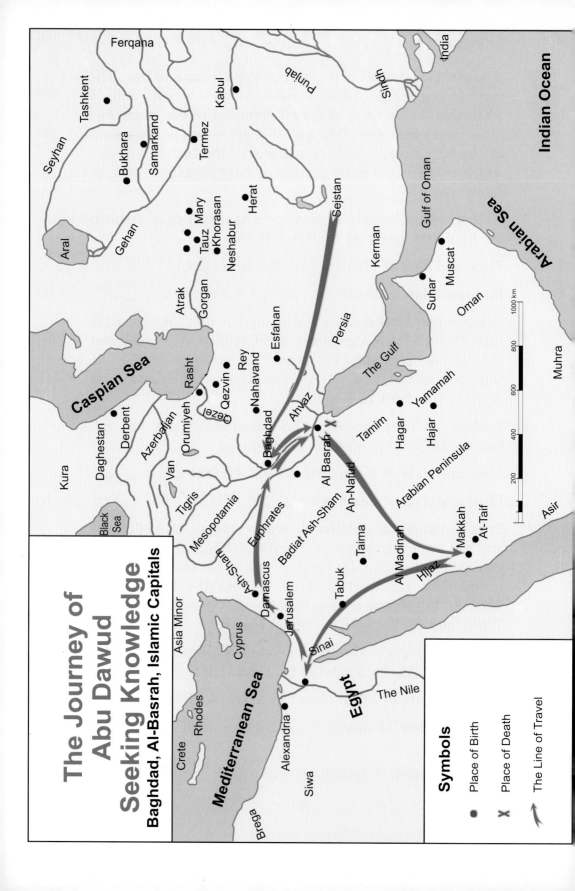

The Journey of Abu Dawud
Seeking Knowledge
Baghdad, Al-Basrah, Islamic Capitals

Symbols

- • Place of Birth
- ✗ Place of Death
- ↗ The Line of Travel

Ferqana

Tashkent

Samarkand

Bukhara

Seyhan

Gehan

Aral

Kabul

Termez

Punjab

Sindh

India

Mary

Tauz

Khorasan

Neshabur

Herat

Sejstan

Indian Ocean

Gulf of Oman

Kerman

Muscat

Suhar

Oman

Arabian Sea

Muhra

Atrak

Gorgan

Esfahan

Persia

The Gulf

Caspian Sea

Rasht

Rey

Qezvin

Nahavand

Qezel

Baghdad

Ahvaz

Al Basrah ✗

Tamim

Yamamah

Hagar

Hajar

Arabian Peninsula

Derbent

Daghestan

Kura

Azerbajjan

Orumiyeh

Van

An-Nafud

Tamim

Tigris

Mesopotamia

Euphrates

Badiat Ash-Sham

Makkah

At-Taif

Asir

1000 km
800
600
400
200

Black Sea

Ash-Sham

Damascus

Jerusalem

Taima

Al Madinah

Hijaz

Tabuk

Sinai

Asia Minor

Cyprus

Mediterranean Sea

Egypt

The Nile

Crete

Rhodes

Alexandria

Siwa

Brega

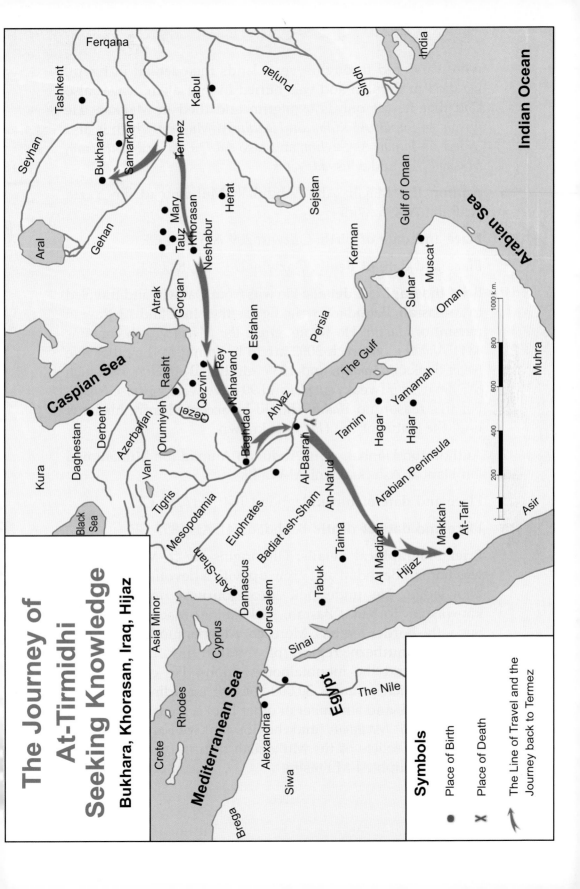

The Journey of At-Tirmidhi Seeking Knowledge

Bukhara, Khorasan, Iraq, Hijaz

Ferqana

Tashkent

Seyhan

Bukhara

Samarkand

Kabul

Termez

Punjab

Sindh

India

Indian Ocean

Aral

Gehan

Mary

Tauz

Khorasan

Herat

Neshabur

Sejstan

Gulf of Oman

Arabian Sea

Muscat

Suhar

Oman

Atrak

Gorgan

Esfahan

Persia

Kerman

Caspian Sea

Rasht

Rey

Nahavand

Ahvaz

The Gulf

Muhra

Derbent

Orumiyeh

Qezvin

Qezel

Baghdad

Al-Basrah

Tamim

Hagar

Yamamah

Hajar

Daghestan

Azerbaijan

Van

Tigris

Mesopotamia

Euphrates

Badiat ash-Sham

An-Nafud

Arabian Peninsula

Makkah

At-Taif

Kura

Black Sea

Ash-Sham

Damascus

Jerusalem

Taima

Tabuk

Al Madinah

Hijaz

Asir

Asia Minor

Cyprus

Sinai

Mediterranean Sea

Egypt

The Nile

Rhodes

Crete

Alexandria

Siwa

Brega

1000 k.m.

800 600 400 200

Symbols

● Place of Birth

✗ Place of Death

→ The Line of Travel and the Journey back to Termez

who wandered through several lands then settled in Egypt. He died in Ramlah and was buried in Jerusalem. It was also said that he set out as a pilgrim and died in Makkah. He wrote *As-Sunan Al-Kubra* on *Hadith; Al-Mujtaba* which is also called *As-Sunan As-Sughra*; and also *Ad-Du'afa' wal-Matrukun, Musnad 'Ali* and *Musnad Mâlik*.

6. **Author:** Ibn Mâjah: Abu 'Abdullâh Muhammad ibn Yazid Ar-Rab'i Al-Qazwini

   Place and date of birth: Qazwin 209 AH/824 CE

   Place and date of death: Qazwin 273 AH/887 CE

   Brief biographical details: He was from Qazwin and traveled to Al-Basrah, Baghdad, Syria, Egypt, the Hijâz and Ar-Rayi in pursuit of *Hadith*. He wrote *Sunan Ibn Mâjah* which contains 4341 *Ahâdith*, of which 3002 are to be found in the other five *Sahih* books of *Hadith*, and 1339 additional *Ahâdith*, of which 613 have *Da'if* (weak) *Isnâds*, and 99 have weak or false *Isnâds*. For this reason no *Hadith* should be accepted from his book until the status of the *Hadith* is known.

7. **Author:** Ibn Hanbal. Abu 'Abdullâh Ahmad ibn Muhammad ibn Hanbal Ash-Shaibâni Al-Wâ'ili

   Place and date of birth: Baghdad 164 AH/780 CE

   Place and date of death: Baghdad 241 AH/855 CE

   Brief biographical details: His origins lay in Marw but he was born in Baghdad and grew up with a devotion to seeking knowledge. He undertook great journeys in pursuit of knowledge, to Kufa, Basrah, Makkah, Al-Madinah, Yemen, Syria, the border regions, Morocco, Algeria, modern-day Iraq and the southern region of modern-day Iran, Persia, Khurasan and the mountainous regions. He compiled the *Musnad* which contains 30,000 *Ahâdith* including those that are repeated, and a number of other books. He is the Imam of the Hanbali *Madhhab*, and he took a well-known stance against the beliefs of the Mu'tazilah during the reign of the Abbasid Caliph Al-Mu'tasim.

8. **Author:** Ad-Dârimi. Abu Muhammad 'Abdullâh ibn 'Abdur-Rahmân ibn Al-Fadl ibn Bahrâm At-Tamimi Ad-Dârimi As-Samarqandi

   Place and date of birth: Samarqand 181 AH/ 797 CE

   Place and date of death: Samarqand 255 AH/869 CE

   Brief biographical details: He heard *Hadith* from many people in the Hijâz, Syria, Egypt, Iraq and Khurasan. He was mature and of a noble character, deeply versed in knowledge. He wrote *Al-Musnad* on *Hadith*, and *Al-Jâmi' As-Sahih*, which is called *Sunan Ad-Dârimi*. He also wrote *Ath-Thulâthiyyât*.

9. **Author:** Mâlik. Abu 'Abdullâh Mâlik ibn Anas ibn Mâlik Al-Asbahi Al-Himyari

   Place and date of birth: Al-Madinah 93 AH/712 CE

   Place and date of death: Al-Madinah 179 AH/795 CE

   Brief biographical details: The Imam of Al-Madinah, one of the four Imams, after whom the Mâliki *Madhhab* is named. He was solid in his religious commitment. He compiled *Al-Muwatta'* and also wrote an essay on preaching and exhortation (*Al-Wa'z*), another book entitled *Al-Masâ'il*, another essay entitled *Ar-Radd 'ala Al-Qadariyyah*, and books entitled *An-Nujum* and *Tafsir Gharib Al-Qur'ân*. And Jalaluddin As-Suyuti wrote a book entitled *Tazyin Al-Mamâlik bi Manâqib Al-Imam Mâlik*.

There are other great books of *Hadith* besides those mentioned here, also known as *Muwatta*, *Musnad*, *Mustadrak* and *Mu'jam*, such as those written by Al-Hâkim An-Nesaburi, Ibn Hibbân, Ad-Dâraqutni, Al-Baihaqi, Al-Baghawi and At-Tabarâni.

***

The writing of the *Seerah* (biography) of the Messenger of Allâh ﷺ and his *Maghâzi* (military campaigns, battles) is a genre that stands alone. The *Hadith* scholars included his biography in their books, for

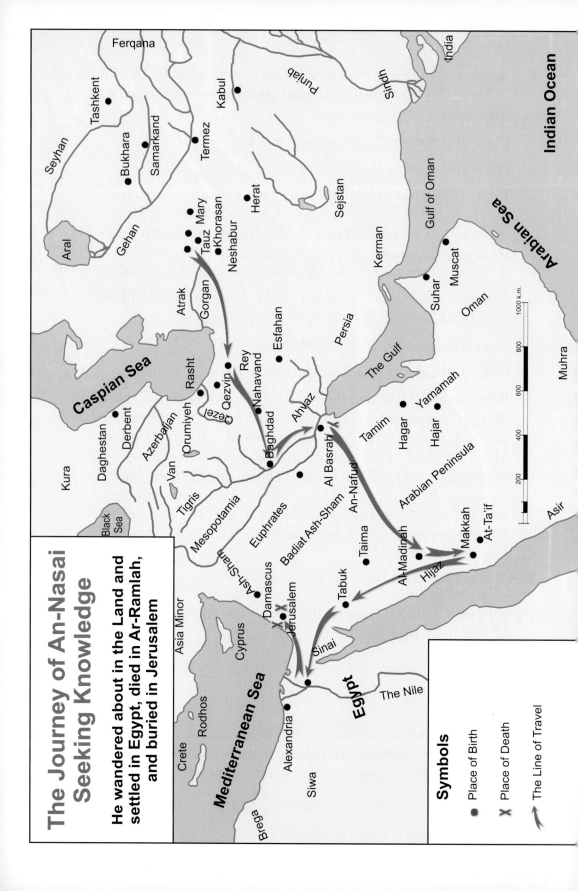

The Journey of An-Nasai Seeking Knowledge

He wandered about in the Land and settled in Ar-Ramlah, died in Egypt, and buried in Jerusalem

Symbols

● Place of Birth

✗ Place of Death

➤ The Line of Travel

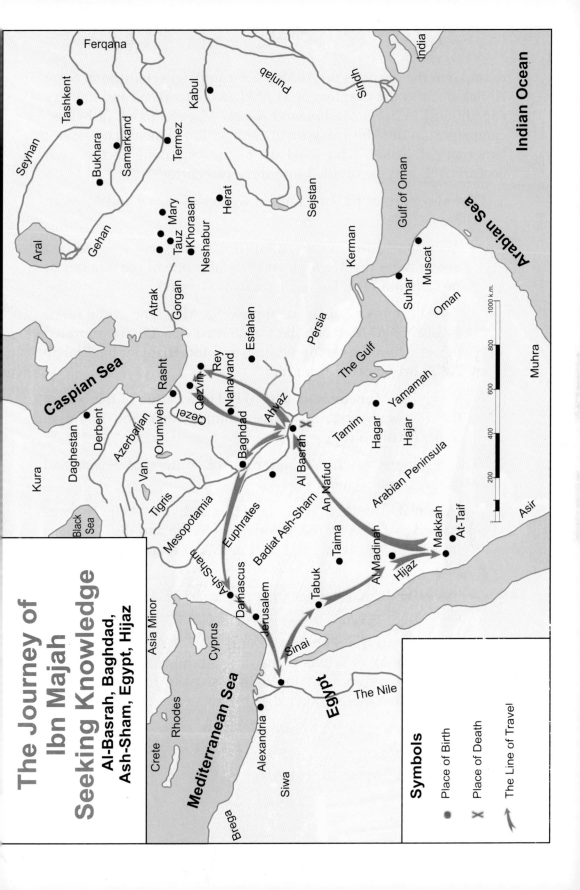

The Journey of Ibn Majah Seeking Knowledge

Al-Basrah, Baghdad, Ash-Sham, Egypt, Hijaz

Symbols

● Place of Birth

✕ Place of Death

→ The Line of Travel

example in the chapters on *Al-Maghâzi* (campaigns, battles) in *Sahih Al-Bukhâri*, and the chapters of *Al-Jihâd was-Siyar* (*Jihad* and military expeditions) in *Sahih Muslim*, and *Kitâbul-Maghâzi* (book of battles, campaigns) in the *Musnad* of Imam Ahmad ibn Hanbal. The earliest historians of *Seerah*, who lived up to the beginning of the third century AH, may be divided into three categories:

1. The historians of the first rank of writers of *Seerah* and *Maghâzi*. These include:

   - Abân ibn 'Uthmân ibn 'Affân (d. 105 AH). He was the first one to write the *Maghâzi*, and was also one of the scholars of *Ahadith* and *Fiqh*. He is *Thiqah* (trustworthy).

   - 'Urwah ibn Az-Zubair (d. approx. 92 AH). One of the seven *Fuqaha'* of Al-Madinah, he transmitted *Ahâdith* and narrated reports from the senior *Sahâbah*, and Ibn Hishâm, Ibn Shihâb Az-Zuhri reported from him.

   - Wahb ibn Munabbih (d. 110 AH). He was one of the best of the *Tâbi'in* (Successors of the Companions), and is *Thiqah Saduq* (trustworthy).

2. The historians of the second rank of writers of *Seerah* and *Maghâzi*. These include:

   - 'Abdullâh ibn Abu Bakr ibn Hazm (d. 135 AH). He was classed as *Thiqah* by the historians of *Seerah* and the historians in general. Ibn Ishâq, Ibn Sa'd and At-Tabari reported from him.

   - 'Asim ibn 'Umar ibn Qatâdah Al-Ansâri (d. 120 AH); he was classed as *Thiqah* by the scholars of *Hadith*

   - Muhammad ibn Shihâb Az-Zuhri (d. 124 AH), a *Muhaddith* and historian of whom 'Umar ibn 'Abdul-'Aziz wrote to the regions: I recommend Ibn Shihâb to you, for you will not find anyone more knowledgeable about the *Sunnah* than he.

3. The historians of the third rank of writers of *Seerah* and *Maghâzi*. These include:

   - Musa ibn 'Uqbah (d. 141 AH).

- Mu'ammar ibn Râshid (d. 150 AH)

- Muhammad ibn Ishâq (d. 152 AH): the Shaykh of the historians of the *Seerah* and *Maghâzi*, from whom two great scholars learned: Ziyâd Al-Bakkâ'i and Ibn Hishâm.

- Muhammad ibn 'Umar Al-Wâqidi (d. 207AH): he was regarded as *Da'eef* (weak) in reporting *Hadith* by Imam Ahmad ibn Hanbal, among others.

- 'Abdul-Malik ibn Hishâm ibn Ayyub Al-Himyari Al-Basri (d. 218 AH). He transmitted the *Seerah* of Ibn Ishâq from the latter's student Ziyâd Al-Bakkâ'i.

- Muhammad ibn Sa'd ibn Mani' Al-Basri Az-Zuhri (d. 230 AH), the scribe of Al-Wâqidi. He surpassed his teacher and is *Thiqah* (trustworthy). The greatest of his books is *At-Tabaqât Al-Kubra*, which is one of the main references for this book, especially concerning military campaigns and expeditions, as well as *As-Seerah An-Nabawiyyah* by Ibn Hishâm.

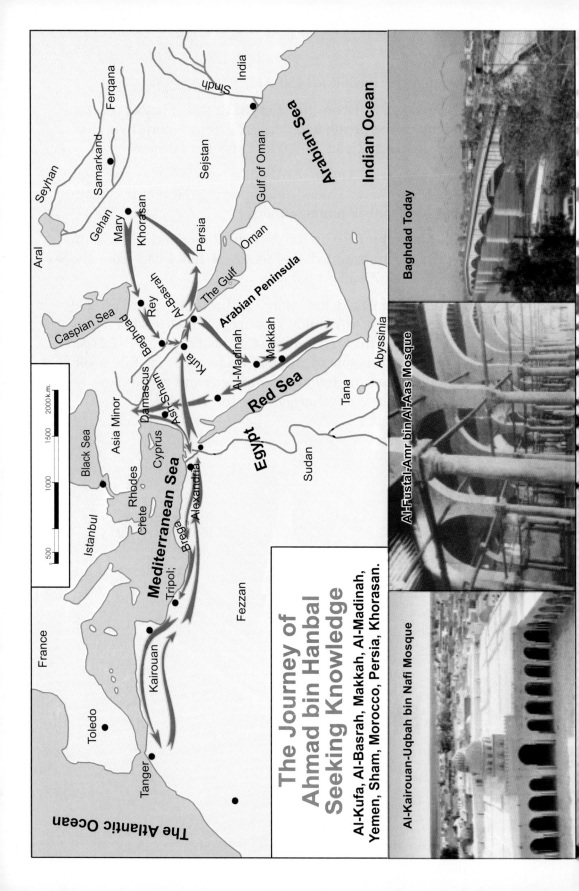

The Journey of Ahmad bin Hanbal Seeking Knowledge

Al-Kufa, Al-Basrah, Makkah, Al-Madinah, Yemen, Sham, Morocco, Persia, Khorasan.

Al-Kairouan-Uqbah bin Nafi Mosque

Al-Fustal-Amr bin Al-Aas Mosque

Baghdad Today

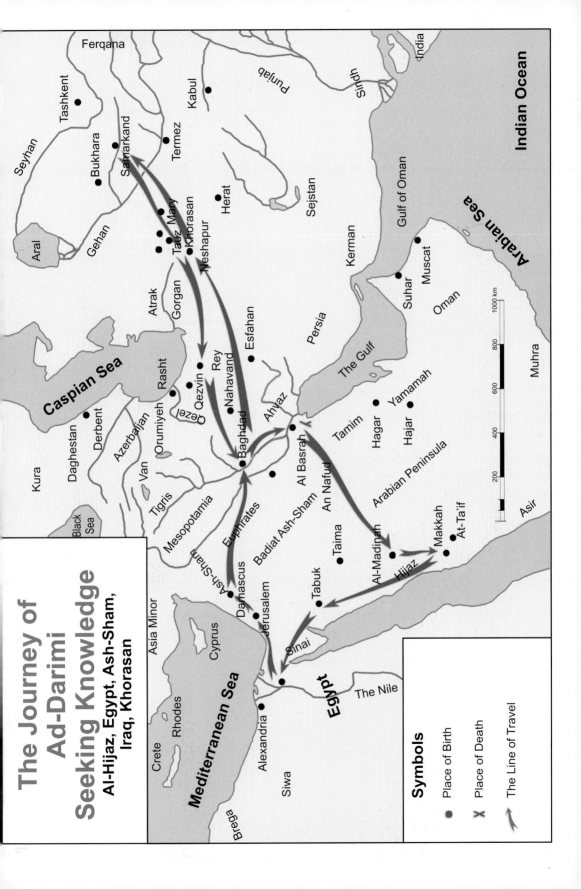

APPENDIX

APPENDIX

The Holy Ka'bah
(The House, the House of Allâh, the Sacred House, the Ancient House, the Qiblah (direction of prayer)

Approximate distances between Makkah and the *Mawâqit* (points at which pilgrims must enter *Ihram* before proceeding to Makkah):

- Qarn Al-Manâzil 80 km *Miqât* for the people of Najd and neighbouring regions.

- Dhât 'Irq 90 km *Miqât* for the people of Iraq and those who pass through it.

- Yalamlam 100 km *Miqât* for the people of Yemen.

- Al-Juhfah 187 km *Miqât* for the people of Egypt, Syria and those who pass through them.

- Dhul-Hulaifah (Abyâr 'Ali) 410 km *Miqât* for the people of Al-Madinah

Approximate distances between Al-Masjid Al-Harâm and some of the boundaries of the *Haram*[1]

- At-Tan'im (where the Mosque of 'A'ishah ﷺ is located) 7.5 km This is the closest point of the boundary to the Mosque

- Nakhlah 13 km Between Makkah and At-Tâ'if. This is Nakhlah Al-Yamâniyyah; as for Nakhlah Ash-Shâmiyyah, which is called Al-Madiq, it is 45 km away.

- Adâtu Laban (Al-'Ukaishiyyah) 16 km

---

[1] From: *Târikh Makkah Al-Mukarramah Qadiman wa Hadithan* by Dr. Muhammad Ilyâs 'Abdul-Ghani, 1st Edn, 1422 AH/2001 CE, Al-Rasheed Press, Al-Madinah.

- Al-Ji'rânah (Al-Mustawfirah)   22 km
- Al-Hudaibiyah (Mawqa' Ash-Shamesi)   22 km
- Jabal 'Arafât (Dhâtus-Salim)   22 km

The first one to define the boundaries of the *Haram* was Ibrâhim ﷺ, on the command of Jibril, and he set up stone markers for them. After the conquest of Makkah, the Messenger of Allâh ﷺ sent Tamim ibn Asad Al-Khuzâ'i to renew them.

Area and capacity of Al-Masjid Al-Harâm

	Details	Area Sq. Meters	Total Area	Capacity	Total Capacity
1	Area of the Mosque before the first Saudi Expansion (the Matâf + Ottoman construction)	29,000 sq.m.	29,000 sq. m.	50,000 worshippers[1] (before removal of the buildings in the Matâf)	72,000 worshippers (after removal of the buildings in the Matâf)
2	The First Saudi Expansion (a basement, ground floor and upper floor)	131,000 sq.m.	160,000 sq.m.	327,000 worshippers	399,000 worshippers
3	Addition of a roof to the first expansion where people could pray 1406 AH	42,000 sq.m.	202,000 sq.m.	105,000 worshippers	504,000 worshippers
4	The Second Saudi Expansion (a basement, ground floor, upper floor and roof)	76,000 sq.m.	278,000 sq.m.	190,000 worshippers	694,000 worshippers
5	Preparing open areas for prayer surrounding the Mosque	88,000 sq.m.	366,000 sq.m.	220,000 worshippers	914,000 worshippers

At peak times more than 1 million worshippers may be accommodated.

---

[1] Capacity is reckoned on a basis of 2.5 worshippers per square meter. It may be noted here that only 50,000 worshippers could be accommodated in the past because there were buildings in the Matâf such as the four Maqâms, the structure over the well of Zamzam, Maqâm Ibrâhim, the Minbar, Bâb Bani Shaibah. When these were removed later on, the capacity increased to 72,000.

The number of boundary markers surrounding the Haram reached 943 markers on top of the mountains, hilly paths, and the highlands. Most of these markers were ruined. The area of the Haram is 550 sq. kilometers.

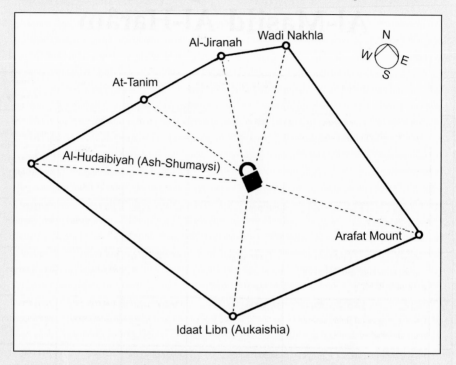

Expansions of Al-Masjid Al-Haram throughout the Islamic History

1- Expansion by Umar bin Al Khattab (ﷺ) on the 17 A. H. / 639 A. D.

2- Expansion by Uthman bin Affan (ﷺ) on 26 A. H. / 648 A.D.

3- Expansion by Abdullah bin Az-Zubair (ﷺ) on 65 A.H. / 685 A. D.

4- Expansion by Al Walid bin Abdul-Malik on 91 A.H. / 709 A. D.

5- Expansion by Abu Ja'far Al-Mansur on 137 A.H. / 755 A. D.

6- Expansion by Muhammad Al-Mahdi Al-Abbasi 160 A.H. / 777 A. D.

7- Expansion by Al-Mutadd Al-Abbasi on 284 A.H. / 797 A. D.

8- Expansion by Al-Muqtadir Al-Abbasi on 306 A.H. / 918 A. D.

9- Ottomanic Construction on 979 A.H/ 1571 A. D.

10- Expansion of King Abdul-Aziz Al Saud on 1375 A. H. / 1955 A. D.

11- Expansion of the Custodian of the two Holy Mosques, King Fahad on 1409 A. H. / 1988 A.D.

An Approximate Drawing of the Holy Kabah Building and a Demonstration of its Dimensions

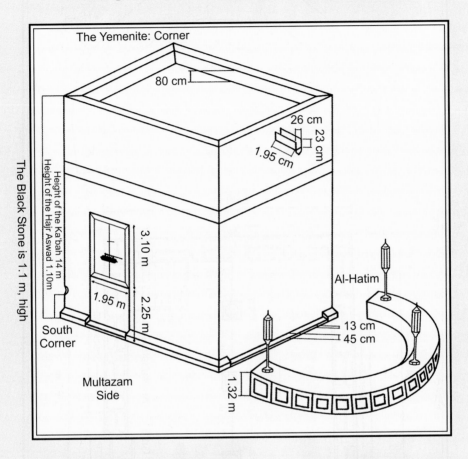

1- Height of the Holy Kabah   14 m

2- Its Length on the side of Al-Multazam   12.84 m

3- Its Length on the side of Al-Hatim   11.28 m

4- Length Between Yemenite Corner and Al-Hatim   12.11 m

5- Distance Between the two Corners   11.52 m

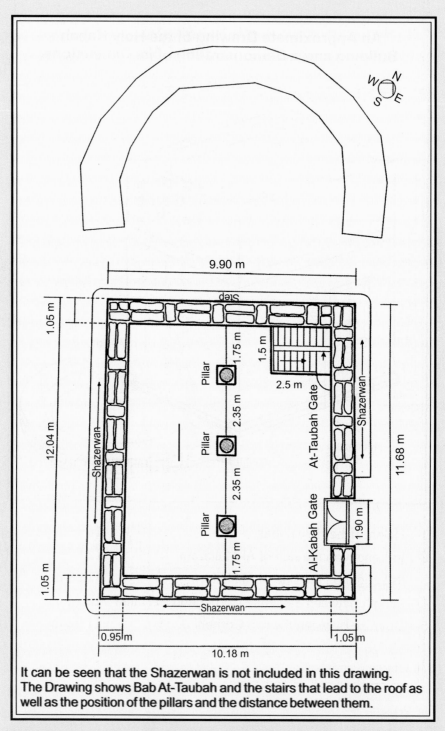

It can be seen that the Shazerwan is not included in this drawing.
The Drawing shows Bab At-Taubah and the stairs that lead to the roof as
well as the position of the pillars and the distance between them.

Dimensions of the Wall of the Holy Ka'bah and its total area.

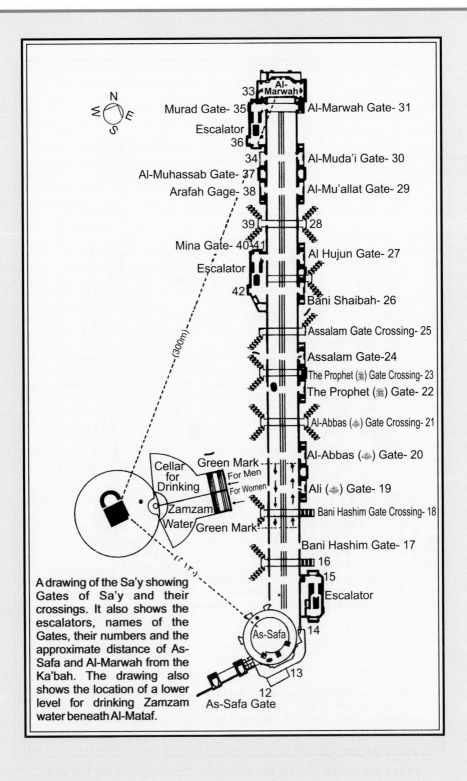

A drawing of the Sa'y showing Gates of Sa'y and their crossings. It also shows the escalators, names of the Gates, their numbers and the approximate distance of As-Safa and Al-Marwah from the Ka'bah. The drawing also shows the location of a lower level for drinking Zamzam water beneath Al-Mataf.

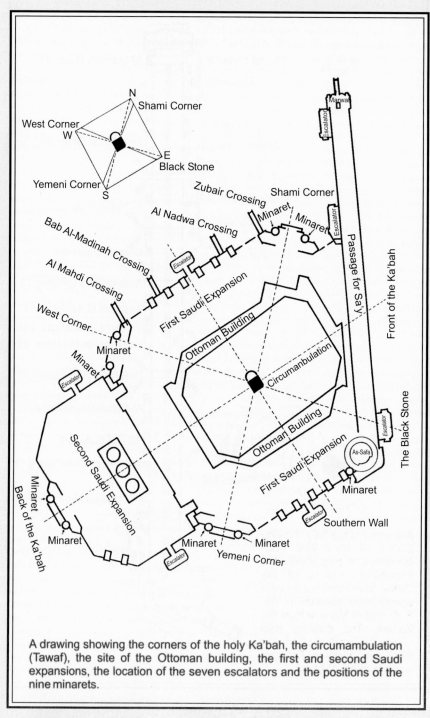

A drawing showing the corners of the holy Ka'bah, the circumambulation (Tawaf), the site of the Ottoman building, the first and second Saudi expansions, the location of the seven escalators and the positions of the nine minarets.

Recent expansions (During the time of the Ottomans and the first and second Saudi Expansions.)

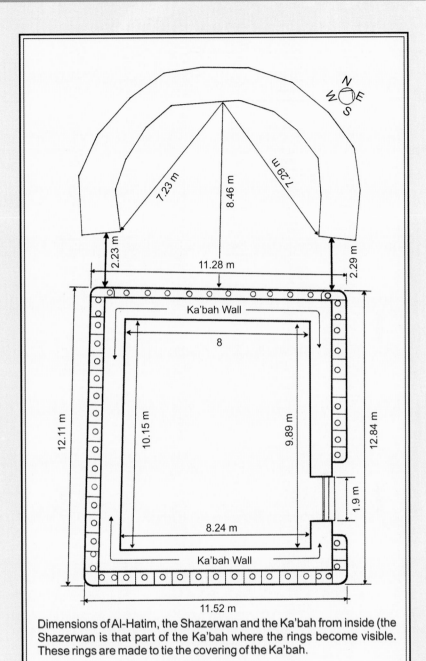

Dimensions of Al-Hatim, the Shazerwan and the Ka'bah from inside (the Shazerwan is that part of the Ka'bah where the rings become visible. These rings are made to tie the covering of the Ka'bah.

Zamzam Well Dimensions

The well opening	= 1.56m	Distance from springs to	= 17m
Depth of the well	= 30m	The bottom of the well	
Water level from the opening	= 4m	Diameter varies between	1.46-2.66m
Depth of the supplying springs	= 13m	Distance from the Black Stone	= 21m

References

- *Al-Iktifa min Maghazi Syedina Rasulillah wa Maghâzi As-Sâdalith-Thâlathatil-Khulafa' Abi Bakr As-Siddiq wa 'Umar Al-Fâruq wa 'Uthmân Dhun-Nurain* (Satisfaction from the Expeditions of the Prophet and the Expeditions of the three Caliphs Abu Bakr As-Siddiq, 'Umar Al-Faruq And 'Uthman Dhun-Nurain): Sulaimân ibn Musa ibn Sâlim ibn Hassân ibn Sulaimân ibn Ahmad ibn Abdus-Salâm Al-Himyari Al-Kulâ'i Al-Balansi, Manuscripts # 4810 and # 4811, the National Public Library, Damascus.

- *Usdul-Ghâbah Fi Ma'rifatis-Sahâbah* - Another Study of the Prophet's Companions: 'Izzuddin Ibn Al-Athir Abul-Hasan Ali ibn Muhammad Al-Jazari. Printed at Dârush-Sha'b, Cairo, Egypt.

- *Al-Isâbah Fi Tamizus-Sahâbah* (Correctly distinguishing the Companions): Shihabuddin Abul-Fadl Ahmad ibn 'Ali ibn Muhammad ibn Muhammad ibn 'Ali Al-Kin'âni Al-'Asqalâni (Ibn Hajar, author of Fathul-Bâri). Maktabah Al-Muthanna, Beirut, Lebanon. First Edition, 1328 H.

- *Al-Isti'âb Fi Asma' Al-Ashâb* (A Comprehensive Study of the Names of Companions): Abu 'Umar Yusuf ibn 'Abdullah ibn Muhammad ibn Abdul-Barr ibn 'Asim An-Namari Al-Qurtubi. This book consists of the footnotes from *Al-Isâbah Fi Tamizis-Sahâbah*. Maktabah Al-Muthanna, Beirut, Lebanon. First Edition, 1328 H.

- *I'lâmus-Sâ'ilin 'An Kutubi Syedil-Mursalin* (Informing Questioners about Books of the Master of the Messengers): Shamsuddin Muhammad ibn Ali ibn Tulun Ad-Dimashqi. Manuscripts # 263 and # 2122, the National Public Library, Damascus.

- *Istinzâlun-Nasr Bit-Tawassuli Bi-Ahli Badr* (Asking Victory through the intercession of People of Badr): Shihabuddin Abul-Abbas Ahmad ibn 'Ali At-Turabulusi, Manuscript # 10412, the National Public Library, Damascus. (Printed with Explanation Notes with the title: *Sharhus-Sadr Bi-Sharh Urjuzah Istinzâlin-Nasr Bit-Tawassuli Bi-Ahli Badr)*

- *Al-A'lâm* (From the best of the important people of the religion): Khairuddin Az-Zirikli. Dârul-'Ilm Lil-Malâyin, Lebanon. Sixth edition, 1984.

- *A'lâmun-Nisa'* (Great Women) In the Islamic and Arabic world: 'Umar Rida Kahhâlah. Ar-Risâlah Corporation. Third edition, 1397/ 1977.

- *Ayyâmul-Arab Fil-Jâhiliyyah* (Arab Days during the Time of Ignorance): Muhammad Ahmad Jad Al-Mawla, Ali Muhammad Al-Bijawy and Muhammad Abul-Fadl Ibrahim. Dâr Ihya'ul-Kutub Al-Arabiyyah, published by Al-Bâbi Al-Halabi. Egypt.

- *Al-Bidâyah wan-Nihâyah* (The Beginning and the End - famous history book): Abul-Fida' Al-Hâfiz Ibn Kathir Ad-Dimashqi. Maktabah Al-Ma'ârif, Beirut and Maktabah An-Nasr, Riyadh. First edition, 1966.

- *Târikh Ar-Rusul wal-Muluk (Târikh At-Tabari* - History of At-Tabari): Abu Ja'far Muhammad ibn Jarir At-Tabari. Dârul-Ma'ârif, Egypt. 1963.

- *Târikh Khalifah ibn Khayyât* (History of Khalifah ibn Khayyât): Abu 'Amr Khalifah ibn Khayyât ibn Abi Hubairah Al-Laithi. Dârul-Qalam and Ar-Risâlah Corporation. Second edition, 1397/1977.

- *Târikhul-Islam* (History of Islam, political, religious, cultural and social): Dr. Hasan Ibrahim Hasan. An-Nahdah Egyptian Library. Sixth edition, 1961.

- *Târikh Makkah Al-Mukarramah Qadiman wa Hadithan* (History of Makkah - Past and Present): Dr. Muhammad Ilyâs Abdul-Ghani. Al-Rasheed Press, Al-Madinah Al-Munawwarah. First edition, 1422/2001.

- *Jâliyatul-Kurab Bi-Ashâb Syedil Ajam wal-Arab* (The Community of the Companions of the Master of Arabs and non-Arabs - a Thesis in the Names of the Companions who witnessed Badr and Uhud): Zainuddin Al-Barzanji A manuscript # 9066 in the National Public Library, Damascus.

- *Al-Harb 'Abrat-Târikh* (War through History): Field Marshall Viscount Montgomery. Anglo-Egyptian Library. 1971.

- *Duwal Al-Islam* (Countries of Islam): Al-Hâfiz Shamsuddin Abi 'Abdullah Muhammad ibn Ahmad ibn 'Uthmân Adh-Dhahabi, with the addition of Critical Notes by Hasan Marwah. Dâr Sâdir, Beirut. First edition, 1999.

- *Ad-Da'wah Ilal-Islam:* Sir Thomas Arnold, An-Nahdah Egyptian Library, Second edition, 1957.

- *Dhakhâ'irul-Uqba Fi Manâqib Dhawil-Qurba:* Muhibbuddin Ahmad ibn 'Abdullah At-Tabari, Darul Ma'rifah, Beirut. 1974.

- *Ar-Raudul-Unuf* - a book on the Prophet's Biography: Ibn Hishâm, Abul-Qâsim 'Abdur-Rahman ibn 'Abdullah ibn Ahmad ibn Abul-Hasan Al-Khath'ami As-Suhaili. Dârul-Fikr, Beirut.

- *As-Seerah Al-Halabiyyah:* 'Ali ibn Burhanuddin Al-Halabi Ash-Shâfi'i. Al Maktabah At-Tijâriyyah Al-Kubra. 1382/1962.

- *As-Seerah An-Nabawiyyah wal-'Athârul-Muhammadiyyah* (Biography of the Prophet and the Muahammadan Tradition) - Footnotes in As-Seerah Al-Halabiyah: Ahmad Zainy (Dahlan). Al Maktabah At-Tijâriyyah Al-Kubra. 1382/1962.

- *As-Seerah An-Nabawiyyah* (Biography of the Prophet): Abul-Fida' Isma'il ibn Kathir. Dârul-Fikr, Beirut. Second edition, 1398/1978.

- *As-Seerah An-Nabawiyyah* (Biography of the Prophet ﷺ): Abu Muhammad 'Abdul-Malik ibn Hisham Al-Ma'âfiri Al-Basri. Dârul-Jeel, Beirut. 1975.

- *Sharh Asma' Ahl Badr* (Explaining the Names of People of Badr): Collected by Abdul-Latif ibn Ahmad Al-Baqâ'i in 1164 H, and explained by Taha ibn Muhammad Al-Jibrini Ash-Shahir (Ibnul-Muhanna), who died in 1178/1764. Manuscript #5151, the National Public Library.

- *Sahih Muslim:* Abul-Husain Muslim ibn Al-Hajjaj Al-Qushairi An-Nesaburi. Dâr Ihya' Al Kutub Al-Arabiyyah, 'Isa Al-Bâbi Al-Halabi. 1374/1955.

- *At-Tabaqât Al-Kubra,* Abu 'Abdullah Muhammad ibn Sa'd ibn Mani' Az-Zuhri. Dâr Sâdir, Beirut. 1388/1968.

- *Uyun Al-Athar Fi Funun Al-Maghâzi wash-Shamâ'il was-Siyar* - basically, a compilation of narrations that have to do with famous battles and famous figures: Fathuddin Abul-Fath Muhammad ibn Muhammad ibn Muhammad ibn 'Abdullah ibn Muhammad ibn Yahya ibn Syedun-Nâs Al-Andalusi Al-Ishbili. Dârul-Jeel, Beirut. Second edition, 1974.

- Al-'Ibar wa Diwan Al-Mubtada' wal-Khabar Fi Târikh Al-Arab wal-'Ajam wal-Barbar: (Examples and the Book of Information about the History of Arabs, Persians and Berbers): Waliuddin Abdur-Rahman ibn Muhammad ibn Muhammad ibn Khaldun Al-Hadrami. Darul-Bayân.

- Futuhul-Buldân (Conquering of the Lands): Abul-Hasan Ahmad ibn Yahya ibn Jâbir ibn Dâwud Al-Baghdâdi Al-Balâdhuri. Al-Maktabah At-Tijâriyyah Al-Kubrah, Egypt. 1959.

- Al-Qâmus Al-Islâmi (Islamic Dictionary): Ahmad 'Atiyatullah. Maktabah An-Nahdah Al-Misriyyah, Cairo, First edition 1386/1966.

- Al-Kâmil Fit-Târikh (A Complete Account of History): Abul-Hasan 'Ali ibn Abul-Karam Muhammad ibn Muhammad ibn 'Abdul-Karim ibn Abdul-Wâhid Ash-Shaibâni ('Izzuddin Ibn Al-Athir Al-Jazari). Idâratut-Tibâ'ah Al-Muniriyyah, Cairo, 1348 H.

- Kitabul-Ansâb (The Book of Lineage): Abu Sa'd Abdul-Karim ibn Muhammad ibn Mansur At-Tamimi As-Sam'âni. Published by Muhammad Amin Damj, Beirut. Second edition, 1400/1980.

- Kitab Ash-Shajarah An-Nabawiyyah Fi Nasab Khairil-Bariyyah (The Prophetic Lineage of the Best of the Creatures): Ibn Al-Mabrad. Verified by Muhiuddin Deeb Mastu, Darul-Kalim At-Tayyib, Damascus, Beirut. First edition, 1414/1994.

- Kitabul-Muhabbar (The Book of Muhabbar): Abu Ja'far Muhammad ibn Habib Al-Hâshimi Al-Baghdadi. New Horizons Publishing House, Beirut. (Corrected by Dr. Elza Lekhten Eshteter)

- Murujudh-Dhahab wa-Ma'âdin Al-Jawhar, 'Ali ibn Al-Husain ibn 'Ali Al-Mas'udi. Dârul-Fikr, Beirut. Fifth edition, 1393/1973.

- *Mizânul-Itidâl Fi Naqdir-Rijâl* (Men's Moderate Criticism): Abu Abdullah Muhammad ibn Ahmad ibn 'Uthmân Adh-Dhahabi, Dâr Ihya' Al Kutub Al-Arabiyyah, 'Isa Al-Bâbi Al-Halabi and Partners. First edition 1382/1963.

- *Mu'jamul-Buldân* (Lexicon of Countries): Shihâbuddin Abu 'Abdullah Yâqut ibn 'Abdullah Al-Hamawi. Dâr Sâdir, Beirut.

- *Muhammad Rasul Allâh* (Muhammad the Messenger of Allâh): Muhammad Rida. Dârul-Kutub Al-'Ilmiyyah, Beirut. 1395/1975.

- *Mu'jam Qabâ'ilil-Arab* (Arab Tribes Dictionary): 'Umar Rida Kahhâlah, Dârul-'Ilim Lil-Malâyeen. Second edition, 1388/1968.

- *Nata'ijul-Afhâm Fi Taqwimil-Arab Qablal-Islam, wa Fi Tahqiq Muwlidihi wa Umrihi Alayhis-Salâtu was-Salâm* (Understanding the Arabic Calendar before Islam and verifying His Date of Birth and His Age (ﷺ): Mahmud Pasha, the Astronomer, Dârul-Bashâ'ir Al-Islamiyyah, Beirut. First edition, 1407/1986.

- *Nasamâtul-Ashâr, wa Nafahâtul-Azhâr Fi Fadâ'il Al-'Asharatill-Abrâr, Ashâbin-Nabi Al-Mukhtâr* (A Book on the Virtues of the Ten Pious Companions of the Chosen Prophet ﷺ): Muhammad Al-Kailâni. Manuscript # 8763, the National Public Library, Damascus.

- *Al-Wafâ Bi-Ahwâl Al-Mustafa* (A Full Description of the Prophet's Affairs): Abul-Faraj 'Abdur-Rahmân ibn Al-Jawzi. Dârul-Kutub Al-Hadithah, Egypt. First edition, 1386/ 1966.